A Sensible God

A Sensible God

Seán ÓLaoire

To order additional copies of this book, contact:
Xlibris Corporation
1-888-795-4274
www.Xlibris.com
Orders@Xlibris.com
53239

Contents

Foreword

*"The goal of human life is to realize God,
and the purpose of religion is to teach one how to manifest the divinity within."*
Vivekananda

When religion takes you to a truth beyond its own, it has done its job. It is important to remember that Jesus said, "Seek the truth and the truth shall make you free." It is also important to have the proper perception of this truth path, as well as its goal, when embarking on one's spiritual journey toward the truth.

Seeking that goal, we often find books that save us some of the effort and suffering that accompany our experiences as well as deepen our understanding of the purpose of our lives. Our spiritual journey is enriched and nourished by books that share the spiritual musings of a deeply mystical and loving heart.

In *"A Sensible God,"* you may find these rich Irish stories, deep poetic musings and nourishing homilies food for your journey to the truth you seek. May this book also become part of your path to the truth of your perfect Self, the *mystic within,* waiting for discovery.

Once again it has been my great pleasure to assist in the publication of this book. And, once again, Seán has allowed me to include some of my favorite aphorisms. I hope the reader will enjoy them and be nourished by them.

Love, light and peace,

Mary Burns

Introduction

This is a book that has been harvested from two very different fields. One is the community of Companions on the Journey, in Palo Alto, California. Each Friday, Saturday and Sunday, I have the privilege of celebrating mass with them. As I meditate on the scriptures, Judeo-Christian and Gnostic, I try to plug into the universe so that I become a nursery for Spirit-seeds that I attempt to grow and cross-fertilize with my own lived experiences. Then I get to deliver thirty-minute homilies in which I can distill them.

The other field is my home, Tír na nÓg, in Healdsburg, California. I live among the mountains and forest, at the end of a five-mile dirt road, and my nearest neighbors are redwoods, madrona, oak and manzanita; coyotes, mountain lions, bob cats, wild pigs, wild turkeys, deer and rabbits. I can hear the music of Pena Creek from my bedroom and, occasionally, smell the salt in the air from the ocean 17 miles to the west.

I spend countless hours trekking here, walking silently and mindfully as my dog, Kayla, has taught me. Here, nature is my teacher. And it is from this field that I have harvested all of the short stories and poems that are contained in this volume.

Every second chapter of this book is either a story/poem conceived in Tír na nÓg or a homily conceived in Palo Alto. All of the homilies were delivered between June 2006 and January 2007. The short stories and poems were written over a period of eleven years, from September 1997 to February 2008. I have left the date of composition on each of these stories and poems.

They come to you with love that they may help stoke the fire of your God-self as you, too, give words to your deepest knowing.

Seán ÓLaoire—Tír na nÓg, July 24, 2008

Acknowledgements

For the average moviegoer, the focus is on the story and on the actors; particularly the lead actor. The aficionado, however, sees who the real creators are, the "backroom people;" those in charge of locations, costumes, script, plot, production and direction. It's the same with a book. The author's work is supported, pruned and developed by many people whom the audience never gets to meet. So, allow me to introduce them.

First, Mary Burns has, once again, devoted hundreds of hours to editing this material, at every stage of its growth. She interfaced with publishers and set up talks in bookstores all over the Bay Area. The reason Mary is such a great resource for this book, is that she is one of the busiest people I know, with significant roles in several international social justice projects. The old adage is very true here, "If you want something done well, ask a busy person."

Her husband, Bob, is the powerful, quiet Jaguar engine that purrs humbly as it holds 550 horsepower beneath its hood. And her son, Pat, the founder and president of *Still N' Motion* did the cover design, in between juggling a host of much more important and profitable jobs. Thanks, also, to his very competent assistants Rose Lee and Sara Burns.

David Carkeek has joined Michael Choy and Ron Alves in recording and reproducing the Sunday homilies, which were the seeds for many of the chapters in this book. To my beloved Companions on the Journey, sincere thanks for providing the venue and encouragement for these sorties into theological and mystical musing.

I am grateful to my uncle Noel, my first friend and an ongoing exemplar of life lived in God's blessed NOW. During a visit to California in March 2008, Noel took the photo, which Pat Burns masterfully included on the cover of *A Sensible God.* And, finally, to my Anam Chara, Dr. Arlen Brownstein whose practiced eye did a second edit on this book, as she does on my health and on my living.

May God continue to hold you all tenderly in the hollow of Her hand.

Seán ÓLaoire—Tír na nÓg, July 24, 2008

1

A Sensible God
(12/18/2007)

My God used to be very sensible. But, of course, I was really too young to understand. As a boy I saw him frequently, got the scent of his fragrance, heard his voice, tasted his words in my mouth and reached out to curl my small hand around a single finger of his. Every one of my five senses connected me to him.

I made the mistake of talking to adults about this. They mussed my unruly mop of hair and smiled indulgently at my naiveté—that is everyone except my great-grandmother who had managed to survive into old age without ever losing her mystical ability and my grandfather who was a life-long druid. A second, even bigger, mistake was made on my behalf; I was sent to school, initially to the nuns and later to the Christian Brothers. They told me that God wasn't sense-able but rather that he was sensible, as in he followed common sense. And I believed them, because they wore the insignia of God and the important adults in my life all deferred to them.

For the next 13 years, I was meticulously versed in this sensible God, this down-to-earth, commonsensical divinity, who wore sensible brown shoes and created people to be sensible plodders. Sure, he did produce the odd mystic, but they were all safely dead. For the rest of us, the advice was to keep our heads down and measure out our lives in teaspoonfuls; dull, pain-filled, anxious lives that were best navigated by common sense, old wives' tales and Old Testament examples. For God was a commonsense God, even when he consigned unbaptized babies to Limbo or sent sinners into everlasting flames for missing mass on Sundays or eating sausages on Fridays. This, too, made sense.

At age 18, I entered the seminary, and God became even more sensible. In exquisite detail, Dogmatic Theology, Sacramental Theology and Moral Theology constructed a fully consistent, logical framework, backed by scriptural references that made it madness to be agnostic let alone atheistic.

That is until I started at the university and majored in mathematical physics and pure mathematics. I was introduced to the "God of the gaps." He was slowly being edged out by science and given increasingly unimportant portfolios until such time as science itself had enough manpower and evidence to give him a golden handshake (with the presentation being made by Nietzsche) and retire him to an Old Folks' Home.

Religion reacted by either vigorously defending the commonsense God of the scriptures or deftly surfing the scientific waves, remaking God to survive the Copernican Revolution, Darwinian Evolution, Relativity Theory and Quantum Mechanics. The more creative theologians even managed to find scriptural references that foretold all of these discoveries. These religious thinkers claimed that God is still really sensible and predicted that real scientists would eventually see the light.

At age 26, I landed in Kenya in a remote area without phones, electricity or companionship. So I did the reasonable thing, I began dabbling in mystical ideas, radical new cosmologies and in thinking-for-myself. We all have mystical experiences, but typically we regard them as unsubstantial, like the dreams of the night. So I began recording and working with the dreams of the night and also with the visions of the day. I had an aha experience when I read that in Hebrew "vision" and "dream" are synonyms. So when the prophet Joel said, "In the days to come I will pour out my Spirit on all humankind; your young men shall see visions and your old men shall dream dreams" he wasn't discriminating against the senior citizens; for dreams are visions you have while you are asleep, and visions are dreams you have while you are awake.

God was very sensible again; but now he made sense because I experienced him by transcending my five senses, commonsense, theology and science but, instead, utilizing the soul.

And then, today, the 18th of December 2007, something else happened. It has been raining heavily for three days and the forest is spectacular during the rainy season; and my dog Kayla needs to walk. We set off, me in my rain gear and she in her house clothes; and we bumped into God—again and again and again.

First, I tasted Him on pearl-shaped droplets of water that hung on each twig. Every leaf on every tree was a chalice of God-life. I stuck my tongue out under a broad leaf and reverently received communion; the blood of God from a Eucharistic minister called Madrona. It was as ecstatic a moment as my First Holy Communion at age seven.

Then I saw Him. He sat astride a faery horse that wore green, gossamer-thin garments of ferns about its fetlocks. God's long flowing locks were made of light-green lichen, and each strand was a lace lattice for catching dreams and attracting visions. His steed was planted upon the hillside with its powerful limbs soaking up energy from the earth as he rested on his journey. We saw each other and each whispered, "Namasté."

As I continued to walk, I realized that each time I dug my sturdy staff in the ground I touched an acupuncture point on the skin of Gaia, and she responded by sending shivers of Earth energy up my spine.

Then I smelled Him, fleetingly. I had walked through a power spot! I stopped, backed up, and moved my head from side to side and sniffed like Kayla taught me. There it was again. I stood absolutely still and sniffed again. I had it! An entire shelf-full from the Akashic Records tumbled into my brain releasing a myriad of memories from many lifetimes on this planet. They danced like children newly reunited with long-lost parents.

It was evening before I returned home; all was still in the forest. I listened more silently than before and then I heard it, the sound of the sunset. It resonated in every cell of my body; light vibrating with light. After a few moments it was utterly quiet again; and then a new song sounded; it was the slow sensual symphony of the moonrise, a half-moon teasingly concealing the left side of her face. This song would last for the entire night. And the stars responded with a poem of their own; a poem crafted by the genius of a Yeats, in the language of a Rilke and spoken in the mystical tones of a Rumi.

Finally, I climbed to the top of my shrine, the place I call, "Cnochán Dara na Naomh" or "The Hillock of the Oak Tree of the Avatars." An ancient Scrub Oak rests there, a garland on the crown chakra of that sacred space. It is always the culmination of my daily pilgrimage. I rested my right hand on the weather-beaten bark and through my now-sensitized palm I could feel the heartbeat of the acorn that begot it; the slow powerful thump-thump-thump of the druid-tree.

So today I came full circle. Today, as I had done in my childhood, I smelled God, I felt God, I heard God, I saw God and I tasted God. After 61 years in this incarnation, I can say once again, "My God is a very sensible God!"

2

How God Flunked Law School

"If you judge people, you have no time to love them."
Mother Teresa

In the summer of 1965, I was temporarily possessed by the spirit of King Solomon, the wisest man who ever lived. I didn't seek out this gift, it was thrust upon me. I had just finished my first year in the seminary and was on summer vacation. It was that year, also, that saw the conclusion of Vatican II, but most of its decrees had not yet been promulgated. In particular the magic thinking about who could receive the consecrated host at mass and how to do it, was still in place.

It started one Sunday afternoon when our second-next-door neighbor, Hannah Donovan came to our house in a complete panic. She had her son, Paul, in tow. Paul was five years old and was constantly in trouble of one kind or another. But now he had really blown it! He was a big kid for his age, but it would be two more years before he would be prepared by the teachers to "make his First Holy Communion." That felt to Paul like a long time to wait. So on this Sunday morning, as pious parishioners lined up to approach the altar rails, where they would kneel with eyes closed, mouth open and tongue stuck out to receive the Jesus-filled wafer, Paul decided to join their ranks. He had seen the drill countless times and figured he had it down pat. So he took his place, stood on the kneeler to elevate his stature advancing his age a few years, closed his eyes and stuck out his tongue. Bingo! Pay day! He processed back to his seat, hands held in a holy steeple, while Jesus dissolved in his mouth. All of his family had gone to an earlier mass, so no one noticed the blasphemy until it was too late. A neighbor woman was the first to spot it. She grabbed his head and pried his jaws apart. Too late, Jesus had already disappeared down his gullet! No sign. So she marched him home and told the awful truth to his mother. They sat in horrified silence for several minutes, trying to estimate whether or not God's outrage at this blasphemy would be visited on all of Mayfield, or merely on the Donovan family. They thought about going to the priest, but feared automatic and immediate excommunication. Then, Hannah had a brain wave, "I'll bring him up to Seán ÓLaoire, he's on his way to becoming a priest. He's a neighbor we've known since he was a child and has known Paul since his birth. Maybe he'll be able to advise us." So that was why a procession of neighbors was now coming in our front gate with an unrepentant Paul being prodded along ahead of them.

My mother made tea for them while they poured out their distress. A secondary concern, it appears, was that, based on past performance, Paul was very likely to repeat this sin. When they had spent themselves and had finally run out of words, I asked if I could see Paul alone. So he and I retired to the back garden.

I asked him, "What did it taste like? He said, "It was kinda stale." I said, "You're absolutely right. Here is a chocolate, it tastes much better. Stay away from communion until they improve the recipe. I'll give you the nod when they do." He simply replied, "Okay." It made perfect sense to him. And it solved the possible recidivism, for he didn't attempt any more Eucharistic encounters until he was formally prepared for it two years later.

The news spread, so exactly two weeks later, May Crowley, who lived nearby came determinedly across the park with her eight-year-old son, Colm. Colm, it seems was also guilty of a Eucharistic mortal sin. He had been at communion that morning, as he was entitled to, having been prepared officially and having "made his First Holy Communion" a year before, but on the way back from the communion rail it was noted by several parishioners and his own family that he was having an oral wrestling match with the Messiah. Jesus was stuck resolutely to the roof of his mouth and no amount of tongue-twisting or jaw-gymnastics could dislodge him. Colm's face was going through all kinds of contortions and his head was jerking from side to side, like somebody with advanced neuropathy, but all to no avail. Jesus was hanging on for dear life like a rock climber on the face of the Eiger. So finally Colm did the only thing possible; a thing however which was mortally sinful; a thing that could speed his immortal soul to eternal perdition. He stuck his right index finger in his mouth and forcibly ejected his Lord and savior and swallowed him live. And the entire congregation had witnessed this sin.

So here they were again in our living room. May Crowley gave us all the graphic details as the mandatory tea was being prepared. What fascinated me most, however, was that throughout the entire proceedings she had a firm grip on Colm's right hand in such a way that his index finger stuck out on its own, separated forcibly from its fellows. It was as if she were afraid that this erring digit which had sinned by illegally touching the body of Jesus was now being held in solitary confinement lest it touch any secular object and thus compound Colm's error. By now his finger was bright red, partly from the pressure his mother was exerting on it, and partly, I suspect, through the nocebo effect (it you believe bad things will happen, they do) as a result of the dire predictions being enunciated by his terror-gripped mother. I asked him, "How does your finger feel?" He said, "It's hurting like crazy," as he turned a pained, fear-filled countenance on me.

I had another brainwave. So I announced to his mother, "Let's go down to the church, I know how to solve the problem." The church was only a two-minute walk from our house, so we set off in procession, me in the lead, followed by Colm and May Crowley, the latter still clamping her son's right index finger in a death grip. My own mother brought up the rear. We entered the side gate of the chapel yard and ascended the steps to the entranceway in front of the big swinging doors. At each side of these doors was a stone holy water font. I now took control of Colm's right hand and dunked it devotionally three times, with great solemnity into the font as I intoned, "In the name of the Father" (dunk) "and of the Son" (dunk) "and of the Holy Ghost" (dunk). The mothers responded, "Amen!"

I released Colm's hand and asked again "How does it feel now?" A very-much relieved Colm replied, "It's grand now; it isn't hurting me at all, at all!"

So we all went back to my house for more tea. And King Solomon went back to building temples, offering to bifurcate baby boys and to entertaining his locally grown and imported wives and countless concubines.

All of this begs the question, What happens when divine law gets mixed up with human laws and when human laws fossilize.

(A) God's Great Inferiority Complex

An inferiority complex can manifest in one of two ways, "straight-forwardly" as poor self-image, lack of self-esteem and self-deprecating hand-wringing Uriah Heep style protestations of unworthiness. Or it can appear in an over-compensatory fashion as arrogant, boastful self-promotion. The God of the Torah suffers from the latter form. Again and again he blows his own shofar, making promises that he cannot keep and claims that he can't substantiate. All in all he is a paper tiger, with a huge ego, bad temper and a pitiful track record as a provider.

He seduced the highly impressionable Abram from Ur of the Chaldees with promises of a land flowing with mild and honey. So Abram, at the tender age of 72, left his idol-maker father's house and followed this promise. Twice within his own lifetime, Abraham had to leave this "land flowing with milk and honey" because of famine and go elsewhere to avoid starvation. Not on milk and honey alone doth man live. It appears he also needs bread. Then in the days of Abraham's grandson Jacob, another famine drove the entire family to seek food and refuge in Egypt. The Egyptians welcomed them at first and then enslaved them for 450 years. In the 600 years between the times Abraham flourished (1850 BCE) and Moses flourished (1250 BCE) God was unable, 75 percent of the time, to protect his "chosen people." Over the next 1,300 years up to the time of Jesus, he didn't improve a whole lot on this dismal record; 40 years wandering in the desert complaining of lousy grub and bad water; 200 years trying to conquer the "promised land;" a civil war in 930 BCE, on the death of Solomon, which divided the country into two, Israel in the north, consisting of 10 tribes, and Judah in the south consisting of two tribes; 721 BCE the northern kingdom is wiped out by the Assyrian Empire, the 10 tribes deported and never heard of again; in 598 BCE the southern kingdom is overrun by the Babylonian Empire, Jerusalem ransacked, the temple destroyed and the two remaining tribes exiled; in 529 BCE they are allowed to return when the Persian Empire overran the Babylonians; they had some semblance of autonomy until Alexander the Great's armies conquered all before them beginning in 333 BCE and instigated Greek rule; in 187 BCE the Maccabees revolted, and self-rule was initiated until two warring brothers invited the Romans in to settle their dispute; the Romans obliged in 70 BCE and stayed for a few hundred years. And from the time of Jesus, to our own times, God's record is even more pathetic: in 133 CE the Bar Kokba revolt was put down viciously by the Romans (who had flattened Jerusalem and the second temple 62 years before); the Jews were in exile up until the founding of the modern state of Israel by a United Nation's vote in 1948. No sooner had they achieved nationhood again after a 2,000-year-long period of foreign rule or exile, than they were attacked by five Arab armies who vowed to drive them into the sea. This effort was repeated in 1967 and in 1973. And very recently we've had the Intifada and the war with Hezbollah.

All in all, this God is a pathetic, little loudmouth with a batting average in the low teens. But here he is in today's reading from Deuteronomy, Chapter 4, offering his "new deal" to Moses and his people. First, he boasts, "I am more powerful than any other God; I am wiser than any other God; I am more just than any other God; I am closer to my people than any other God to his people." Then the empty promises, "I will give you a land of your own; and I will protect you forever from all of your enemies. Finally, the payback, "You have to keep my law and promise never to attempt to change any part of it."

(B) The Fossilization of Law

It's bad enough that we bow the knee to this caricature of a God whom we ourselves have created; it's bad enough that we really believe that the laws we find in the bible actually emanated from the intelligent ineffable source of all that is; but the final indignity is that we fossilize these laws by elevating the letter while ignoring the spirit. Religions of all stripes are replete with ridiculous examples of this. For example, a Jewish hen who lays an egg on the Sabbath has thus broken the injunction against servile work, and therefore whoever eats this egg is an accessory to her crime.

Saint Paul, who was never renowned for his retiring, self-effacing personality, claims that his version of law and gospel is the only authentic one, and if anybody else (even an angel) comes preaching a different line, people are to refuse to believe.

But the Roman Catholic Church is in a class of its own when it comes to turning human precept into divine decree. So, from the people who gave you the "how many angels can dance on the head of a pin?" debate, here are some beauties: Limbo, a place or state of natural happiness where un-baptized babies spend eternity, bereft of the vision of God. Presumably they are fed intravenously and wear self-cleaning diapers. Purgatory, a spiritual de-lousing facility, where you can get into the express line, if somebody on Earth gains a plenary indulgence coupon and names you as the beneficiary. Hell for all eternity for knowingly eating a hotdog on a Friday. Hell for all eternity for failing on any given Sunday to attend a mass in a language you don't understand, celebrated by a priest who has his back to you. Hell for all eternity for the failure to be born Catholic, or willfully refusing to become a Catholic once you learned of it's divine hegemony.

And then there was the fine print. Take respect for the consecrated host, for instance, to revisit crimes and situations similar to those of Paul Donovan and Colm Crowley. Every Catholic Church had, outside the door of the sacristy, a pipe (perhaps six inches in diameter) sunken in the ground with the top four inches showing. It was called the sacrarium. If a sacred cloth (e.g., a purificator or a stole) needed to be put out of commission because of stains or tears, it would be ceremoniously burned and the ashes placed in the sacrarium.

One day in a theology class, the Reverend Professor asked one of the students, "Mr. Murphy, what would you do if you were an ordained priest who had just pronounced the words of consecration over the bread "Hoc est enim corpus meum," only to have a mouse climb onto the altar, steal the consecrated host and escape into his mouse-hole?" Without batting an eye, Mr. Murphy, who was an even more dedicated comic than myself, replied, "I would burn down the church, father, and put the ashes in the sacrarium!"

There was a morbid fascination with protecting the consecrated host from mishap, with all kinds of delicate situations being prophylactically prepared for e.g., "What would you do if, while giving communion to a woman with a low cut neckline to her blouse, the host were to fall into her cleavage?" Or, "suppose, just as you were pronouncing the sacred words of consecration over the wafer, a bread truck were to pass by the open door of the church?" To safeguard against this Eucharistic-meals-on-wheels scenario it was decreed that only a bread container (paten or ciborium) that was actually sitting on the corporal (a roughly 12" by 12" cloth placed atop the altar linen) was impacted by the words of consecration; so, no sourdough Jesus or sweet baguette savior.

Each group attempts to retrofit great teachers from the past with its present set of prejudices, beliefs and dogma. I recently came across a new-age community based on Hindu teaching but with a great regard for Jesus—*their* Jesus, a Jesus who, they tried to convince me, was a vegan and non-drinker. When I quoted passages from the gospels in which Jesus coached his disciples how to fish, cooked fish for them and ate fish with them (John Chapter 21); they told me I was making it up. When I pointed out to them that Jesus not only drank wine, he made wine on one occasion, 180 gallons of it! (John Chapter 2), they told me it was non-alcoholic wine. A typical case of "Here's my belief, don't bother me with facts."

It seems to me that there are four main reasons why the spirit of the law gets calcified into mere human commandments. Firstly, it happens academically, or out of necessity and soon becomes a tradition, then a *sacred* tradition and finally an immutable divine decree.

Let me give you two examples of this. A friend of mine, Maureen Locke, as a young girl was being groomed for domesticity by her mother. This involved, as part of the syllabus, learning how to cook. Maureen progressed quickly, so soon her mother felt she was ready to learn how to do the Sunday roast. Each Sunday the family had potatoes, cabbage and a hunk of beef. Her mother took the hunk of beef, snipped off the two ends and then placed all three pieces on the cooking tray and slipped it into the oven. "There," she said, "That's how it's done!" Maureen asked, "Why did you snip off the two ends?" To which her mother replied, "That's how you have to cook roast beef!" "But why," insisted Maureen, "they're all on the same tray?" "Child," her mother patiently and patronizingly intoned, "When you are cooking roast beef you have to snip off the two end pieces. That's how you have to do it." "But it doesn't make any sense to me" Maureen protested. "Who taught you how to do it like that?" "Why, your grandmother did," replied her mother. "I'm going to ask grandma, then" said Maureen. "Go ahead," said her mother. "She'll tell you exactly what I told you." A few weeks later, Maureen paid a visit to her grandmother and explained her predicament, finally asking in frustration, "So why grandma, do we have to snip off the two ends before we cook the roast beef?" "Well, it's very simple, child, when I was teaching your mother how to cook, we were quite poor. We only had a tiny oven. So in order to get a piece of roast beef into it, I had to snip off the two ends and arrange the three pieces on the tray, so they could all fit in!" Problem solved—necessity, in this case was the mother not only of invention, but also of tradition.

Here's another example for you. The ordinations in Kiltegan, where I trained for eight years to be a priest, used to be held on Easter Sunday each year. The newly ordained priests, however, remained in the seminary until June, and at that time they were given their mission appointments (Nigeria, Kenya, Brazil, etc.) by the Superior General. So they said their masses daily in the seminary. Now before the decrees of Vatican II were promulgated there was no such thing as con-celebration, rather each priest said his own mass with a congregation of at least one—typically an acolyte (altar boy). So your typical church had 15 or so little chapels, each with an altar, and between 7 a.m. and 9 a.m. daily all of the priests said their "private" masses. Since these chapels abutted each other, there would be a constant hum of priests audibly intoning the ancient Latin rubrics. Lots of altar servers were needed. In April of 1965, as I was finishing my first year in the seminary and just a few months before my King Solomon experiences, it fell to me to assist the newly-ordained Father Frankie McAuliffe in his daily masses. The first day, I laid out his vestments for him, set the altar, arranged the sacramentary and the lectionary, prepared the wine, water and bread, and put my little bell in position. Frankie bowed, kissed the altar and began, "Introibo ad altare Dei . . ." (I will enter unto the altar of God.) And I responded, "Ad deum qui laetificat juventutem meam" (To God who gives joy to my youth) and we set off at a healthy gallop. There were no incidents until we had finished the offertory prayers and then Frankie, noticed with deep consternation that I had forgotten to light the two altar candles before we began the mass. He looked furtively around to see if any of the other priests had spotted this grievous error. Apparently they hadn't. Each one was bent to his task, engrossed in the mystery. Frankie whispered to me, "Light the candles, we have to start again." Blushing deeply, I got the taper and matches and we fired up the two candles. "Introibo . . ." said Frankie once again "Ad deum . . ." I replied with relief and conviction.

Now Frankie was a very bright man, a very good theologian and deeply spiritual to boot, but in 1965 he was still stuck in the magical thinking of the theological times. The church had very definite requirements about the conduct of the Eucharist. And one of these requirements was that you had to have two *lit* 65 percent bee's wax candles, in order to celebrate a valid mass. One candle would *not* do; candles whose composition was less than 65 percent bee's wax would not do; and 140 *unlit* candles, even if they were 92 percent bee's wax would not do.

Why candles at all? Because, presumably, long before electricity or gas or even hurricane lamps had been invented, priests needed light to read the sacred texts. Necessity once more had birthed twins, and one of the twins, law, had become divine decree.

I think that the second major reason for the calcification of law is simple hygiene. In the case of the ancient Israelites, their 613 laws were composed at a time when they were newly escaped slaves, living in the desert for 40 years. They were visited by all manner of medical and sanitary issues, with infectious conditions being the primary killer of those who survived the frequent violent clashes with desert tribes. So Moses, practical man that he was, created a "community-based health-care" system with an emphasis on preventive medicine. It was a stroke of genius and saved countless lives. It may well be the origin of the adage, "cleanliness is next to Godliness." But good and effective and life-saving as these decrees are/were, they did not emanate from the ineffable Godhead as mandatory injunctions carrying huge criminal penalties if ignored. You may as well claim that the precept "Thou shalt wear condoms for all acts of intercourse" is a divine decree, because with the AIDS epidemic it could save millions of lives today. That is one medical safeguard that the Catholic Church is *not* likely to insert into its slate of divine commandments.

Many of these sanitary and medical issues, of course, carry moral content, which is not the same as insisting that they are divine decree with eternal punishment for the offenders.

The third major reason, I believe, for how law is abused is the will to control. Despots, oligarchies and pyramidical systems learned a long time ago that if you can convince the "massa damnata" of the divine origin of a precept, you can impose it on them, no matter how difficult, demeaning or enslaving it might be. This insight has been cynically employed in all of the successful institutions of history—political, economic and religious. The "divine right of kings" is such a concept. It matters not that historically, every royal lineage is a product of the "satin shoe coming down the stairs and the hob-nailed boot going up the stairs." In other words, each of those ruling families were once bloodthirsty commoners who violently wrested control from earlier blue-blooded aristocrats. But once the commoners can be convinced that kings are appointed by divine will, revolts against their excesses are less likely to happen. The United States of America of 2006 is still suffering majorly from this syndrome in its support of the current disastrous political and economic regime.

And the fourth great reason for law degradation is, I believe, a fundamentalist mindset that interprets metaphoric musing as literal legislation. I remember once going into a shop in Nakuru, Kenya and seeing a white-turbaned man of the Wakorino. The Wakorino is a very fundamentalist African Christian sect. As almost everybody does in Kenya, I reached out my hand in greeting. He quickly shoved his hand behind his back and said, "No! I cannot greet you." "Why?" I asked. "Because" he said, "the bible says, 'greet nobody on the way.'" I was well aware of this statement. It was part of Jesus' instructions to his twelve disciples, when, while he was still alive, he sent them out on a trial missionary run. He wanted to impress several things upon them. Firstly, to trust in God, so there was no need to take a lot of money, food or spare clothes, but rather expect that their listeners would meet their needs. Secondly, he insisted that they not put a lot of energy into trying to convince individuals and villagers who were inimical to their message, but rather to move on to greener pastures. And thirdly, not to waste time dawdling along the road chatting about the weather or politics with strangers, but rather to stay focused, because the time was short.

In typical Jesus fashion, he enjoined these parameters in wild exaggeration. And in typical fashion the synoptics all reported different and contradictory versions of these commands.

Mark (the earliest writer) says, "You can take a walking stick and sandals, but you may not take a bag or food or a second tunic with you." Matthew (written ten years later) says, "no" to everything—no walking stick, sandals, money, bag, food or second tunic. Luke (written 10 years after Matthew) agrees fully with Matthew—no's across the board. And he adds a special "No" all of his own—"No greeting people on the road." Obviously, by Luke's time (around 90 CE) there was even more need to hurry and a greater urgency not to waste time.

So I said to my turbaned friend, "Where in the bible does it say you should not greet people?" He replied, "I can't remember, but I know it's there." "Well," I said, "I can make it easy for you. You'll find it in Luke Chapter 10. So go home and read it for yourself, and you'll find that according to Luke, Jesus *also* said you must not carry a walking stick, you must not wear sandals and you must not carry money. So what are you doing in this shop with 10 Kenya shillings in your hand? And why are you wearing sandals? And why are you carrying a walking stick? The shopkeeper, a Sikh gentleman was greatly amused at this exchange, and my poor Wakorino was utterly confused. His stance is typical of what fundamentalist thinking does to "the word of God."

Each group wants to believe it has the final version of God's law, which is given in a special language, to a chosen people via the final prophet. But, of course, there is no final version of God's law or word; there are only more elegant and adequate versions of how infinite, unfathomable mystery walks among peoples at subsequent stages of evolution.

And there is no special language—though each has its strengths and weaknesses. Each language is capable of articulating the full range of human experiences. God does not have a mother tongue nor did she have to take a course in English-as-a-second-language. In spite of attempts to claim it is Sanskrit or Hebrew, Greek or Latin, Arabic or Tibetan, each of these is equally incapable of encompassing the mystery of which only post-language spirituality is an adequate medium.

And there is no final prophet. "God" will continue to send new ones as long as the manifest realms exist; and they will always be counter-cultural and upsetting to us; and we will probably continue to vilify and kill them.

And there are no chosen people because all peoples and all species and all creation are equally precious to spirit.

(C) Jesus Gets Really Upset

In today's gospel, I think that Jesus' choice of words shows that he was really upset at this deification of human precept. The context is the following: His reputation as a preacher and as a healer was beginning to spread, so the theocratic authorities in Jerusalem send emissaries to investigate him. What the investigators immediately saw was that Jesus' disciples were not keeping "the law." In particular, they saw the disciples eating with unwashed hands. For his non-Jewish readers Mark goes on to explain that Jews always wash their hands as far as the elbows before eating or after coming from the market; and that they wash cups and jugs, kettles and beds. All of which is very good, hygienic and healthy, but none of which is attributable to divine Obsessive Compulsive Disorder. They come to Jesus to reprimand him for his disciples' behavior, and he flips his lid. He calls them a bunch of hypocrites and brings out the big gun, scripture itself. Quoting Isaiah he says, "These people honor me with their lips but their hearts are far from me. They teach mere human precept and ignore the weightier things of the law—justice and compassion." He goes on to cite a specific practice in which these lawyers have set aside a divine directive to honor and support parents in favor of a clergy-friendly precept to support the temple. In this twist, a person mandated by God to look out for his mother and father could declare his money and possessions "Korban," that is "dedicated to the Temple" and then he could dodge his obligation to his parents. There was a further loophole, that even Enron would have been proud of; after his parents died, and his "obligation" to them was ended, he could then rescind the "korban" and keep all of his wealth to himself. This could be called "eating your korban and having it, too."

So Jesus went off on them. The gospel accounts of this incident are written, of course, in Greek. Jesus probably was using Aramaic, but Mark, in order to show Jesus' outrage uses very strong language. When Jesus went on to proclaim, "It is not what goes into a man that makes him unclean, but what comes out of him e.g., murderous, lustful, rapacious thoughts. What a man eats goes into his stomach and from there gets dumped in the "aphedon." Now Greek had many words signifying a latrine, long drop, toilet, water closet etc. But "aphedon" is none of these prissy words; "aphedon" literally translates as "shit house." Mark was a soldier so the crudity may have been his; or Jesus may have actually used an equivalent crudity in Aramaic to signify the depth of his frustration with what the lawyers had done to the spirit of God's word.

His insight, of course, was spot-on. It is from the individual heart that egoic thoughts, addictions and evil intentions come forth. It is from the heart of a culture that oppression and discrimination, caste and class systems come forth. It is from the heart of nationalism that conquest and prejudice and the notions of chosen and damned peoples come forth. And it is from the heart of the species that our savage exploitation of nature and the animal kingdom comes forth.

(D) The Law Verses the law

In California a new law (AB32) has just been passed. It mandates the toughest guidelines in the entire United States on the reduction of agents and activities that produce global warming. It is a good law.

In the United States right now we labor under the Patriot Act, which has gutted humanity's greatest experiment with democracy. It is *bad* law.

So what constitutes good law and what constitutes bad law. Here are a few ideas. There are universal laws, laws which long preceded the advent of the human species on the cosmic scene. I believe they are of three types: first, the laws that governed creation, the big bang and the beginnings. In Hinduism this would be the domain of Brahma, the creative aspect of God. Second, are the laws that regulate and sustain the universe as we know it; these strive to maintain homeostasis. In Hinduism, this work is done by Vishnu, the sustaining principle of God. And third, there are the laws governing ongoing evolution and change. This, in Hinduism, is the function of Shiva, the "destructive" face of God, the one who radically reconfigures.

Having said that, I want to propose that human laws are only valid to the extent that they, firstly, are in alignment with these cosmic laws; secondly, assist humans in coming into alignment with their own inner divinity; thirdly, entrust humans with the responsibility of being stewards of creation; and, fourthly, attempt to end suffering, for all species, in our world.

There is increasing evidence that cosmic laws themselves may be evolving. It's not just that the universe is evolving, but that the very principles themselves that shepherd that process may also, be changing. If that is so, how very important then that we have the courage to examine and if necessary, change our perceptions of divine laws and human precepts. So Jesus proclaimed much to his listener's horror, "the son of man (i.e. a human being) is lord even of the Sabbath. This "Law of the Sabbath" is, among the 613 laws of Torah, the single most important. And here is Jesus proclaiming, that not even the Sabbath law is above the human.

The history of humanity, however, has been a grudging, kicking-against-the-goad, petulant attempt to prevent all such re-perceiving. It was "in spite of" not because of religious law that slavery was ended; and it was "in spite of" not because of religious law that women, in the United States, got the right to vote. And it is because of religious law that Roman Catholic women are still barred from priesthood. In Maggie Thatcher's inimitably strident and arrogant words, "The law is the law is the law."

In the hands of fearful, small-minded bureaucrats, cosmic law quickly became a plethora of paranoid precepts. But the universe cannot be thwarted, Spirit cannot be blocked, and evolution will inexorably overcome even the most intransigent of obstacle-makers. So human laws are good when they are in alignment with life; and they are bad when they obstruct evolution's dance with light.

I want to examine the connection between morality and law. It strikes me that spirituality is frequently reduced to religion, religion in turn is reduced to morality, and morality fixates on sexuality. This is obvious even with a cursory glance at human history; and it is a glaring fact in what happened in the 2002 elections in our country. We saw what happened when unscrupulous politicians got in bed with fundamentalist Christians: the great issues facing our country were reduced to "gay marriage." This was then piously called a "faith-based response." When have you ever heard right-wing Christians, those who want to make us a "Christian nation once again," when have you ever heard one of them yell, "Help us get back to the teachings of Jesus who said, 'Love your enemies, do good to those who hate you and pray for those who slander you?'" No, it will be statements like, "God has withdrawn his protection from America because we have permitted gay rights and abortion . . ."

That said, sexuality, reproduction and the human life span are important moral issues whether they involve artificial contraception, abortion, stem-cell research, right-to-die, gay marriage or pre- or extra-marital sex. And we need legislation to guide us in all these arenas. But they are *not* the great moral issues of our times. The truly great moral issues of our times, I believe are: ecology—protecting and nurturing the planet that protects and nurtures us; dealing with overpopulation, before we rip each other apart for dwindling resources advertised by a growing consumerism and hoarded by a diminishing oligarchy; warfare, a 5,000-year-old obsession with violence as the way to end violence; poverty, the shameful sight of hoarding food, at a cost of billions of dollars, when it could, in the immortal words of Martin Luther King, Jr., "Be stored for free in the wrinkled bellies of the starving babies of the world."

The truly huge moral issues of our times are healthcare, housing and education for all human beings without regard to color or creed, nationality or language.

The application of cosmic law, in our times, is the enactment of regulations governing all of these concerns. Lesser moral issues will easily fall in line and be attended to in this model. And health issues will flow from that, but will not be given the force of divine decree.

True human law will attempt to end suffering for all humans at all stages of life, from conception to excarnation. Truly compassionate law will attempt to end suffering for all the species on the planet. And truly divine law will attempt to end the suffering of the planet itself which is gasping for air and sweating to death.

It, will, in a single statement, raise the spiritual consciousness of the children of Adam from magical and mythic, from dogmatic and sectarian, from nationalistic and tribal beliefs to full cosmic, mystical union.

3

The Time Before . . .
(October 23, 2001)

God began to dim the lights in my outdoor bedroom at precisely 6:05 pm this evening. I watched His retreating figure make its way down behind the western mountains. It would be another hour before total darkness engulfed me. In the meantime, I could see the ever-diminishing glow of His sun-lamp. He did, however, leave me the half-moon as a night light.

I stood up, on my outdoor bed, atop Meditation Rock, raised my arms aloft and soulfully sang The Lord's Prayer in my Mother Tongue:

> Ár nAthair
> atá ar neamh.
> Go naofar t'ainm,
> go dtaga do ríocht,
> go ndéantar do thoil ar an dtalamh,
> mar a dhéantar ar neamh.
> Ár n-arán laethiúil
> tabhair dúinn inniu.
> Agus maith dhúinn ár bhfiacha
> mar mhaithfimidne dhár bhfichiúna féin.
> 'Is ná lig sinn i gcathú, ach saor sinn ón olc.
> Amen.

Then I shouted after Him:
Tell me a bedtime story!?

He chuckled, and over His shoulder He said:
I'll send you a dream instead!

Promise?
I pleaded.

As sure as God is my witness!
He fired back.

And He was as good as His word. Here is the dream He sent me:

I am a newborn human infant, gurgling happily in awe of this new home of mine. The oceanic bliss of the uterine darkness has become a fairyland of lights and sounds, tastes and smells, feelings and emotions. I am lying on my back; four long tentacles are waving above me, each of them ending in five lesser tentacles; they are fascinating! They seem to be dancing to some divine music, weaving and undulating to an inaudible melody. Every so often one of them approaches me and I grasp it in my mouth and suck appreciatively. But the music demands that it eventually be released to join its fellows in the wild.

Now, I am suddenly caught in a time vortex that plummets me back at dizzying speed into an earlier era of my DNA.

I am a newborn plant, smiling ecstatically at the sun, in awe of this new home of mine. The oceanic bliss of the subsoil's darkness has become a fairyland of light and sensation. I am standing erect, having pushed myself aloft from rooted legs. Many long tentacles are waving above me, each of them ending in green heart-shaped petals, whose cores are yellow flowers. They are fascinating! They seem to be dancing to some divine music, weaving and undulating to an inaudible melody. Every so often one of them approaches me and I smell its fragrance. But the music demands that it eventually be released to join its fellows in the wild.

Once again, I am suddenly caught in a time vortex that plummets me back at dizzying speed into a still earlier era of my DNA.

I am a newborn sea anemone, moving sensually in the warm waters, in awe of this new home of mine. The fairyland of the Life-smith has become an oceanic bliss of deep, silent ecstasy. I am holding tenaciously to a rock. Silk-sided tentacles choreographed by invisible currents are waving above me, each of them ending in multicolored finger tips. They are fascinating.

They seem to be dancing to some divine music, weaving and undulating to an inaudible melody. Every so often one of them approaches me, bearing a gift which I pop into my mouth. I lick the residual taste on the generous finger-tip. But the music demands that it eventually be released to join its fellows in the wild.

For the third time, I am suddenly caught in a time vortex that plummets me back at dizzying speed to the earliest era of my DNA.

I am a newborn star, beaming brilliantly into the pristine darkness, in awe of this new home of mine. The fairyland of the Sun-smith has become the interstellar void of deep intergalactic space. I am pulsating with light and with life. Million-mile-long tentacles, obedient to the baton of the wind-master of the cosmos are waving above me, each of them ending in rainbow-colored solar flares. Waving lengths of light, wavelengths of light. They are fascinating. They seem to be dancing to some divine music, weaving and undulating to an inaudible melody. Every so often one of them approaches me, and I wrap it comfortingly about me. But the music demands that it eventually be released to join its fellows in the wild.

For the final time, I am suddenly caught in a time vortex that plummets me back at dizzying speed to the earliest era before there was DNA.

The last splink of light from God's retreating lamp went out, on my bed atop Meditation Rock. There was utter silence and total darkness.

Then God whispered:
Now, do you see!?

4

Pat the Yank

"It is in the shelter of each other that the people live."
Irish Proverb

For almost 150 years Ireland's three main exports were people, potatoes
and priests—in descending order of importance! Beginning with the "Great
Famine" of 1845, 1846 and 1847, the population of Ireland plummeted from
eight million to four million people, through starvation and emigration.
The infamous "Coffin Ships" took the travelers across the Atlantic in the
dark bowels of vessels which had long since passed their prime. Many did
not survive the trip, but for those who did, "Amerikay" was the land of
freedom and opportunity. The vast bulk of them never again saw Ireland;
hence, the invention of the "American Wake." We Irish have long been
famous for our wakes, three-day affairs that snubbed the nose at death
and defied it to do its damnedest; we would not be cowed, demoralized or
beaten into submission. Nay, rather, we would celebrate death with music,
food, clay pipes, alcohol and dancing, and even the corpse was expected
to participate in that latter activity. "Breakfast at Bernie's" is but an insipid
imitation of an Irish wake.

When it became obvious that emigration to America was a final farewell
to the "Emerald Isle," we came up with the American wake. It had all the
trappings of your normal wake, except that the "corpse" (emigrant-to-be)

was expected to participate in the music, the food, the clay pipes (dudeens) and alcohol, and not just the dancing.

Almost none of them ever came back. Instead they would regularly send letters and money to support the family at home and to pay the ship's fare for the next wave of emigrants. They wrote songs and poems, short stories and novels about the "auld sod," and they cried salty tears into pint glasses of brown ale, but almost none of them ever came home again. None, that is, except "Pat the Yank." Pat the Yank was in his late 70's when I first met him, at age four in 1950. He lived on our street, and was only called "Pat the Yank" behind his back, though I suspect he knew about it and wouldn't have minded particularly if his birth certificate were altered to reflect this new sobriquet. Pat had gone to America at the turn of the century when he was in his 20's. They gave him one hell of a wake, and off he went to vomit up his guts in the belly of a tramp steamer and make his fortune where the very streets are paved with gold. And he did fairly well, but a year was enough for him, and home he came shortly after the first anniversary of his wake to settle down and spend the rest of his life in the town of his birth. He quickly established himself as the resident guru on all things American. Whether your question was about politics, geography, history, style of clothes or modes of transport, at the other side of the Atlantic, Pat was your man. And so he became known as "Pat the Yank." This started off as a cynical comment on the fact that he wasn't able to survive the States, but as his audiences grew in size and longevity, it was spoken with genuine admiration.

A typical evening would find Pat seated at his own fireside, pipe in mouth, his wife sitting across the hearth from him knitting a "gansey" (sweater) for one of their 35 grandchildren, and 12 or 15 locals on chairs, stools or haunches listening to his stories and plying him with questions.

I remember one such evening. Somebody asked, "Pat, tell me this and tell me no more, is the pace of life very fast in America?" Pat threw the questioner a pitying glance, took the pipe out of his mouth, squirted tobacco-colored spittle into the glowing turf, where it sizzled like a newly-arrived sinner in hell, and replied, "Fast? Fast is it, you ask? I'll tell you about 'fast.' It's not like us here, God love us. Take the Cork County Council for instance. You see a pothole in the road, small enough to step over. The Council sends out five men to review the situation. These boys will convene around it, discuss it, debate it, draw sketches with their shovels and then break for tea. After an hour, they'll assemble again and approach the problem from another angle, discussing the pros, but mainly the cons. Then they'll break for lunch. Lunch is always a leisurely affair and could take up to two hours to let the repast settle comfortably in the stomach. Then they're back at their task tackling some heretofore un-recognized difficulty in the job. Everybody will have to have his say, and that will carry them comfortably to the afternoon teatime, which will last for another hour. By the time that break is over, 'tis hardly worth getting serious about the job, cause now 'tis only half an hour to quitting time. So, reluctantly, they gather up their shovels and bid a good evening to the pothole, promising to 'be back bright and early tomorrow morning.' True to their word 'bright and early' at 9:45 a.m. they're at the task again, brainstorming, pooh-poohing each other's suggestions and determined not to actually begin filling in the pothole until they achieve consensus. This process will take all of the first week. Now they're ready for action. They spit in their hands, grab their shovels and to a man they agree it's now time to go fetch the gravel and the tar. Bringing these items to the site, however, is never straightforward. The size of the gravel has to be calculated depending on the number of donkey-and-carts that use that particular section of roadway; the prevailing winds have to be taken into account; and the altitude factored in. But definitely by the end of the second week all materials have been assembled. Now it's a 'flurry-of-activity' time. The pothole is so small that only one man can work at a time while the others lean on their shovels, shouting advice, criticism and encouragement—all at the same time. In the course of these exertions, one of them is bound to 'put out his back,' and the job abandoned while they all take him down to the 'North Infirmary' debating the likely 'workmen's compensation' that will come of it. The hole may now stand abandoned for several months, welcoming cart wheels into its ever-burgeoning maw. Eventually, the original group may come back, only to decide that it is now far too big a job for a team of five. Intense negotiations with 'the gaffer' over the next week will finally result in a generously increased bunch of commandoes, fortified by 'danger money,' because anything could happen in attempting to tackle a chasm of this size. Six months have now gone by and all the gravel has been stolen by little boys as ammunition for their catapults. Hanam an diabhail (my soul to the devil) but a Council worker's job is never done!"

Here Pat the Yank spat once more into the fire, sucked a few times on his pipe and then continued, "Well, I can tell you one thing for nothing, it's not like that in the United States of Amerikay." I remember one morning, 'twas about 6:20 a.m. and I was passing through Manhattan on my way to work. There was an almighty gang of men digging a hole in the ground. They told me 'twas the foundations for a brand-new skyscraper. They had diggers and dumpsters, excavators and lorries, trucks and wheelbarrows, steel cables and cement bags, lumber (that's what the yanks call timber), hosepipes and concrete blocks. There were guys scurrying up and scurrying down, gaffers (a whole bunch of them), shouting orders in several different languages and one geezer with a set of plans that looked like the Book of

Kells. I'm telling you I was impressed, but I couldn't stand idly about for hadn't I work to do myself? So off I went, and that day I got some overtime, so I didn't get home until nearly 10 o'clock that night. I passed along the same street in Manhattan and I declare to the Lord God almighty, they had the skyscraper finished! Done; all 100 floors of it! There were even people already *living* in it. Well, just as I was passing the front door of it, I saw this poor "angashore" (pitiful type) being thrown out on the sidewalk. I sez to him, 'whazza matter, buddy?' He sez, 'Oh, I'm after getting evicted because I'm in arrears with my rent.' That's America for you! Fast? You have no idea in God's green Earth what fast is, until you spend time in the States!"

And he stuck the pipe in his gob and looked nostalgically into the flames, imagining, no doubt, how his fortune might have grown to millionaire proportions, if it weren't for the fact that he had chosen instead to come back to Erin to educate the natives.

(A) What Shape is this Universe of Ours?

There are two answers to that question. God lives in a three-cornered universe, while we live in an L-shaped universe. The three corners of God's universe are Being-Knowing-Bliss, or the Isness of God, God's total self-knowledge, and the utter contentment God experiences in Herself. Put another way the three corners are the Creative, Sustaining and Destructive aspects of God's relationship to His own handiwork. Hinduism calls these Brahma (the creator), Vishnu (the sustainer) and Shiva (the destroyer.) Physics might refer to these as the laws of evolution, homeostasis and entropy.

All life, as we understand it, comes from light, and light is an emanation of love. So *we* live in this L-shaped universe; Love, Light and Life. If we inhabit the same universe as God, then, perhaps it's a three-cornered, L-shaped universe.

Beginning with God, who is the Primal Energy, the ineffable, in-articulateable, transcendent ground of all being, there is an emanation that becomes the void, the pregnant womb of the unmanifest. This, in turn, gives birth to all the manifest realms, which I could divide into three categories; physical realms e.g., planets, asteroids, rocks; non-physical realms e.g., the states of angelic beings, pure intelligence; and "mixed-realms," which are partially physical and partially non-physical e.g., the realms of extra terrestrials or extra biological entities, as well as Earth beings. This latter group (Earth beings) emerged about 3.7 billion years ago from a realm that up to then was "merely" a physical realm (the third rock from the sun). First this rock produced single-celled organisms, and, later, multi-celled organisms. Then about 700 million years ago came the great sea creatures that explored and played in the murky depths until 400 million years ago when some really intrepid explorers among them took the first tentative steps onto terra firma. Mostly they stayed, though some (e.g., dolphins) eventually (like Pat the Yank) decided to go back home. These land creatures went through lots of incarnations from reptiles to birds to mammals. The mammals experimented further, throwing up the primates, then the hominids, then homo erectus, homo sapiens and, about 200,000 years ago, in East Africa, anatomically modern humans, who today number 6.5 billion members.

To revisit the course of this journey, we might employ a telescope to trace the vestigial evidence of this void-emanated, big bang. But just as easily we might choose to use a microscope. The human organism consists of a bunch of organs (heart, liver, lungs, eyes . . .), all of which are composed of cells, consisting of molecules made up of atoms, containing a nucleus which "reduces" to pure energy again. So if you start with a human and go up, using a telescope, or go down, using a microscope, you arrive at the very same energy field. Truly we live in a system whose center is everywhere and whose perimeter is nowhere.

(B) Why Travel, You're Already There!

So, we can start anywhere, and then head off in any direction; either way we always arrive at God. In fact "arrive at" is actually a misnaming of the facts, because at every step of the journey there is *only* God manifesting; and the traveler, herself, is also a manifestation of God.

God was in the place you left, as you began your search for God. In fact God *was* the place in which you began your search for Him. And God was in all of the way-stations you passed as you continued on your God-seeking safari. In fact God was all aspects of all of those places. And God was in the destination, where your pilgrimage ended and where you declared, "Ah, here She finally is!" In fact, God *was* that place and all of its facets. There was never any need to set out on the search; if you had the eyes to see, She was there from the beginning, and from before the beginning of your quest. In his Gnostic gospel, Thomas says, "Lift a stone and I am there; split a log and I am there."

The journey, then, is merely a metaphor for the process of waking up to the preexisting and always existing reality that God is, and that only God is. The eye that is looking for God is God's own eye—and *you* are that eye.

5

Chapman Creek
(November 17, 2003)

I have picked my way laboriously up the steep newly greening hillside, using my walking staff to gain purchase in the freshly moistened soil. The chemise is prickly, but my jacket is bearing the brunt of the assault. Occasionally, however, it offers an impenetrable wall, and then, humbly, I crawl underneath, between its unyielding legs. I always wear gloves for these safaris, because I frequently have to pull myself upwards, and many a thorn and many a poison oak leaf would be happy to repay my grasping.

It finally rained last week, so at least I can gain a foothold. I am aiming for a clearing halfway up the hill, which I spotted from the trail by Chapman Creek. A little winded, I am now arrived. It was well worth the effort. I am looking southwest. To my right the sun is hovering about an hour above the horizon and, in a shaft of light, an utterly invisible angel is juggling 25 almost-invisible gnats in an excellently crafted piece of choreography. Not to be outdone, several more equally invisible angels are imitating this performance with troupes of 20 and 30 gymnast-gnats.

The brook is chatting noisily to itself, commenting on the rocks it is rounding, and the willow branches that bob and weave and dip into its waters. It is talking quite loudly about a huge redwood tree, which fell across it several years ago, and that still straddles its banks and lies embedded up the entire side of the hillside to the trail, which I left some 15 minutes ago.

It is a fascinating dialogue: the water-ahead forewarning the water-to-come of the sights that await it, and the water-to-come comparing notes with the water-ahead to ensure that nothing was missed. They will keep up this chatter until they reach the great Pacific Ocean, and then go speechless with awe.

To my left is the ramrod-straight shaft of a naked tree, rising out of the soil near the creek like the mast of a stranded schooner. Not a branch, nor a twig, nor even a leaf interrupts its bare skin. It hasn't been alive for years, and red-crested woodpeckers feast on its colonies of grubs and worms, but nobody told it that it is dead, so it stands proudly erect like an old veteran of the Great War standing to attention in his underwear while the radio plays his national anthem.

6

Are You Ready for Your Earth Mission?

"It is good to have an end to journey toward;
but it is the journey that matters in the end."
Ursula K. LeGuin

Once I got to be present in the launching area, to see the launching pad, all of the instruments, mission control, engineers, even the astronauts. It was actually on Monday, January 30th 2006, and I was there for nearly four hours. But it wasn't in Houston, or Cape Canaveral or in the wastelands of a super-secret Siberian site. It was in Berkeley, in a four-hour hypnotic regression conducted by a psychologist friend of mine, one of the founders of the Haight-Ashbury Free Psychological Clinic. And for most of the regression I was in a bardo state, the state between lifetimes. While I was in this state, I asked to visit the launching area and my request was granted.

The excitement there was greater than anything I have ever experienced: souls about to "depart" for planet Earth, and their well-wishing soul-mates and soul-groups as well as mentors who had prepared them for the trip. But the most imposing figure of all was the coordinator, a being of such light that all who witnessed "him" (for in truth this being was genderless) were swept into boundless, endless, limitless love. This being had "teleconferenced" the minds of all those present, so that an idea originating in any one mind instantly became fully available to all other minds in the launch area.

Their mission was "Incarnation on Gaia."

(A) The Body as Sacrament of Incarnation

I differentiate between signs, symbols and sacraments. Signs are when one physical object stands for another physical object e.g., a rectangular piece of metal with paint on it stands for a tarmac road 200 meters farther on. A symbol has one foot in physicality and the other in non-physicality, for example a kiss, where the physical part is the lips that meet and the non-physical part is the love it conveys. A sacrament is a special kind of symbol. Ordinary symbols can be made to lie, like Judas betraying Jesus with a kiss. But a sacrament actually causes to happen the very thing it points to, for example, the focused intentionality of a community during a Eucharistic liturgy causes Christ consciousness to occur among and within the members.

I believe that there are two kinds of sacraments; firstly, orchestrated rituals that celebrate movement from one stage of incarnation to the next, in other words, rites of passage; and, secondly, significant, spontaneous "leakages" from beyond the veil into this world of form.

In orchestrated rituals of all cultures, both secular and sacred, this has been a constant. A few simple examples will suffice to illustrate this.

Within the Native American tradition, the number four is sacred, and so, things tend to happen in fours. There are four primary directions, four vocations (visionary, healer, teacher and warrior); and the four eras of childhood development (lying, sitting, standing and walking) are ritualized. They have many other sacraments as well, for example, the medicine wheel, the peace pipe, the sweat lodge, and the vision quest.

Among the Kalenjin peoples of East Africa, the four main rites of passage are, the naming ceremonies of the newborn; circumcision of boys and girls at puberty; initiation into warriorhood; and initiation into elderhood.

In the Roman Catholic tradition, there are seven sacraments; baptism (mainly of newborn infants, though it can be done at any age); reconciliation (done for the first time around age seven) as the child reaches the use of reason. This sacrament can be repeated throughout life because it celebrates the movement into full alignment with the community, which has been impacted by "sin"); First Holy Communion, representing a conscious choice to be in spiritual communion with the church community; Confirmation typically received at age 11-14 at a time when she is sexually maturing and also developing the ability to think self-reflexively and thus be able to critique both her own values and actions as well as those of the culture; the Sacrament of Matrimony, which is the religious symbol of marriage; Ordination, the induction into priesthood; and finally, the sacrament of Anointing of the Sick, a celebration of healing or of transition into the afterlife. Each of these seven is tied to a chronological transition of the individual but always involves community.

However, I believe that there are many other sacraments or passages. I claim there are, at least, seventeen such passages and each passage has its own symbolic rites.

The first sacrament is the one I witnessed at the launching area. This is truly, the most courageous. Here the individual soul that has volunteered for incarnation finally "takes the leap" and this great event is witnessed and celebrated by a heavenly host. I want to paraphrase a statement of Jesus and say, "Truly, there is more joy in heaven over one soul who incarnates than over 99 souls who do not yet incarnate!"

The next sacrament occurs when the soul merges with the fetus or embryo. I don't believe that conception and soul-arrival are time-synched. The parents build a spacesuit on the understanding that "If you build it it will come." All physical species are endowed with a natural intelligence, which includes the ability to replicate their bodies. Some variable time later, a soul may choose to merge with it. If not, the embryonic spacesuit will be shed by the mother, and so nearly a third of all pregnancies end with miscarriages, mostly at such an early stage that the mother doesn't even know she is pregnant. This merging process is not easy; two vastly different kinds of intelligence are attempting to align. Sometimes it proves so frustrating that the soul may decide it can't go through with it and it aborts the mission and returns "home." However, when a final commitment is made to the merger, a second sacrament is celebrated.

Sacrament number three: the birth and the first breath (in many languages, a single word does triple duty for breath, life and spirit e.g., ruakh, in Hebrew; pneuma, in Greek; pepo, in Swahili; prana, in Sanskrit; and inspiratio, in Latin. Now the community really gets involved in the sacrament to welcome the newborn into its culture. However, this is, as yet, not a final commitment on the part of the soul. I believe that Sudden Infant Death Syndrome (SIDS) is sometimes evidence of the soul finding the confinement of the child's body and brain too taxing and waves the white flag. In other cases, it may be that that was its contract with the souls that inhabit the bodies of its parents and family and community and so does NOT represent a surrender.

The fourth sacrament is the development of the ego; now the "child" has a new sense of self, a CEO of consciousness and a center of operations. It will prove a mixed blessing. While being a vital part of the evolution of its trajectory on planet Earth, ego will prove its single biggest cause of suffering.

Then, number five; the child will stand up and begin to walk. It's getting more control over the spacesuit, the merger is progressing nicely and the "oohing and aahing" of the parents is the ritualized blessing. It is the first self-propelled journey since the great one on the launching pad and highly symbolic of the safari of incarnation.

The sixth sacrament is celebrated when the child learns to talk. Symbolic of all communication, though infinitely inferior to the telepathic communication in the bardo state, it represents the beginning of the search for meaning and for remembering the mission. Mostly, cultures completely misread this and, instead, seduce the child into the societal trance of forgetting even more deeply. But with great glee the parents celebrate this sacrament while missing the real purpose of it.

Around age seven, the child will begin to be able to reason; now he is fit for rules and roles. Age seven and sacrament number seven go together. By now his official "education" will have begun and he will have been introduced to a wider community than the family and the ego will take a significant bruising as "little Johnny" realizes that every family in his neighborhood has produced its own crop of "little Johnnies" all of whom are laboring under the mistaken notion that they are the center of the universe. Weird! Here, he will recapitulate what his very first parents experienced when they got kicked out of Eden for exercising the gift of discernment.

By age 12-14 most children are beginning to become sexually mature. Their own bodies will baptize them in a waterfall of biochemicals, which will bring energy, excitement and very mixed messages from society. This is their eighth sacrament. Now the spacesuit is able to reproduce itself and the culture will have to exercise great pressure for holding that in check.

Nature helps some here by conferring the ninth sacrament at almost the same time. Through it the child learns to think self-reflexively; to hold a mirror up to his own thoughts, values and actions and, also, those of his culture and of the world community. He will discover lots of hypocrisy in society, lots of competing and, sometimes, anti-thetical tendencies in himself.

Number ten prepares him for the first significant friendship in which peer pressure, more than society in general, is the yardstick of behavior and the sacramental-minister. The agony and the ecstasy of romantic love will leave its mark on the quantum leaping evolution of personality, which will happen to him at this stage.

In turn, this will lead to sacrament number eleven which is a serious commitment to a long-term relationship. Society will mark this with some kind of marriage ceremony. As in other sacraments, this understanding will vary significantly among cultures and from era to era in human history. There is no divinely revealed version of it, I believe. In Papua New Guinea, among its 700 tribes, before it was "discovered" by the West, every imaginable model of "marriage" was practiced; some of which would curdle the stomach of any God-fearing born-again Christian. But marriage always involves some combination of companionship, sexuality, romance, child-bearing and child-raising, intratribal agreements, intertribal alliances and contra-gender modeling to promote healthy individuation and balancing of the male and female energies in each of us. Quite a tall order here for number eleven.

Sometime around this period, and sometimes predating it a little, is sacrament number twelve, which ritualizes the adoption of a trade, profession, occupation or vocation. It will be the "graduation" ceremony coming at the end of schooling and specialized training. Here, individual members will take different roles in providing for the community its basic needs and discretionary desires. Between us we manage to muster whatever it takes to live a full human life.

Most cultures insist on initiating its members into sacrament number thirteen, which is calculated to instill unquestioning loyalty to the tribe or nation. Its motto is, "My country right or wrong" and it demands not less than everything, whether that be killing or dying for the group. It is the sacrament of Ethnocentrism. And for most individuals and most cultures in our world it's the last sacrament they administer. The four remaining sacraments are viewed by these as flakey at best or dangerous at worst (and they represent about 70 percent of the world's population.)

But here they are, anyway. Number fourteen is the shift from ethnocentric to world-centric thinking and moral action. Now, "my neighbor is all mankind, even those who are my enemies or differ from me in religion," as the Baltimore Catechism said in a moment of elegant theology; alas more honored in the breech than in the observance throughout the course of Christian history. Once you remember the launching pad, this makes absolute sense, since gender, ethnicity, socio-economic status, denominational affiliation etc. are merely artifacts of the spacesuit and have nothing to do with the essence of the spirit within. But it represents a huge leap in the evolution of human society, with only 30 percent of the population having arrived at that knowing.

Beyond that is sacrament number fifteen in which our concern and compassion embrace all living things. Now we see clearly that Earth is our mother who has fashioned us from the very molecules of her body, and continues to re-create our bodies, from her own, by giving us food, water and air. And when we die and "shuffle off these mortal coils" she graciously receives back the molecules for which we have no more earthly use. The trick is to also remember that she has other children, most who significantly predate our species, and who she loves equally. These are our brothers and sisters, as Native American wisdom says, "the stone people, the four-leggeds, the winged . . ." This sacrament awakens us to our covenant with all of these and our concern to share our mother's resources with them.

The penultimate sacrament is Enlightenment, the coming into full alignment with our essence and the end of the amnesia for our true nature. Very few have received this sacrament, as yet. It has only been available for about 2,500 years and been savored by some avatars e.g. Lao Tzu, Gautama Siddharta, Mahavira, Zoroaster, Jesus, Socrates and, perhaps, some modern saints. But it is our birthright and more and more of the human family are destined to undergo this transformation.

Finally, sacrament number seventeen is the taking of the bodhisattva vow. Having reached enlightenment and therefore not needing to visit the launching pad anymore, some loving beings promise to keep returning until all living beings are free from the illusion of separation. These combine the great courage of the volunteers on the launching pad with the limitless love of the enlightened. Aching to be fully merged with God and so end all separation, they choose instead to incarnate in order to guide the rest of us away from separation and into unity, stage by stage by stage until all of us are ready to dissolve into the ineffable mystery of God out of whom emanates all forms. Then we can all cross the finishing line together.

Which brings me to the second kind of sacraments, the spiritual "leakages" from the other side. These appear to be spontaneous occurrences, but, in fact, they are meticulously orchestrated from beyond the veil with our own previous but forgotten connivance. Before we entered the launching area, we spent significant energy planning all manners of hints which we built into incarnation as clues to help us to wake up and remember.

Some of them are the following: intuitions, which Carl Jung defined as "perceptions via the unconscious." Of course, we need to exercise discernment. Not every stray thought is divinely inspired. On the other hand, we can develop this intuitive faculty and, thus, have a whole other resource available. New-agers wildly exaggerate the frequency of these intuitions, while a materialist mentality denies their very existence.

Déja vu experiences are not just weird time distortions or brain hiccups, but planned interventions to trigger remembrance. We have "googled" the outline of this life before we committed to it, and now we are having a flashback of that preview. This one causes lots of laughter back home.

Then, there are the moments of awe, a spectacular sunset, a timeless interlude in the company of a beloved, watching the sleeping face of your infant, a lightning storm, hearing a Beethoven symphony, listening to the subterranean, rippling growling of an earthquake, smelling freshly baked bread outside a confectioner's shop, eating a pan-fried trout at 10,000 feet altitude after a long day's trek in the mountains; they come in all guises.

Or the leaks may happen in the dreams of the night, the big dreams of which Jung and the shamans and the scriptures spoke; ones that you can recall years later around the campfire, when the glowing faces and the encircling darkness draw us into a deeper communion and render censorship unnecessary. Sometimes, these dreams come in waking consciousness. In truth, the ancients did not distinguish between dreams and visions, both were God-talk, the normal way in which She spoke to us. Meditation and time spent in nature are fertile breeding ground for these incursions.

On occasion, spontaneous psychic phenomena occur; a precognitive "knowing" that Aunt Julia, who you haven't heard from in seventeen years is going to phone you; a telepathic communing with another across a room; an image of the exact location in which my roommate hid the apple pie, so that I can walk directly to it and put my hand on it, as her mouth drops open. All these are invitations to think outside the box and see into different dimensions of reality.

Brushes with death or significant illnesses can quickly and dramatically startle us out of our soporific mediocrity and get us shifting the paradigms that define our "reality" and our priorities.

These leakages don't just happen to individuals. On occasion, entire groups can experience them. The feast of Pentecost is a case in point. When a critical mass is reached (the mythological 100th monkey syndrome), or the morphogenetic field has been established, the leap becomes easier and easier. Within months of Roger Bannister's famous sub-four-minute mile in 1954, dozens of other athletes managed a task that until then was deemed impossible. Each quantum leap in human evolutionary history (agricultural revolution, industrial age, information age) has been ushered in by some group leakage. They are always fragile, however, and the gains can sometimes be lost. Our history is fraught with great breakthroughs that have not been maintained. I call it the concertina effect, this oscillation between hard-won gains in freedom, equality and awakening on one side and fear, stultifying tradition, hierarchy and xenophobia on the other. For instance, the honoring of women that were hallmarks of early Christianity and Islam soon gave way to new waves of misogyny and oppression.

In truth, however, these gains are never really lost, even if the culture temporarily swallows them up and covers them over. In time they will once again bubble to the surface and become a dominant meme for the group.

(B) Pain as the Price of Incarnation

Of what does pain consist? I believe there are four sources: first from the effort to merge eternity with temporality the timeless nature of the bardo state and of the soul is now squeezed into time frames. The ability to view the entire gestalt is fragmented into thousands of pieces and run chronologically. It's the equivalent of cutting up a masterpiece into hundreds of shards and then trying to identify the artwork by viewing the pieces sequentially. Or it is like trying to view a movie by visiting the projectionist's box and going through the celluloid roll frame by frame; boring and very frustrating.

The second source of pain is stuffing the intelligence of spirit into a three pounds organ we call the brain. The newly arrived soul immediately runs into this problem as it attempts the merger with the spacesuit. Trying to dock two very different kinds of intelligence is difficult in itself, but when the soul's intelligence is forced to downgrade to the body's version, that is REALLY frustrating.

The third source comes from cramming spacelessness into a confined physical location. The free, untrammeled spirit, which used to think itself into situations is now weighted down with a dense, heavy, unwilling spacesuit. The first shock here is the womb and, in particular, the tiny claustrophobic embryo or fetus. We have this sensation sometimes when we are dreaming of running or swimming and it feels as if we are trying to move through treacle or molasses. More typically, we have the opposite sensation during dream sleep as we fly or just change locations by thinking of them. And this feels like the most natural thing in the world because it is. But it's not really in the world, rather it's before the world, after the world and in the worlds of altered states of consciousness.

The fourth source of pain is the greatest: the radical amnesia created by the very act of incarnating. It is far more disabling than Alzheimer's and induces similar kinds of "personality change." We walk around in a daze that hides reality from us and persuades us to believe in the wasteland of "waking consciousness," which is anything but wakefulness. Is it any wonder that as soon as he became enlightened, Gautama Siddharta, when asked who he was and why he was preaching a new philosophy, said simply, "I am the Buddha; the one who is awake." What we misname as "waking consciousness" is the deepest sleep of all because in it we are most stuck in the illusions of separation from God, self, other and nature.

It is small wonder that some people find this so frightening that they commit suicide. Most of us opt for a less radical self-offing: we resist the invitation to wake up and become enlightened, choosing instead to dedicate our lives to mediocrity, TV and beer.

But pain is the least of our discomfort. Pain is just the price of admission here. We know the cost before we come. So we really become masochistic by adding suffering to pain. Suffering was not part of the bargain; this is something we have created by ourselves for ourselves.

Suffering is always the result of inadequate cosmologies, interpretations, stories, self-talk and cultural trances. It is the addition of countless layers of forgetting to the original amnesia of incarnating. The more our models tell us we are separated, the more suffering we sign up for. A bodhisattva, on the other hand, suffers very little, because though compassion, which is her hallmark, does involve "suffering with" the pain and the suffering of others, it is always done with a transforming aspect which radically re-contextualizes it. The pain of compassion can always be held in the greater container of an adequate cosmology that gives a meta-perspective on both the pain-provoking situation and on the entirety of an incarnation. It is the ability to weep during the movie of incarnation while remembering that outside the theatre is our real life of never-beginning and never-ending bliss.

And this is where sacraments, leakages and Pentecost help to sometimes gently dissolve and other times violently explode these layers of forgetting.

(C) Enlightenment as the Fruit of Incarnation

The very good news is that incarnation is NOT a punishment from God, like the myth of His throwing the "bad angels" out of heaven, or Adam and Eve out of the garden. Planet Earth is not a correctional facility, nor yet is it a testing ground. It is not even a place to grow, evolve, discover or learn. Rather, it is the "sine qua non" of realizing enlightenment. In fact, without incarnation, enlightenment is not possible. Incarnation is part of Lila, the divine game, whereby God plays hide-and-go-seek with God. Incarnation is that which allows us to plumb the very depths of the illusions that we are separate from God, separate from others, separate from nature and, ultimately, sinners who, at worst deserve hell (the eternal state of separation) and, at best, earn redemption through the sacrifice of a Jesus or the intercession of a Buddha. Once we have experienced this deepest of all forms of separation, we are ready for the return journey into the fullness of remembering. And that is enlightenment!

So thanks be to God for the gift of this "precious human body" which is the vehicle for that awesome safari. And that human body is not just my individual spacesuit, but the body of Gaia, my mother, the Earth, the ultimate organ-donor agency. I contain molecules in my body that once belonged to Jesus or Mahatma Gandhi or you, and when I have danced with them, I pass them on to other souls on safari, in a steady stream of gift-giving while I am still incarnate, and in an orgy of love-bestowing when I die and through burial (a slow, teasing release of the gift) or cremation (the overwhelming, immediate and total distribution of the gift.)

And when I reincarnate, either to continue the journey of remembering or because I am a fully awakened bodhisattva, Mother Earth will fashion me a brand new spacesuit or, if she is in a playful mood, give me a whole bunch of molecules that I had during a past incarnation.

Either way, if I am awake, I will smile in recognition and say, "Shall we dance?"

7

Cousin of Oisín
(9/7/1997)

I'm sorry you had to die like that.
I'm really, really sorry you had to die like that.
How long ago did it happen? And how long did it take?
I'm sure you were scared; terrified!
Did you slowly starve to death?
Or was the panic so bad that your heart quickly stopped?
You couldn't even look around you!
Did the night noises frighten you?
Did you imagine that each time the dry leaves rustled, some predator was
about to savage you?
I can see that you really tried to escape, but you just entangled yourself
some more.
I am so sorry that you had to die like that.
Did you think God had abandoned you?
Did you curse Her, and then immediately feel guilty and vulnerable
and beg Her to forgive you and set you free?
Did you exhaust yourself in your efforts for liberty, so that you finally
submitted and let your spirit go where your body could not?
Were there long cold moonlit nights and hot turgid days to your agony?
Or were you mauled to death in the first few hours?

I am so sorry.

Did you have a family?

Was someone anxiously awaiting your return?

Is there a broken heart that still wonders if you simply left, or if you are dead?

And did you think about that, then?

Did you find a way, later, to give that special one reassurance?

I am so, so sorry for you and for that someone.

I am staring up at the skull of a deer, enmeshed in section of downed fence wire. I have been laboriously climbing this 60-degree forested hillside, since I left the stream twenty minutes ago. It's been almost a crawl. When I stopped to draw breath, and stand upright I found myself on eye-level with a bleached, big-antlered skull. The lower jaw and the rest of the body was missing, but the skull had a full complement of upper teeth—and two large, pathetically vacant eye-sockets.

I can see exactly what happened. You were browsing on this very steep hillside, foraging at the foot of a large Madrone. Sometime before, another Madrone had fallen in a storm and flattened the mesh fence. Somehow you got your antlers caught in the fence. In struggling to free your head, you lost your footing and fell down the hillside. Your entire body-weight conspired to tighten the wires around your antlers. You didn't have a chance. I am so sorry, that it had to be like that. It was your crown of horns that trapped you. Now all that is left of your spacesuit is this bleached skull, with green mold growing on the antlers. As a gesture to your spirit, long since set free, I now free your skull too, and place it proudly on the hillside, overlooking the stream below, and facing tomorrow's rising sun.

You know I just remember that I found the rest of your body 6,000 miles away. It was the autumn of 1968 and I was in the mountains of County Wicklow one Sunday afternoon. This time the fence was upright and you had attempted to jump lithely over it. The fence was only about four feet high and I know that you could easily have cleared it. But you miscalculated, and your left hind leg slipped in between the two top parallel wires which were only three inches apart. Once more your momentum and body-weight conspired to twist these wires around your ankle, while your head crashed to the ground on the far side. There was no way you could undo it.

When I found you, the entire body (flesh and skin and all of the internal organs) was present, but the head was missing. It looked like the work of weasels or ferrets, or perhaps a badger.

Isn't it strange that it took me thirty years to find all of you?

I hope you didn't suffer greatly.

I'm really sorry you had to die like that.

Twice.

8

The Great Soul Who Volunteered To Be Gaia

"From all eternity God lies on a maternity bed giving birth.
The essence of God is birthing."
Meister Eckhart

On Friday night last, September 22, 2006, I had dinner with my friends Connie and Ed Vincent, at their home in Menlo Park. After the meal they invited me to watch a documentary that a friend of theirs had recently made. It is entitled, "Recycled Life," and is the story of the "Guajeros," people who live in the municipal dump of Guatemala City. At two-and-one-half miles in diameter, it is the biggest land-fill/dump in all of Central and South America. There is a continual stream of municipal trucks bringing refuse and large bulldozers constantly moving it about.

But the "Guajeros" are not merely professional scavengers who raid the landfill in nine-to-five daily sorties; they *live* there. In some instances they are third generation residents, with 60 years of an unbroken family domicile right on top of this quaking methane-oozing, utterly toxic and foul-smelling dump. They have built their cardboard-and plastic homes on site, and have married, given birth, lived and died without ever leaving. As you can imagine, they suffer from very high rates of cancer and respiratory illnesses.

As each new truck arrives, about ten of the Guajeros place a hand on its side and "escort" it to its particular dumping spot. This appears to be a well-defined work ritual: they are spaced about two paces apart on both sides of the truck and when it comes to a halt and begins to tip its load these ten people have the scavenger rights. Since there are trucks arriving by the minute, there's "plenty for everybody."

Of course, with all of this traffic and the huge bulldozers constantly reconfiguring the dump's topography, accidents happen. On one occasion two children got caught under a "landslide" as a bulldozer did its job. All work ceased as the cry went out and the entire encampment set about feverishly trying to unearth them. No luck. Panic! The army was called for and they sent in troops to swell the work force, but the children were never found. The theory was that the chemicals, gases and liquids saturating the debris are so corrosive that they literally vaporized the children, bones and all.

But life goes on. Each week this colony of workers retrieves one million pounds of recyclables, which are bought by vendors who arrive in convoys one day a week. A really good week is when a person earns $16 for his labor.

One day in January 2005, all hell broke lose. The methane gas, that underlies the dump and constantly oozes out, caught fire and the entire dump went up in flames and burned non-stop for a week, clouding Guatemala City with toxic fumes from which there was no escape.

Since then the city has fenced off the entire area; erstwhile "residents" who want to continue to work there are issued with identity tags and can only be on site from eight o'clock in the morning to four o'clock in the afternoon. No children under 14 are allowed on site; and many parents, who didn't see the point in sending their little ones to nursery school, which was started some years ago for the Guajeros, have finally agreed to do so.

Some really poignant "human moment" images from the movie were the following: a year-old baby sitting patiently in a cardboard carton for hours at a time, as her mother worked the dump; a ten-year-old fatherless boy reporting matter-of-factly that his mother threw him out to fend for himself after she remarried; and a toothless thirty-something man, grinning from ear to ear as he spoke of his good fortune when he found a pizza "that wasn't even cold yet!"

That night, after I left the Vincent's home, I had a powerful dream, in which I experienced how Mother Earth groans in compassion for her little ones. It was a long dream and I saw levels of Earth-life and experienced the history of Gaia's preparation for its mission this time around.

(A) Human Body Building

We are Gaia-nauts, all 6.5 billion of us humans, who have agreed to plumb the depths of the illusion of separateness. Through incarnation, tribalism, theology and fear we have "descended into hell" even going so far as to formally preach the existence of eternal states of separation from God, designed for those outside our chosen group who do not merit salvation. This, truly, is "the pits" of the illusion of separateness. But it is in this same crucible that the great mystics and visionaries, the Christs and the Buddhas, have honed their skills, rolled back the amnesia, seen the light, become enlightened and offered a way for the rest of us to also remember. Heaven is the pearl in the oyster of Earth buffeted by the ocean of hell. Incarnation can only remember and retrieve nirvana if it's prepared to safari through Gehenna (to mix several theologies and four languages in a single statement).

In this process, then, the gateway to all the virtues is "awareness." Waking up is the "sine qua non" of any serious quest. Once the journey has begun, compassion is the summit, the queen of all the virtues on which we must set our sights. And compassion is really only possible after awareness has been achieved. What passes for compassion before we are aware is mere mawkish sentimentality or highly infectious and utterly disabling pity. Because true enlightened compassion is not just "suffering with" another, but the ability to feel the other's pain *while simultaneously* knowing and offering an entirely new explanation. This new explanation elevates the suffering to its eternal, voluntarily-embraced purpose. True compassion is to suffering as the miracle of childbirth is to the agony of labor.

This growth into enlightenment is a long complex process for which our divine mentors have done excellent preparation. And the vehicle for this entire journey is the precious human body. Our job is to build it. In order to build it, however, we first need to know what "body" actually means. And here, in the West, we are at a major disadvantage. Our model of body is woefully inadequate. Since the time of Descartes we have careened down the slippery slope of confusing body with physicality. In our time we have reduced it, in computer terms, to a WYSIWYG (What You See Is What You Get) notion. We think that "body" is synonymous with flesh, blood, bone, sinew, nerves, cells, hormones and tendons. And this impoverished model is the basis of our medicine; which is why, in 2004, doctors (iatrogenesis) were the leading cause of death in the United States, outscoring cancer, strokes or heart disease. Hopefully energy medicine is an attempt to undo that.

Other cultures and other eras had much more adequate models, though they certainly lacked the technology which is the major contribution of the West.

Ancient Persia, for instance, spoke of "ka" and "fravashi"—the physicality of body and the energy template that underlies physicality. The Greeks fine-tuned it some more, with three categories sarx (the physical body), soma (the energy body) and pneuma (the spirit body). This had huge consequences for Saint Paul's notion of resurrection, when he stated, "What is sown is not the same thing as what grows." In other words you don't sow an apple, expecting to grow more apples, you set a seed that will become a tree that will birth apples. But what you sow (a tiny seed) doesn't look anything like what grows (a tree). By the same token, you don't plant a daffodil to grow daffodils. The bulb you put in the ground doesn't look anything like the yellow petals on a long elegant green stalk that grows. So, Paul goes on to state, "Sarx (the physical body) cannot inherit the Kingdom of God." Only pneuma (the spirit body) can do this. Most Christians do not realize this very powerful insight and teaching of Paul on life-after-death.

But the Hindus, as in many other areas of philosophy, medicine and spirituality, take "body" to a whole new understanding, differentiating among seven distinct levels.

The base level, which they term "the gross body," is the one that Western medicine thinks is the whole megillah. It's vibrating between 400 and 700 nanometers (red to violet) and so is visible to the human eye. It is composed of molecules (carbon, hydrogen, oxygen and nitrogen mainly) which are replaced regularly through food, water, air and sunlight as well as elimination, sweating and exhaling. When a person dies, this level of body is recycled back into the ecosystem to be used by all creatures that have physical bodies.

Above the gross body is "the etheric body," vibrating at a level which renders it invisible to the normal human eye, unless you have the ability to see auras. This energy template is the blueprint used to build the physical body, just like a building contractor uses the architect's plan to know where to put the various physical components he has assembled (cement, steel, lumber, glass etc.). All physical illnesses manifest here first, and true prophylactic medicine must also begin here. It would be as foolish to attempt to reconstruct a house that was seriously damaged in a fire without consulting the original blueprint as it is to attempt to cure a serious physical illness without advertence to the etheric template. But that is precisely what Western medicine has been attempting for the last 500 years.

This energy-body, I believe is the morphogenetic field of which the English biologist, Rupert Sheldrake, speaks. In other words it is a blueprint honed, over time, by nature that allows a new species to enter the evolutionary picture and then, subsequently, makes it much easier for later individuals, within that species, to physically come into the fullness of the plan.

When the physical body dies, this etheric body is given back to the universe as free energy to be employed in any way it sees fit. Perhaps it's to invigorate later members of the species, or, perhaps, to set up brand-new templates for the advent of a hitherto non-existent species.

The third level is called "the astral body" and it has three functions. Firstly it is the dream body, literally the vehicle "you" inhabit each night when you dream. It carries you into places and dimensions in which your education and evolution continue as you sleep because not a second of time is wasted in this elegant system of training. Secondly, it is your emotional body; it is the level of you from which you access the energy of your feelings; it houses your repertoire of preverbal and pre-rational responses. Thirdly, at death, it becomes the repository of all of the experiences of your entire incarnation; the library of your lifetime.

The fourth level of body, in this Hindu model, is "the mental body," somewhat akin to Plato's "Ideal Realm." It is the place that allows you to know *that* you know something, even before you know *what* it is you know. For instance, someone asks you a question and you say, "There are three things I want to say in response . . ." Now you haven't yet had time to think about the question, but you already "know" that you have three responses. Only as they begin to "come through" will you actually know what they are; but part of you already knows that there were going to be three, and what those three are. This part is the mental body. And from here you "download" insights, mentation, ratiocination, ideas. True "education" then, from the Latin 'e-ducare' (to lead out from within, or as Jesus would say of the wise householder, "To bring forth from his storehouse things new and old") is accessing this treasure trove of wisdom.

The fifth level is "the causal body" and it vibrates at a still higher level. This is the master archives containing all of the experiences of all your incarnations on the planet or in any other realms you have visited or lived in. It is the wellspring from which the mental body draws, and that is what accounts for the mental body's near-omniscience. It is not just your retirement account which you can enjoy when you are done with incarnating, but it is the lifeline that feeds you continually right now.

The sixth level is "the Soul body." This has twin components, Atman and Jiva. The image Hinduism uses is of two birds sitting on a tree. They are experiencer and witness. Occasionally one swoops down onto the ground of incarnation while his comrade watches. At the end of the incarnation, Jiva, for it is always he, flies back up and they compare notes until Jiva is ready for the next swoop. I had an interesting experience of this a few weeks ago. Some years back a friend of mine lost his wife to cancer. Sometime later, their daughter, a woman who is now in her 30's was visiting her mother's gravesite and conversed with her as she is wont to do. The mother answered that she had already incarnated as a Chinese child. Then, a few short weeks ago, the husband who was also in the habit of visiting and speaking with his "dead wife" asked her, "How can you be talking with me if you are already incarnated?" She replied, "Because part of us never gets incarnated, ever, and what energy we do commit to incarnation can actually split into simultaneous, parallel Earth lives; and sometimes several souls can agree to inhabit a single Earth body."

Her husband was intrigued and sent me an email asking for my comments. I replied, "I agree fully with the first two parts. The third part (several souls in a single Earth body) I have never heard of, but I find it fascinating and will think some more about it. I have been convinced for many years that a soul (atma) does not commit all of its soul-force to any particular incarnation, but retains a portion in the soul-state. What it does commit, Hinduism will call Jiva, what it does not commit they will call Atma. In the same way when you sleep at night and "lose consciousness," all of your energy does not depart, some is needed to keep your physical being "ticking over" e.g., heart beat, respiration, blood pressure, hormones etc. So part of us is always in the presence of our soul group, while the rest is on safari on planet Earth or elsewhere. And secondly, I have also felt, for many years, that the soul-force dedicated to incarnation may well choose to speed up its learning by inhabiting several different Earth bodies, at possibly a different era of human history, simultaneously. So I may, right now, be Seán ÓLaoire an Irish priest penning these words in my home in Healdsburg, California at 2:39 p.m. on the afternoon of September 27, 2006 and be experiencing, at the same timelessness, life as an 11th Century African slave girl in Nigeria.

In fact, dreamtime may well be a device to allow us a few parallel and simultaneous learnings. It may allow us to visit "ourselves" in parallel or previous Earth lives; or it may allow us the opportunity of visiting with and learning from other beings in other dimensions of the astral planes. The esoteric literature speaks of at least two levels of the astral plane—a higher level where we might encounter angelic beings; and a lower level where we might meet discombobulated entities or the Earth-locked "dead" who have yet to find the light. On either of these planes we might also encounter other "sleeping" astral travelers like ourselves! You've heard of speed-reading? Well here are techniques of speed evolving.

The seventh level of body, in the Hindu model is called, "Brahman" or cosmic consciousness. At this level "I" am united with all that is, that was, that will be, or that could be. This is the level at which Jesus-who-grew-into-Christ-consciousness could say, "I and the father are one," or "Before Abraham came to be I Am." At this level, we are all God because we do not identify any more with any of the lower bodies, though we may continue to use them for purposes of experience. Loving my neighbor as myself or forgiving my enemy make absolute sense here, because my neighbor *is* myself and my enemy is my shadow self. Both enemy and friend are merely manifestations of "me," the "God me" who is not Seán or Gandhi or Hitler.

This realization of cosmic consciousness is possible at each of my deaths; at the end of each incarnation; but only on condition that "I" drop all of the other mis-identifications. Two conditions prevent most of us from taking this step: on the one hand, fear and fixation and addiction to these lesser "selves" or, on the other hand, an overwhelming compassion which results in the bodhisattva vow to keep reincarnating until all sentient beings realize the illusion of clinging to any of these lesser selves.

Of course, it doesn't take death of the gross body to make this choice available; any death will do, especially the death into non-dual mysticism, where, as a bodhisattva I can live in compassion for all of my brothers and sisters, while simultaneously operating out of this cosmic consciousness. This is the apotheosis of parallel lives.

(B) Planetary Body Building

This is where my dream kicked in on Friday night. I saw that the planet itself also has seven levels of body and that just as "ordinary souls" (the ones like us who incarnate as individual humans or animals) volunteer for their mission, so also do extraordinary souls, or mahatmas. Except these volunteer for missions as planets, galaxies (really GREAT souls) or universes (the cream of the crop). I saw that there is a "planetary training school." Just as we humans, on death, take our Earth energy back to our soul pods to debrief with our heavenly mentors and continue our education to prepare for the next incarnation, so, too, do the planet-to-be souls. They have their own launching pad as they excitedly gather with kindred spirits and coaches to begin new missions.

Like us they do not commit their entire soul-force to any incarnation, and like us they enjoy parallel, simultaneous incarnations. And, of course, they may take the bodhisattva vow until it is opportune to merge with the ultimate, ineffable ground of being.

There is one big difference, however. Planets (and even more true for galaxy-souls and universe-souls) have much bigger visions than we do, for three main reasons. First, they are much more advanced souls to begin with. Second, their incarnated lifespan is in the region of 10 billion years with the resultant wealth of experiences. Third, they birth many more life-forms. Humans merely birth other humans, though we play host to many parasites, viruses and bacteria that use us as transport and food. But mostly these passengers existed long before us and will outlive us, as individuals and a species. Planet Earth, on the other hand, has birthed over 10 million different species. This allows her to have 10 million perspectives—just on biological life, let alone on emotional, mental and spiritual life. An increasing ability to take other perspectives is regarded, by many spiritual teachers, to be the hallmark and touchstone of true spiritual evolution.

Unlike materialist evolutionary biologists, I do not believe that Earth is merely the staging ground for random developmental processes operating by chance mutation, survival of the fittest and natural selection. I believe this apparent randomness has a deeper archetypal patterning-for-creativity and that far from being a dead carcass on which parasites feast and breed and mutate, Earth responds to, guides and learns from the efforts and lives of all her children, since she first produced life some 3.7 billion years ago. She is unswervingly focused on her primary task of throwing up a species that will recognize its innate "I Am-ness" and thus recognize the divinity in all things, from rocks to angels.

In my dream, I went on to be taught how the seven levels of Earth's bodies operate. First, Earth has a gross body, vibrating between infra-red and ultra-violet that the human senses can detect. This gross body was inhabited by Gaia-soul almost five billion years ago and probably has an expected life span of another five billion years. Then, like our gross bodies, it will die and be recycled as cosmic dust, perhaps to be swept up by some asteroid belt and re-used for a similar or quite different purpose—just like the carbon of your physical body may wind-up in mine, or in that of a field mouse.

Second, it has an etheric body. This is composed of, among other things, the four forces modern science identifies, namely: the strong force, the weak force, electro-magnetic and gravity. Most humans cannot sense this subtle body of Gaia, but very many animals *can* sense it. With ability to see into the infra-red end of the color spectrum, for instance, snakes can see some aspects of this level, not to mention dragonflies with 2,700 facets to each eye. And bats, of course, who can hear up to 100,000 hertz, have an acoustic image of this body that we can't even begin to imagine. There is lots of evidence that animals can detect Earth tremors even before they register on our Richter scales. A shiver in the energy body of the planet is detected kinesthetically by creatures who are more in tune with their own subtle bodies and that of their mother. When Gaia sheds her gross body in "death," this subtle body is given back to the universe as free-to-be-used-anywhere-you-need-it energy.

Earth has an astral body, which is the instrument for the same three activities that our astral bodies perform. First, it is the Gaian dream body. Given how advanced she is, Gaia-soul has the capability of consciously inhabiting all levels of her body simultaneously and with unbroken awareness. She does not, as we do, have to "go to sleep" to access her dream state. So while she goes about all her other chores, she dreams of her mission and how to optimize it. She travels in this astral body visiting with the astral bodies of beings on the higher and lower astral planes, and learning from and helping in all of these encounters. This allows her to use "cross-over" knowledge from her parallel lives on other planets and in other dimensions.

Second her astral body is her emotional body, which we humans get to recognize by its physical symptoms, just as we can read in peoples' bodies the physiological evidence of anger, depression, joy, nervousness and bliss. For the astute observer of nature, the Earth's astral body is seen in the seasons, in sunshine and storms, in tornadoes, hurricanes, blizzards and blistering heat, as well as in the still, breath-holding silence of a sunrise or the hypnotic lapping of gentle waves on a golden beach. However, like a mother that has to deal not only with her own emotions but with those of her children, Gaia deals with and sometimes manifests the trials, tribulations and triumphs of each individual entity among the 10 million species she has conceived, birthed and continues to nurse. In fact, this was the entry point of my dream last Friday night after I had seen the Guajeros movie. The deep realization of how Gaia feels as she watches a one-year-old baby sit placidly for hours at a time in a crumpled cardboard carton while its mother scavenges. As she hears a ten-year-old boy nonchalantly tell the interviewer that his mother kicked him out to fend for himself when she remarried; as she hears the toothless 30-something man grin hugely at the incredible windfall of a pizza that "wasn't even cold yet!" I felt her grief as she watched rivers be polluted, mammals suck on toxic air, and animals become refugees as their habitat gets demolished. This pain I felt in my dream became the prelude to this education-about-Gaia that I am attempting to put into words.

A third function of her astral body is that, on her demise, it will become the repository of 10 billion years of awesome experiences, each a precious multi-media snapshot of her time as Earth.

The fourth body of Gaia is her mental body. Teilhard de Chardin called this the Noosphere or sheath of deep knowing. It is her connection to her still-higher self; that part of her that knows *that* she knows even before she knows *what* she knows. From here she derives her inspiration. Moreover, she has one further aspect to this level of body that the rest of us do not directly have. From the sun which spawned her during its own birth, she receives a continual stream of information which she passes along to us as DNA snippets. These are the "missing links" that account for both the gradual development and the occasional quantum leaps in evolution. Carl Sagan once calculated that all of the information in all of the libraries and archives of the planet is 10^{17} bits, but, he estimated, sunlight beams 10^{25} bits at us every five minutes! Gaia's mental body is a very busy body.

Her fifth body is the causal one. As with us, it is the major archive (what esoterica would call the Akashic records) of all Gaia-soul's experiences in all of her incarnations as planets or as any manifest form. What a wealth of experience she now brings to bear on her present mission, for, unlike you or me, she is consciously able to access all of that in order to deal with any situation or envisage any great new creative possibility.

Body number six is her Atman, or in her case her maha-atma (great soul): her great-soul body. Like us, there is both a Jiva and an Atma aspect to this. Part of her is eternally in God-presence while the rest is committed to incarnation in one or many guises sequentially or simultaneously. She can "hang out" with kindred spirits of comparable spiritual development, her great-soul-group and be a missionary into manifestation in this divine choreography of remembering.

And, finally, there is her Brahma-body, the meta-cosmic consciousness that allows her to realize that she is one with all other planets, with all other galaxies and with all other universes. Moreover, in this self-identification she realizes that neither a frog nor a spider's web is less fully a physicalization of the divine than she.

Younger planet-souls or planet-souls having their first or second incarnation may occasionally feel fear or anxiety, but it quickly (15- or 20-billion years), passes and gives way to the bodhisattva vow to forego merging until everything goes "Aha!"

(C) I'm Afraid You've Got Cancer!

The insidiousness of cancer is that it is a murder-suicide—the diseased cells eventually kill off the very host they themselves need if they are to continue to live and to propagate. So the host dies and then, shortly after, the cancer cells die. Humans are the cancer of the planet. But not only are we the cancer of the planet, we have preformed surgery on her with our strip mining and wanton deforestation; we have subjected her to radiation through the hole we have created in the ozone layer and through global warming; and we have subjected her to chemotherapy by poisoning the land, the air and the waters. And like all victims of chemotherapy she has lost her hair—the verdant trees and foliage. The good news is that no matter how aggressive we are, and no matter how much disease we cause our mother, she will survive—but we may not. The bad news, however, is that before we manage to wipe ourselves out, we will first have destroyed hundreds of thousands of other species, our brothers and sisters birthed in compassionate creativity by our own mother. Once the suicide is done, Gaia will shake off our effects like a puppy coming out of a pond, and immediately set about repairing herself. Then, when she is good and healthy once more, she will lovingly and imaginatively set about evolving another species which will truly recognize its own divinity, recognize the divinity of all other life forms as well, and live in harmony with all God's family on planet Earth.

Nature is the most resilient factor in all of creation because it is the physical manifestation of the eternal Spirit of God. It is life's love affair with life.

Some years ago I had a powerful vision in which I saw, in profile, a heavily pregnant woman. I could see into her belly and I realized she was the cosmos pregnant with planet Earth. As I watched, there were times when the mother appeared wan and listless and other times when she looked healthy and vibrant. Then I noticed that instead of being attached to the fetus by a single umbilical cord, she was attached by six billion umbilical cords; and I could see liquid coursing through them. Now the umbilicus has two functions: firstly, it brings food from the mother's body to the unborn; and, secondly, it takes away waste matter that the fetus is eliminating. In my vision I could see that when the liquid in the cords was clear, the mother looked vibrant, but when the liquid was gunky-looking she became ill and haggard. And I got it: the liquid represented the thoughts, the words and the actions of each human. These have the power to destroy or the power to heal. When there is a critical mass of good thoughts, words and deeds, then our mother beams brightly, is alive and healthy and therefore capable of carrying us safely; but when there is a critical mass of negative thoughts, words and deeds, then she is nauseated, has constant morning sickness and is unable to nurture her unborn.

(D) Give Me Your Poor . . .

A soul volunteers for an Earth mission and the price of this incarnating process is pain. There are four kinds of pain: first, the pain of having to cram spacelessness into space; second, having to cram timelessness into time; third, having to cram near-omniscience into a three-pound brain; and fourth, and most devastatingly, the creation of amnesia, so that I forget my origin, my true nature and my purpose. This results in suffering which is the consequence of inadequate stories, cosmologies and interpretations of my experiences during incarnation. The end result is that I become a human who acts out of love, compassion, resilience, hope, faith and a sense of humor, or else out of fear, anger, hatred, prejudice, despair or even catatonia. Most of us act out of a combination of these.

In fact, all mammals suffer from having limbic systems and thus the ability to feel emotions, all mammals are able to foist an interpretation on their experiences, tell themselves stories. Animals without a limbic system do not suffer, because they don't have emotions and they don't create explanations for their experiences. But they do feel *pain*, real pain. It is not fun for a snake to be hit over the head with a stick, or for a chicken to be caged all of its life.

And the planet, too, experiences the pain of incarnation for three of the four reasons that humans do. The exception is that, as a great soul, it never forgets its true nature, its origin or its purpose. But it does operate under the constraints of space, of time and of cramming super-intelligence into a physically dense and cramped body, even if it is 8,000 miles in diameter.

And, as I saw in my dream of Friday last, the planet does suffer, but it is not the suffering of inadequate stories, cosmologies, interpretations or explanations, rather it is the suffering she feels for her ten million species, the children of her own fertile womb. She groans from witnessing the struggles of all the non-human species, and from watching the schizophrenic struggles of humans as we vacillate between:

> Love and fear
> Compassion and depression
> Peace and violence
> Hope and despair
> Awe and exploitation

There is some relief for her, however. There are those among her human children who seek to share her burden of suffering. Some time ago I came across an article in the magazine, *SHIFT* which is put out by the *Institute of Noetic Science*. The author was proposing a new syndrome for the *American Psychological Association's Diagnostic and Statistical Manual (DSM)* that she called, "border*land* personality disorder." Now there is a well-established pathology called, "border*line* personality disorder" which is the result of very poor or abusive parenting in early childhood that results in the inability to form appropriate boundaries, so that the "world" continually invades and controls. Adults with this condition are very volatile, suffer great mood swings, idolize and then demonize their friends, apparently without good cause, and are often suicidal. It is a very difficult condition to treat therapeutically and can involve many years of very patient ego-building. In the SHIFT article, the author was suggesting that a parallel condition with many similar features might, in fact, be the vicarious manifestation of Gaia's own suffering; that some people were showing signs of pathology not for any personal or historical reasons but because, like the shaman within tribal societies who symbolically acted out, or even temporarily took on, the illness of a "client," they were symbolizing and taking on, in their own personality, the great vicissitude of modern life—for the planet.

I agree with the author. In fact I believe that this has been part of the traditional function of the poet, prophet and artist. These have been called, "the early warning system of the planet."

Hopefully, we will not continue to pathologize these people, lock them up or put them in chemical strait jackets. And hopefully we will not merely smile appreciatively and remark, "What a lovely poem!" or "Isn't that a powerful painting!" Rather, may we be awakened to full consciousness by all of these people.

Conclusion

I want to finish with a comment on a Pauline distinction. Saint Paul in his first letter to the Corinthians Chapter 15, differentiates between the first Adam (the husband of Eve) and the final Adam (Jesus the Christ). In effect, Paul says that the first Adam was vitalized dirt. In fact, the name Adam comes, in Hebrew, from the word, "clay" or "dirt" or "earth." So it's a pun. It's like saying, "the earthling came from earth "or "the human came from humus." Paul is claiming then that originally God made a clay figure, much like children do with mud, and as the piece-de-resistance, he blew on it and filled it with spirit. In Hebrew "ruakh" means "breath" or "wind" or "life" or "spirit." Thus there was clay, then there was a clay-molded figurine and finally God gave it a soul. So the first Adam was an animated lump of clay.

In the case of Jesus, however, Paul claims that he was the incarnated word of God (logos). So the process happens in the reverse order. First there is pure Spirit, God, the second person of the Blessed Trinity. Then this "entity" decides to incarnate on planet Earth, and so it embodies. It is an eternal spirit that fashions for itself a spacesuit. So whereas the first Adam was en-spirited earth, the second Adam is earthed spirit.

I only half agree with Paul's theology. I believe that any spacesuit, whether it is worn by a human or worn by a caterpillar, is the work of God's immanence, whereas the soul, any soul, one that incarnates as a human or one that incarnates as a planet, is the work of God's transcendence.

So mission or incarnation is the "mysterium conjunctionis," the mystical union of God's immanence with Her transcendence; the coupling of soul with spacesuit; the docking of timeless and spaceless intelligence with a time-bound, space-limited mind-body. It leads to the forming of family—Gaia's children who finally understand themselves, their mother and their mission.

Then we who were the Guajeros scavenging on the toxic dump of leftover theologies and polluted politics can discover the light beings we truly are and abandon the "not yet cold pizzas" of old time religion for the soul food of a modern mysticism.

9

My Auntie the Ant
(2/14/08)

I almost stepped on an ant; a small but a very busy one. I stopped, squatted on my haunches and apologized. As ants go she was rather matronly, reminding me of a diligent aunt, so I asked her if it was okay to call her, Auntie. She said that would be fine, since she already has tens of thousands of nephews. I'm not sure if this was a compliment to me or a "pick a number and wait 'till you're called" kind of response. But then, we human beings have a real need to feel special, recognized, different; so I made bold enough to ask her about this.

"Pardon my boldness," I said, "but I have to be honest; all ants look the same to us humans. How do you distinguish yourself from the others?" She laughed uproariously at this. "Why, you silly fellow, is it important to be special? You have 50 trillion cells in your body, all coordinating their activities. Do you think each one of them needs to feel special? Unfortunately for you, occasionally a bunch of them do feel that they are special and declare their independence. You call that, Cancer. We ants have a *group soul*, and each one of us is like a cell of that soul.

"But we are holographic cells, which mean two things: first, each of us contains all the wisdom, information, know-how and Spirit of the soul; and, second, any of us can be done without, and not in any way diminish the soul. When you scratch your nose you kill millions of skin cells, each one containing all the data necessary to reconstruct you. Do the shed skin cells cry, "Murder most foul; desist!"? Your soul is not the less for the loss of the cells, and if it needs them for its mission, it will simply and quickly make some more.

"So I appreciate your apology for almost stepping on me, but really it wasn't necessary. You humans don't seem to get it that you, too, have a group soul as a species, as well as your own individual souls. You are filled with so much fear about losing your life that you kill others to save yours. Don't you see that this is merely the social dimension of individual physical cancer? The inability to hold the group soul as preciously as you hold the individual soul is the reason for the species-wide autoimmune disease you call war.

But let me go back to the holographic piece. Since each ant is a hologram of the group soul, it means that whenever any individual ant gets new information (where food is, a good location for a new nest, a change in the weather) we can immediately upload this information to the soul, which makes it instantaneously available to all of the other ants. Have you seen us touch antennae? Watch us on a trail some day, a single, apparently meandering line of us moving in both directions. Have you noticed how, when any pair meets, they touch antennae? Do you think this is just to gossip about the queen or complain about the minimum wage? No! We are exchanging valuable information about where we've just been, but, and here's the piece that may really interest you, it is not merely ant A giving data to ant B; rather the joined antennae act as a morphogenetic template to upload this information to the field of ant consciousness. Every single ant in the colony is immediately aware of the new information. Cool huh? What you don't realize, however, is that the cells of your own body are doing exactly the same thing. There is instant ongoing communication among all 50 trillion of them. But you want to hear the good news and the bad news? The same thing is also true of your group soul. All information, all wisdom, all thoughts, all words, all actions are immediately uploaded to the field of human consciousness. Teilhard de Chardin called it, the Noosphere. And this field is, at once, the source and the result of all human activity. There is nothing you *do* to another, there is nothing you *think* about another, there is nothing you *say* about another that you are not doing and thinking and saying about yourself. Until you understand that, you will continue to be miserable."

This was really heady stuff, so I needed to take a time out. I said, "Auntie ant, I'm going to have to think about that one. So, can I slow the pace a little and ask you about more down-to-Earth issues?" "Sure" she said.

"Well, I've just finished building my home about a half a mile from here. I had thought about it for years, designed it, drew several versions of the plans, and then, finally, I set about building it. I notice your home right here. It's pretty new; in fact, it seems to me as if it is in the early stages of construction to judge by the small amount of soil you've shifted. Do you just pick a location and start digging and hope for the best?"

For the second time she laughed uproariously. "Heavens, no child. It's nothing like that. When we decide to move and start a new colony, we send out our seismic geologists. They reconnoiter the terrain within a half a mile radius. But unlike your geologists we don't need to dig test pits, because we are in harmonic resonance with our Mother, Gaia. On the 'soles of our feet' we have very sensitive sonar pads that tell us, as we walk over a piece of ground, what the subterranean system looks like. Then we decide on a location. On the designated day we leave the old home and head out for the new one. We already have a mental blueprint of the finished product.

"As you might imagine, given that you've designed and built a lot yourself, we want to make sure it's protected against the elements. We don't just dig a hole in the ground that leads to a large underground chamber; heavens, no, because the rain and the ground water would make it damp and uncomfortable. So we take three precautions. Firstly, we create a very small aperture so that the effects of direct rain are minimized; secondly, as we excavate, we create a circular, conical mound around the aperture so that surface water is diverted away from the opening; and then, thirdly, we dig a diversionary tunnel, so that whatever rain water makes it through the aperture is funneled away from the colony itself. I assure you it's nice and dry down there where we live.

"We also plan our heating, cooling and ventilating system. We mainly heat the living quarters from our own body temperature, which we can regulate pretty effectively. It may get too hot down there, so we always have another funnel to the outside that eliminates unwanted heat. We can open and close this vent to suit our needs.

"Then we set about excavating the living quarters, the queen's bedroom, the food stores, the nursery etc. And the finished product is an exact replica of the design each one of us had in mind the moment we began the trek from the old home. Since we are all holograms, there is no such thing as an unforeseen obstacle causing problems for a crew working in any part of the project. We are all immediately aware of the challenge and all the subcomponents of the home building are immediately readjusted without any confusion among the crews. Each "crisis" is welcomed as an opportunity for group creativity."

At this stage of the dialogue, I was having serious doubts about the human contention that *we* are the apex of creation. So I tried one last time to simplify our discussion even further. I said, "I've noticed how there is always a lush, fresh grassy mound around the entrance to your ant home. Can you tell me about this?"

"Sure" said auntie ant. "Hundreds of millions of years ago we used to be foragers, seeking out food wherever we could find it and bringing it home to the family. But then a long time ago we invented horticulture. So if you watch closely, some day, you can see how it works. Once we've established a new colony, we go out foraging as our distant ancestors did. We like grasses a lot, so we chop the stalks into little pieces and carry them home. The top section of each stalk contains the seeds for making more grass. So we feed on this and then we plant some of the leftovers on the circular, conical mound I mentioned earlier. To the ignorant observer this may look like dumping our waste on our own doorstep. Trust me, it isn't! It is both a spiritual practice and a provision for the future. First, the provision-for-the-future piece: by planting the seeds on the mound we are growing next year's food supply, and now it is far less work; no more long schleps, instead, just a quick visit to the kitchen garden. Moreover, this grass guards against soil erosion of the mound in the event of unusual weather.

"As for the spiritual piece; we are not just planting for the future, we are pouring libations to our ancestors and saying, 'Thank you' to our Mother, Gaia. You lived in Africa; you know the custom, the African version of 'Grace before meals'; it is to pour some food or drink onto the ground before you eat, to bless those who have gone before and to bow in gratitude to the Earth.

"And God responds to us. When the day's work is done, and we have retired for the night, closed the vent to retain the heat and done a final check in with the group soul, then we listen as God uses the blades of grass on the mound by our front door to create flute music to tell us that She loves us."

10

Remembering That You Forgot

"Many people spend their health acquiring wealth,
and then spend their wealth trying to regain their health."
M. Scott Peck

The art of "telling you how to get there" is a highly honed skill which unfortunately is located in a recessive gene among the Irish. In any set of directions, it is mandatory that 95 percent be about what not to do, where not to go, and what you must avoid at all costs. The denouement, when it finally arrives, must be brief and anti-climactic.

Let me give you an example: You're lost in a strange town in Ireland and you approach a native and ask, "Can you tell me how to get to Mattie Murphy's house on Templebryan Road?"

He will take off his cap, scratch his head and say, "To tell you the truth, if I was going to Mattie Murphy's house, I wouldn't start from here at all." You smile indulgently and wait patiently as he rearranges his inner cartography. Eventually he'll say, "Go back the road two miles (this will be a huge understatement, because Irish miles are very different from American miles or English miles) and you'll come to a road goin' off to your left. There's a pub on the corner, and you'll see Tom Dillon's bike parked outside. It's a high Nellie and the saddle is broken. There'll be a dog tied to it. Don't take that road, whatever you do, for it'll get you totally lost. Are you listening to me now?

"Proceed for another half mile and you'll come to a cross road. Straight ahead will be a very steep hill, and there'll be sheep in the field on the left side, with blue and red markings. There'll be 19 or 20 of them; don't take that road either. Off to the left there will be a small bridge, with a little stream flowing underneath, containing the nicest brown trout you'll find in a year's fishing. Beyond the bridge is Kate Mahoney's cottage. It has a blue door and there'll be a donkey in the yard. Kate isn't in great health at the moment; she had to go to Cork for an operation three months ago. Whatever you do, don't take that road to the left. Are you listening to me now?

"At the crossroads, turn right and Mattie Murphy lives in the first house on the right. Good day to you now!" And off he'll go about his own business.

Shakespeare said it far less eloquently with far fewer words in Hamlet where Polonius advises an emissary, "By indirection find direction out."

I want to use today's scriptures in the same way. They are a good map of what not to do, what not to believe and what does not work. After all, I'm Irish, with that same recessive gene.

(A) The Problem

The scripture readings today from Daniel and Mark are redolent with outdated models of relationship. And the presumptions, about how God relates to humans, how humans relate to each other and how humans relate to nature, are old, antiquated and not only irrelevant but positively injurious to our health.

These readings also make false promises and raise false hopes. In speaking of the "end times," Mark has Jesus ominously remark to his listeners, "This generation will not pass away until these things come about!" Was it Jesus who said this or was it Mark? Who ever said it was wrong. Two thousand years later, this and many similar gloomy predictions in the intervening times, have all proved incorrect. Either Jesus was a poor prognosticator or Mark an inattentive note taker, because, however fragilely, we are still here on the planet.

The results, however, of those kinds of models and those types of promises have led to an endless cycle of xenophobia, prejudice, war and violence. It is extremely anachronistic and utterly divisive to continue to use these myths and models to conduct inter-community, interdenominational and international relationships. Old myths, scriptures, theologies and anthems lead to outdated, harmful economic models, stifling political systems and divisive religious attitudes.

This is the prevailing sickness of our species, and so I want to look at this sickness on all levels and suggest a way through.

(B) Six-factored Illness

There is a lot of simplistic thinking about the origins of illnesses, with the preponderance of opinion favoring the mechanistic bacteriological theory, with some token consideration of environmental influence. This is the famous Louis Pasteur vs. Antoine Beauchamp battle about whether it's the invaders or the terrain that are responsible for disease.

I believe it is much more complicated; that it is, at least, a six-factored equation. Depending on the terrain and depending on the invader, these factors will be weighted differently. The first factor is genetic predisposition. Biology has, traditionally, given far too much credit to this factor, making ridiculous claims that we are "victims of our genes," as if genes were determined to impose their will, come hell or high water. Popular books by respected authors with titles like, *"The Selfish Gene,"* and the main presumptions of both psychobiology and sociobiology, would have us believe that we are hapless, hopeless and helpless victims of dictator genetic plans that are determined to have their evil way with us.

In fact, as brilliant researchers like Bruce Lipton have shown, genes are very compliant, malleable and willing servants allowing their resources to be channeled and expressed by information fed to them through the intelligence faculties that lie within the individual cells, among the cells and outside of the entire organism of which the cells are a part.

So the second factor in illness is the environment. And by environment I mean everything from the in utero experience, the birth process, the neo-natal nurturance, the diet, the climate, the culture, the family dynamics, the education, the religious upbringing and the weather patterns. The intelligence agencies of the human organism feed all of this information into its decision center and this part then communicates to the cells that respond very obediently. It's a clear example of "garbage in, garbage out:" If the intelligence is faulty, wrong decisions are made and disease results. Faulty or fabricated information about weapons of mass destruction in Iraq led to an unjust war, the death of hundreds of thousands of innocent people and the sacrifice of American domestic welfare to the insatiable God of warfare. The human body is subject to the same phenomenon.

This points to factor three, which is personal belief system. Information leads to perceptions, perceptions lead to stories, stories lead to beliefs and beliefs lead to decisions. The cells will express themselves as illness, when they are given directions by freaked-out intelligence on the basis of fear-filled perceptions created by wrong data about the inner and outer environments. So it is incorrect to say that we are "victims of our genes." It is far more accurate to say that we are "victims of our beliefs." Biologically and sociologically, wrong beliefs are a major cause of disease and disaster.

The fourth factor is personal lifestyle. I have never seen a person make a significant and sustained recovery from a major illness in the absence of a concerted change in lifestyle. Our diet, sleep patterns, work, exercise regimes and recreation all contribute to the experience of illness or to the process of healing. In the craziness of the whirlwind of modern life, most of our energies go into making us sick while most of our money goes into trying to make us well. We have to work harder and harder to earn more and more so we can afford to spend larger and larger sums on repairing bodies that feel less and less healthy. As a case in point, Americans spend billions and billions of dollars over-eating so they can justify spending billions and billions of more dollars dieting. Over 35 percent of us are obese.

The next two factors are a little more esoteric in nature. Number five is karma. Sometimes we have agreed in the bardo state (the time between lifetimes) to accept an illness in the next incarnation as a way of growing; or sometimes the illness is the residual effect of our experiences during a previous incarnation. This is analogous to what happens even within a single lifetime, where the results of a lifestyle during childhood or early adulthood only become obvious in later adulthood. How often do people in their 60's recall the ridiculously dangerous chances they took in their 20's or the very unhealthy practices in which they indulged during their 30's and proclaim, "I thought then that I was invincible." Like George Burns, at his 100th birthday celebration, we can all proclaim, "If I knew I was going to live this long, I would have taken better care of myself!"

The final factor, I believe, is the "Bodhisattva dimension." I call it this in honor of the Buddhist teaching about the Bodhisattva, that enlightened being, who, free from samsara or the need to reincarnate, vows to keep coming back until all sentient beings are free from illusion. There is a little of the Bodhisattva in every one of us to the extent that we can act altruistically. Illness may be a gift to the scientific community to find a cure, so other sufferers may be helped, or to friends and family who are thus offered the opportunity to respond with compassion.

Any illness, then, is a weighted composite of these six factors. Now, let me tie six-factored illness with seven-level body. An illness can begin at any one of five of these seven levels. It never starts at Brahma and it never starts at etheric, though it always *manifests* first at etheric. Let me expand on that. Whenever there is an "injury" or "insult" to a level of body, information is immediately communicated to the etheric body which reconfigures the energy template to manifest an appropriate response. This response will then be sent out to all five levels, indicating the appropriate symptoms to be produced. Symptoms, then, are the printout orchestrated by the etheric which jiva, causal, mental, astral and gross will manifest.

Some typical ways in which a level of body can begin this process are the following: I step on a banana skin and break my leg. Gross! (I mean that in both senses, as in "bummer dude" and "this injury starts at the gross body level"). I lose my spouse, and the injury begins at the emotional (astral body) level. I read some convincing propaganda and am filled with a whole new prejudice, and the illness begins at the mental level. I experience some extraordinary siddhi (psychic gift/occurrence) and get inflated; now the illness has started at the causal level. Or I lose faith in goodness or God, and the illness begins at the jiva level.

Beginning at any level, and immediately alerting the etheric body, all five levels, including the initially insulted level, will quickly start manifesting symptoms. Typically, healing will be begun by jiva or the mental body. Now spiritual realignment or a different kind of thinking quickly delivers antidotes to the etheric body, which just as impartially redistributes a new set of instructions to all five levels. The etheric body is to the seven-layer system what the cell is to the gross body—an obedient servant, unquestioningly sending out the directives required for expansion or for defense.

Allopathic medicine that only deals with the gross body, thinking that thus it is affecting a cure, is like a person who is being blackmailed for an indiscretion of which there is photographic proof. The blackmailer sends him a print and says, "pay up or else!" And the recipient destroys the print thinking, "that's the end of the evidence." But in reality only when the negative is destroyed, together with all prints, can he rest secure.

In time to come when we finally learn to utilize this energy template with energy medicine, we will look back at the antediluvian medical practice of the 20th century in which the treatments of choice were surgery, radiation and chemotherapy. Imagine your house has been invaded forcing you to take refuge in the attic. So you take out your chainsaw and sever the stairway in order to deny the invaders access (surgery). Then you lob a few grenades into the kitchen to kill the guys hiding in there (radiation). Then you spray Agent Orange into the sitting room to defoliate the indoor plants behind which another group is hiding (chemotherapy). "Finally" you say, "I've licked the bastards." Indeed you have. However, you are now stuck in the attic, you have no kitchen left (if you ever manage to climb down), and meantime toxic fumes are wafting up towards you riding on the hot air coming from the inferno in the kitchen!

(C) Levels of Illness

We tend to think of cancer as a disease of an individual person, as in "John has cancer." And indeed, biological cancers are a stark fact of life, but that is merely one level of illness. I would contend, in fact, that it is the *final* level. But let's begin with that level and call it level one. I have just written about how it is a six-factored phenomenon experienced by a seven-tier being. So let me term it "individual or biological cancer."

The second level I would call, "interpersonal cancer," by that I mean one-on-one crime whether that manifests as physical violence, active prejudice or emotional abuse.

Level three is "inter-group cancer." This gets activated by xenophobic denominationalism, tribalism or nationalism. It is an institutionalized malaise, a societal infection that poisons inter-cultural cross-fertilization, turning the possibility of pollination into the reality of racism or the exercise of excommunication. In its most robust forms it leads to pogroms, ethnic cleansing and international warfare.

The fourth level I call, "inter-species cancer." By this I mean, the intentional or collateral destruction of nature and the extermination of species, all of which had squatter's rights established here millions of years before Adam got bar-mitzvahed. We justify it by everything from the scare tactics that "wolves kill people;" through "we need to trawl fish in order to feed ourselves" to "weeds are stealing sunlight from us." It makes humans the undisputed lords of creation, which is, then, seen as merely a resource to be dominated or exploited—God said so.

And the fifth level I call, "global cancer" by that I mean a finally "triumphant" humanity standing astride the carcass of a dead nature, beating its chest, not realizing that we are not just the big boys in this kindergarten called Earth, but also the freshman class in the university called the Cosmos. Until we act as citizens of the universe we will continue to fall prey to this global cancer.

I predict that unless we first address these "higher" forms of cancer we will not solve biological cancers, because these latter are merely a holographic image of the other four. There will be no permanent "magic bullets to conquer cancer" until we think in relationships and act in relationships to other individuals, other groups, other species and other worlds.

It's as if I saw a spot on a wall, think its dirt and attempt to wipe it away with a damp cloth. No matter how hard I scrub I can make no impression on the stain. And the reason I can't is that it is not a smudge, it's a shadow being cast by light hidden behind an obstacle. When I discover the light and discover the obstacle, I can discover the solution to the stain. The light is relationships of love and respect, the obstacles are our outmoded myths, scriptures, theologies and anthems. And the resulting dirt smudges are the five cancers.

Gestation and healing both operate from the head to the feet and from the core to the periphery, while sickness and dying go in the opposite directions.

Look, then, at how cancers operate. They are always greedy, shortsighted, and in killing the host they trigger their own suicide. They operate from the bottom up, starting with the annihilation of individual people and ending with the "death of God." And they operate from the outside in, starting with the destruction of systems and ending with the annihilation of values and ideals.

On the other side of the equation, healing and evolution are prodigal and generous to a fault since they are limitless spirit-in-action and boundless creativity-in-orgasm. This force cannot be stopped, though it can be temporarily impeded or diverted at huge cost to the obstructionists. Moreover, it is epigenetic, nothing is wasted, rather all subsequent phases incorporate but transcend all previous phases in the same way that a tree calls upon its roots even as it stretches excited twig-fingers towards the sun. It is truly cephalo-caudal, beginning with a remembered God as transcendence and moving seamlessly to God grounded in immanence. And it is proximo-distal, starting with an inner realization and manifesting as external behavior.

To be even more precise, this journey of evolution into enlightenment and illness into healing has three dimensions to it. It has an "outreach" aspect from individual to interpersonal, to inter-group, to inter-species, to cosmic inter-planetary. Then it has an "in-reach" aspect which is the healing of organism to organs to cells to molecules to atoms. And it has an "up-reach" aspect which is the integration of gross to etheric to astral to mental to causal to atman to Brahma bodies.

When we finally understand this we can stop blaming the victims and cease expecting them, on their own, to wipe out biological cancer.

(D) How to Become a Healer

So how do we sign up to be healers? The first art to be developed is discernment. This is the ability to distinguish between the etiology of an illness and the purpose of an illness, between the biological mechanisms and the spiritual intentions, between the "how come" and the "what for?" In the section on the six factors, the first four would answer the "how come?" question, and the last two would answer the "what for?" question. Attempting a healing without first distinguishing among the first four is foolish in its own right. For example, giving "fat reducing pills" to someone who is obese while he lives on a diet of French fries and coke as he lies on a couch clutching the remote-control, is a terrible waste of pills, French fries, coke and time. If the mechanistic cause, the "how come?" of the excess weight is personal lifestyle then healing can only happen when it addresses that issue.

Then we have to distinguish between the "how come?' and the "what for?" Attempting a cure before establishing the cause/purpose discrimination will at worst lead to total failure and, at best, lead to mere temporary symptom relief. It will be back. If I knock over a water glass on the table and it spills onto the floor, there isn't much sense in mopping up the floor until I first stand the glass upright and then mop up the water on the table. And while the "what for?" is mostly a matter of karma or the bodhisattva vow, it will always entail "how come?" etiology. Moreover even the "what for?" is not always about enlightenment. There is also, at times, the hidden motive of "secondary gain." A person can unconsciously identify with or capitalize on an illness, i.e., the little schoolboy who finds that a painful stomach gets him a day at home with mother, comic books and tender loving care has discovered an ally in illness. Jesus confronts this in John Chapter 5. He noticed a crippled man at a healing spa. The problem is he'd been there for 38 years and was still crippled. One Sabbath Jesus confronts him with the question, "Do you *want* to be healed?" The man replied by grumbling that he had nobody to put him into the waters after they were disturbed by an angel. Apparently, the story was that every so often an angel came and ruffled the surface and the first person into the pool would be cured. Obviously, this put cripples at a distinct disadvantage. The man warmed to his excuse-making, I'm sure, and was quite prepared to regale Jesus with a bitter list of complaints, but Jesus cut him off and asked again, "Do you *want* to be cured?" He apparently said, "Yes," so Jesus cured him and then invited him to break the law by carrying his bed home on the Sabbath. The ever-vigilant Pharisees spotted this grievous sin and accosted the man, who was more than happy to pass the blame on to Jesus. I suspect that the guy was really pissed at his change of fortune. Who *was* he, now that he was no longer a cripple? And how would he obtain food now that he no longer had an excuse to beg? "Damn that Jesus guy! Why couldn't he mind his own business?" It was a classic case of being upset because of feeling a lot better. So secondary gain could be as powerful a purpose for illness as karma or the bodhisattva vow; a healer has to learn to discern this.

Then there is the little matter of "prayer and fasting." In Mark Chapter 9, Jesus and three of his apostles have come down off Mount Tabor after the transfiguration event. The other apostles, at the foot of the mountain, are with a father and his epileptic son. Previously, Jesus had commissioned and empowered all twelve to be healers and they had come back from their two-by-two missions with glowing reports and hugely expanded egos; but they had failed to cure this boy. Crestfallen they stood by as the father explained their failure and asked if Jesus himself could do any better. Jesus went on to question this man at some length (to determine cause, purpose and secondary gain?) before he performed the cure. The man went away triumphant with his healthy son, and when he was safely out of ear-shot they asked, "Why couldn't we cure him?" Jesus replied, "This kind is only healed through prayer and fasting." So what's the deal here? I define prayer as the immanent (human) aspect of God talking to the transcendent (divine) aspect of God. And meditation is the transcendent aspect of God talking to the human aspect of God. Thus prayer is about coming into full alignment with Self, the God within. All fasting is a technique to experience an altered state of consciousness and so enter into solidarity with the experience of other hungry persons; so by "fasting" Jesus means coming into alignment with the God in the other person.

Through prayer and fasting then, I am both in alignment with my inner divinity and the inner divinity of the patient whom I want to heal. It's like trying to boil water in an electric kettle. If the electric lead is plugged into the outlet (alignment with Self-God) but not into the kettle (alignment with You-God) then the water will not boil (no healing happens.) Conversely, if the lead is plugged into the kettle but not into the outlet; still no cigar. Only when it is plugged in at both ends does it work. I must be sure, however, not to confuse "alignment with other" and "co-dependency with the other's dysfunctionality." If I do then we are both in hot water, but neither of us is plugged in.

Then there is the question of "faith." Once, when a leper came to him to beg for healing, Jesus asked him, "Do you believe I can do this?" In other words he wanted to know if this man himself could plug into the electric lead. Faith itself is a two-phase phenomenon. Initially, all that is needed is "belief in a powerful other." This is known in medical and psychological research as the "locus of control" question. It is the essence of the placebo effect, which is actually responsible for at least 35 percent of any healing that happens via surgery, radiation, medication or laying on of hands.

Jesus and other healers become the screen onto which the placebo is projected. And that is fine; it works very well, but there is a level of faith beyond that, which is much more effective, and in which the locus of control is shifted from a "powerful other" to one's own core or God image. In my own research on the effects of intercessory prayer-at-a-distance, I found that this inner locus correlated very significantly with higher success rates (ÓLaoire, 1993).

This re-locating of control can normally only happen, however, when the "designated healer" is enlightened enough to get his own ego out of the way; He must go from thinking of himself as the source of the healing, through thinking he is the channel of the healing, to realizing he is merely a mentor encouraging the "client" to heal herself. There is a great story in Matthew 9 that illustrates this. Jesus is on his way to the house of Jairus the synagogue leader of Capernaum whose little daughter is seriously ill. A huge crowd is accompanying him and among them is a woman who has been hemorrhaging continually for 12 years. She suddenly has an intuition that if she can only touch the hem of his garment she will be healed. Very surreptitiously she does so. But Jesus stops in his tracks, whirls about and demands, "Who touched me?" I'm sure Peter snorted and said, "Get real, there's a huge crowd milling about and jostling each other and all of us; so what do you mean, 'Who touched me?' Be reasonable." But Jesus would not be diverted. "No," he said, "somebody touched me; power went out from me." Shamefacedly the woman came forward for not only was her illness an intensely private matter, but she was also breaking the Mosaic Law, since all bleeding women were unclean and had to sequester themselves. Anybody they touched was also deemed ritually unclean. I'm sure the fundamentalists in the group were angry at her, for now they, too, had to go home and purify themselves. So why did Jesus embarrass her? The truth is, he didn't; rather he empowered her because he said, "My daughter, it is your faith that cured you!" And this did not mean, "it is your faith in me, Jesus, that cured you," but rather, "your faith did it all by itself, since you are as much a child of God as I am and when you plug into this realization you don't need the placebo of projecting onto a healing symbol like a curandero, physician or preacher." Christianity however continues to fight on behalf of Jesus' ego by insisting that he healed because he was uniquely the son of God. In this story, Jesus has moved beyond that position, but initially is stuck in the "I am a conduit of God's healing" because the woman is projecting onto him. So he takes a timeout to explain to her and thus empower her, and any of the listeners who had "ears to hear" that a designated healer is merely a mentor-teacher to inspire all of us to plug into our own core divinity.

Building upon this, then, comes the realization that all healers are "wounded healers." And the wounding comes either from a personal illness, experienced either spontaneously, or orchestrated by a society, as in shamanistic initiation or rites of passage, during which serious physical and mental pain occurs naturally or is intentionally built into the ritual. For healers who have not undergone such a naturally occurring illness or been forced through the crucible of initiation-induced illness, their woundedness comes from a real identification with unity consciousness, during which they really feel the pain of the world.

Mostly, our doctors and therapists are trained in the tools of the trade but are not expected to be transformed by the training. They become technicians instead of wounded healers, and we are enamored of their skill set but not healed by their ministrations. They haven't undergone the separation, transition and integration of the shamanistic training or the rites of passage of pre-industrial cultures. The result is technically superb piano players with no soul to their music who leave transfixed but not transformed audiences in their wake. When Jesus quoted the proverb, "physician heal thyself," I believe that is what he meant. In other words, when healers are concerned only with curing physical illness based on inadequate models of body, illness and healing, then they have to heal themselves by radically overturning the old thinking and begin to operate from this new paradigm.

Everything I have written about "how to be a healer" is true not just of those who would be healers of *biological* cancer, but also of those who would be healers of all the other levels of cancer too. In fact the truly great healers of the 21st century will be those leaders who point to, educate us on and help us overcome the upper level cancers. Then the mopping up exercise of healing biological cancers can be left to the medical and therapeutic apprentices.

11

Cosmos 101
(1/30/2001)

They were as cosmopolitan a group as you would expect to find on the New York subway. Engrossed in their own worlds, each one's attire told something of their profession. The young woman with the baby in her arms looked like a hippie from the '60's—definitely an "earth mother." Beside her sat a doctor-type. He was, in fact, a neurosurgeon. On the other side of the surgeon was a dreamy-eyed college girl, a student of goddess-lore, dreaming of love and romance. Across from them sat the psychic who could tell you your past lives simply by looking at your aura. And, finally, beside her, fully awake with the soft embracing gaze of Shakyamuni, was a Zen Buddhist monk.

Standing in the middle was the person who set the whole thing in motion. With one hand he was holding on expertly to the overhead strap, as the train bucked and squealed and tried to throw him. In the other hand he held a newspaper and something in it was giving him great pleasure. He beamed, guffawed, and to nobody in particular announced "Well whad'ya know. So, black holes in space may not be the annihilators of matter they were reputed to be. They may, in fact, be the birth canals for new universes!" Just then the train came to a screeching halt and with a final amused shake of his head, he imprisoned the newspaper under his left arm and disappeared into the milling masses on the station. Five pairs of eyes followed him until he was swallowed up and the train began to lurch away. Then five brains began to muse.

The young mother hugged her baby more tightly, smiled to herself and thought "Of course the mother does not annihilate! Whatever appears to be destruction is but a reconfiguring. What were those scientists thinking about when they claimed that black holes were terminators, annihilators or destroyers? We live in a BrahmaShiva universe. Creation always re-emerges from apparent entropy." She gazed adoringly at the sleeping face of her infant and thought "Perhaps, this universe, our universe, came from a black hole in our mother universe? I'm sure the Big Bang was her joyful shout as she gave birth to this baby universe in which we live. I wonder how many baby universes can a parent universe create?"

She looked out the window as the train shuddered to a halt at the next station. On the platform a group of carolers in Santa Clause outfits sang Christmas songs. The lyrics drifted into the open compartment as it disgorged one group and sucked in a whole new troupe.

"I wonder" she mused "if some incredibly wise beings were watching, billions of years ago, and enquired of the locals 'Where is the new cosmos to be born? We have seen its star in the East and have come to bring it gifts.'"

The train pulled into the darkness again, and now when she looked toward the window she could see her own form. A form that up to two months ago was pregnant. She had feared four months ago that she would go on expanding forever! "Perhaps" she mused "that is what is puzzling the astronomers, who can't figure out whether we live in an ever-expanding universe or not. That's the reason." she felt, with a great surge of discovery. "It only appears to be expanding forever because it has been increasingly pregnant for as long as we have known it. When it gives birth, then it will contract until its next conception. I wonder if post-partum mother universes have to do yoga to get their shapes back." She laughed aloud at this thought, put her hand embarrassedly to her mouth and looked furtively at her companions. Nobody, except the Zen Buddhist monk, seemed to have noticed.

She remembered a lecture she has once heard by an eminent physicist. "What had he said?" She cast about trying to remember the numbers and the statement. He had said something like "For every cubic centimeter of eleven-dimensional primordial space, 10^{27} brand new universes are created every second!" She thought "Wow, what a mouthful. Wow, what prodigality." He had gone on to say that many of them were duds that only lasted nanoseconds. The notion now caught in her throat "Are these, then, still-born universes? I wonder does a mother universe weep when she miscarries?" She hugged her own baby close, and then stood up carefully as the train approached her stop.

The neuro-surgeon watched her go and then went back to his own reverie. "I wonder if black holes are the dendrites and the axons joining the siblings to their parent in the brain of God? Is each universe a single cell in the divine brain? And are black holes the neural pathways which create the network? Are there psychic and literary umbilical cords connecting Shakespeare to all of his creations?; and his creations to each other? The mother of all universes may not so much be a parent, who birthed and is now separate from, though in contact with all of her daughter universes, but a 'suprawomb' in which all the adult-children-universes continue to live and evolve while, themselves, birthing their own baby universes! Rather like an extended, multi-generational family."

For some reason he remembered a nature film he had once seen, in which a water-spider was filmed in a pond. The camera work was superb and it tracked her as she built her underwater home. First she swam to the surface and, somehow, trapped a pocket of air with her two hind legs. She pulled this bubble several feet underwater and fastened it to the stalk of a water-lily. Then she went back to the surface and lassoed some more air. She fused the two bubbles into one, doubling its size. She made several more trips and each time she managed to merge the bubbles, until she had one great bubble attached to the stalk. Then—the piece de resistance—she went inside the bubble without ever popping it! This was her home and she entered and exited at will, without piercing the delicate membrane!

"Perhaps" thought the neuro-surgeon "the pond is like the suprawomb and the bubbles are like the baby universes within it?" Suddenly, he had a vision of a tiny, quivering baby universe, shivering in the palm of God's hand as She crooned "Do not be afraid, little one, because I love you." Quite suddenly a large tear ran down his right cheek. "Did anybody notice?" he thought self-consciously. Nobody had—except the Zen Buddhist monk.

Next to the doctor the college girl, too, was thinking up her own cosmology. She lived to recognize love and sensuality and creativity wherever it could be found. "What if each universe is androgynous—penetrating itself, receiving its own seed into its own womb, expanding and then expelling its baby universe through a black hole!?" The thought gave her goose bumps of pleasure. "Evolution, then, may be the ecstatic love-making of an adult universe with itself, which will eventually, result in a brand new baby universe." She smiled to herself and thought "Gee, I hope the Religious Right doesn't condemn it as a deviant sexual practice!" She remembered that recent astronomical theory had revised the calculation of the age of the universe down from 19 billion years to 13 billion years. "So" she figured "Our pubescent cosmos is just now becoming sexually active. What an adventure lies ahead of it. Pretty soon it will be writhing in the orgasm of conceiving its first-to-be-born."

The college girl hugged herself and sighed aloud in satisfaction. Nobody, except the Zen Buddhist monk noticed.

The psychic was aware that an interesting shift had happened in the carriage since that chance remark of the "newspaper man." She had covertly watched the auras of her companions expand and change colors. Moreover, light seemed to arc from each person's aura to the auras of the others—like cosmic dancers in a creatively choreographed holographic display. Though physically, emotionally and mentally in their own worlds, they were, yet, intertwined at the causal level and together wove a tapestry of beatific insights.

She gave herself up to her own part of the dance. "Just as a cosmos births new universes, does each soul birth new lives through reincarnation?" She had no doubt they did. But what she now wondered was "Since time is an artifact of human consciousness, and really doesn't exist until we manifest on the physical plane, might a soul, who had just finished a lifetime in 20th century America, decide, after a Bardo respite, to incarnate the 'next' time in 13th century Africa? Why not, indeed? If incarnation is the experiment of learning to love in the many configurations of human experience (e.g., gender, ethnicity, skin color, IQ level, religious affiliation etc.), it makes perfect sense that Spirit possesses Fast Forward, Rewind, Cut, Copy and Paste functions."

She smiled in the glow of where the dance was taking her. Another sudden insight gripped her "Oh" she thought "If time is, indeed, part of the illusion of manifestation, why not parallel lives? Why not lives as a female Egyptian slave of 2500 BCE, as a male American politician of 1800 CE, as a gay Italian man of 1960 CE, and as a Celtic Druid of 400 BCE—ALL AT THE SAME 'TIME'? Modern business protocol might call it 'multitasking.' Why not, in fact, as the Hindus taught, an Atma, who remains steadfast and unattached, while its Jiva dives repeatedly into a myriad of simultaneous incarnations? Perhaps there are three levels of the process, all occurring at once! First, the Atma—eternal, unperturbed, unmanifest, disincarnate—watching without attachment or aversion, fear or anger. Second, Jiva, in its bardo states, between incarnations being debriefed and preparing for its next safari. And, thirdly, the time-circumscribed, spacesuit-inhabiting entity, simultaneously learning in parallel incarnations, all at once. Thus, when the heart-broken, bereaved young wife anxiously asks 'Will I see my beloved after I die? What if he has already reincarnated?' the answer is 'Of course you will. You will meet him in the bardo state and in a parallel joint experience.'"

She smiled again to herself and wondered "What if, right now, I could be simultaneously aware of all of the fellow travelers with whom I am sharing parallel bardos and incarnations?" She looked about the carriage. "Is this group" she asked herself "here by chance or by design? How is each of us experiencing ourselves and the others in the parallel situations?" She attempted to radiate recognition to her companions. The Sanskrit phrase "Tat twam asi" (That thou art) leapt to mind. "Of course" she thought "we are all one to begin with, and to end with. But wouldn't it be cool if we could remember that occasionally." From the corner of her eye, she fancied she saw the Zen Buddhist monk nod his head in agreement.

"What would that recognition do to the illusion of separation?" she wondered. "Would it vaporize and dissolve, and extract from it Self-Realized beings?" Her mind went back, once more, to the black-holes-in-space conundrum. "What if, like Self-Realization, black holes are very efficient recycling devices that take a massive physical object, like a planet or a star, and thoroughly pulverize all its matter, reducing it to its DNA, which it then hurls into a brand new environment to begin a whole new evolutionary journey?"

"Is the universe, then, merely birthing itself? Manifesting its own recessive genes? And is each black hole an opportunity to birth a different version of itself? Perhaps, all the black holes in a universe are the channels for it to simultaneously birth the different permutations and combinations of its own DNA? Since the cosmos is the 'manifest' dimension, then each universe is merely the articulation of a different possibility. So the 'original' universe is not a universe at all, but the unmanifest void of all possibility."

Just then the carriage lights went out for a few moments, as subway lights sometimes do in a tunnel and utter darkness enveloped them. The only sensory feedback was the rattling of the couplings between the cars. It was easy to imagine the dark womb of nothingness. She clapped her hands as if to applaud the synchronicity of it. Nobody detected the sound of it, except the Zen Buddhist monk who thought, "What is the sound of one psychic clapping? It would make a good koan."

The monk was as aware of the darkness as he had been in the light. He, too, had been sitting in contemplation of the black hole. "If a black hole cannot be seen in the light, can it be seen in the dark?" He had an image of a black hole. It seemed like a vehicle by which a universe might turn itself inside out, rather like what happens to a glove when you take it off. As he watched the image, he saw the universe re-reverse itself. The question arose "Did it use the same black hole to re-reverse itself as it used to reverse itself?" He sat with that for a while. In his mind, he heard one of his students ask "Master, if that is how it is with universes and black holes, kindly tell me does the re-reversed cosmos go back to where it started or does each folding and unfolding cause new manifestations?" In answer the master peeled off the glove from his right hand. It had fit perfectly. As he retracted his fingers and thumb, all of the sheaths turned themselves inside out. He held it aloft for the students to see. He handed it to one of them, the questioner, and said "Put it on your hand." Since it had been a right hand glove, to begin with, the student attempted to put it on his own right hand. Of course, it did not fit—for now it was no longer a right hand glove but a left hand one.

"What is the sound of one glove clapping?" he asked aloud of his companions in the carriage.

Nobody answered, except the Zen Buddhist monk himself, who said nothing.

12

What I Learned from a Geisha Girl

"All theory is against the will, all experience for it."
Sam Johnson

Her aunt was absolutely shocked! I should explain that her aunt is a 95-year-old Russian émigré who lives on the East Coast. She is a very religious woman who has always been deeply involved in the Russian Orthodox community. One of her spiritual practices is to decorate Easter eggs each year. This is a very intricate process and there are two kinds of decoration, "ordinary" meant for the laity, and "elaborate" made for priests. Since I befriended her niece five or six years ago, the aunt has decorated a "priest's egg" for me each year, even though we have never met, spoken on the phone or even corresponded.

The niece is a first-rate social psychologist, a top researcher in a world-renowned research organization, and occasionally we get together to discuss psychological and spiritual issues. On Friday last she was on the phone with her aunt and the conversation went something as follows;

"What are you doing tomorrow?"

"I'm going to meet with Father O'Laoire"

"What are you going to talk about?"

"Actually, I'm going to bring my computer and show him a movie, so we can discuss it."

"Oh, yeah. What's the movie?"

"It's called, 'Memoirs of a Geisha.'"

And that's when the aunt became absolutely shocked. I'm sure she had an image of a high-hatted, black-frocked, jewel-bedecked, crucifix-carrying cleric being blitzed by a celluloid sensual assault on the senses facilitated by her very own niece.

"What?! You're showing Father O'Laoire a movie about a Geisha?"

"It's because I want his input on a project I'm working on just now and the issues in the movie are relevant."

"Okay, but you must promise me that if he begins to show any signs of discomfort you must immediately turn off the movie."

"Yes, auntie."

So yesterday we watched a 30-minute clip. Then she asked me, "So what do you think? What is your reaction and assessment?" We talked for another half hour, and this morning in my meditation it came up again. I will make four main points: the first one I will call, "Wanna play?" The second one I will name, "If *you* don't believe what *we* believe, we're gonna have to kill you." My third point will be, "Travel broadens the mind;" and lastly "So what can *I* do?"

(A) Wanna Play?

Briefly, since I only saw a half-hour of it, the movie was about parents from a little fishing village in Japan who sold their two daughters aged about nine and twelve. They were then spirited away to the big city, and torn apart, the older one to be pressed into prostitution and the younger one into a Geisha house to begin her long training. It seems that the entire culture—all social classes, both genders and all age groups—conspired to make this "normal." What was most upsetting to me as I watched was that the women also, even the grandmothers, wholeheartedly endorsed and participated in this game.

I began to see that life on Earth is a game; in fact a nested series of games within games. Each family, group and culture creates its own version. And we play several subsets of these games simultaneously.

On a spectrum, these games run the gamut from downright slavery where only a person's vital needs (food, shelter, clothes) are provided (so that he/she remains capable of producing the work), through the geisha, who has standing in the community, but is still "owned" all the way to fully-independent citizens of a participatory democracy, protected by an enlightened constitution and Bill of Rights. This latter achievement is very fragile, and we see in our own country how this has been severely diluted by a regime that seems determined to drag us back to an earlier part of the spectrum where security from monsters under the bed is the reward for trading in civil rights.

Historically most of these games have been pyramid schemes in which the elite at the top dominates the other layers, all the way down to the largest single group which has the least rights and profits least from the arrangement. But it is imperative that even this latter group agrees to the game so, frequently, the priestly caste "discover" revelations that get recorded as "sacred scripture" that, allegedly, mandated this setup. Once people can be educated to believing in a deity, who speaks only to designated seers, then it's a slam-dunk. Now, with promises of a heaven-after-this for people who keep the commandments, it's relatively simple to keep the groaning masses in line. Initially, it may be necessary to keep physical restraints in place, but eventually these can be relaxed once the social restraints have solidified and the psychological acceptance and divine mandate have been impressed on the culture's neuronal circuitry. Now the slight pressure of the mahout's naked heel behind the great beast's ears can create a perfectly obedient elephant.

The game evolves. It is never created, in toto, by a single individual anymore than a single individual sat one day and said, "I think I'll invent a brand-new language, and I think I'll call it English," and then proceeded to invent a grammatical structure, a vocabulary, accents, inflections, cadences, emphases, syntax and semiotics, which he then foisted on a group, so that it became the mother tongue of the next generation. No, each game grows organically, reaction by reaction, response by response, encounter by encounter. Needs meet resources and agendas coalesce. The powerful then begin to nudge it and steer it in particular directions, and eventually you have a full-blown, society-sanctioned game.

Every one of us is stuck in such a game, often with several subplots e.g., as an Irishman I might be playing the game of a Celt, with sub-games of class-consciousness, anti-English prejudice and fidelity to Roman Catholic dogma. As an American citizen I might be playing the game of denizen of the world's only superpower, with sub-games of "the poor are poor because they are lazy" or "we have to eradicate them darned Eye-ranians before they develop weapons of mass destruction" and "marriage is a divinely ordained covenant between one man and one woman!"

This is where enlightenment enters the picture. An enlightenment experience allows me to temporarily rise above the field of play and see the game for what it is—a game. Now I can see its limitations, its flaws and its very human origins. When I come down from this experience, I can never quite buy in again to the illusions of it. Great prophetic figures are those who created cultural earthquakes by recognizing this. Society responds by emphasizing the spiritual restraints. "God decreed it. By opposing it you are a heretic!" When these don't work, they put on the social restraints, "This person is not a patriot." Then the psychological restraints "So you think everybody is wrong, and you're the only one who sees the truth!" Finally, when all else fails, the physical restraints go back on—jail time. If even this fails, then comes assassination/execution. But an idea, whose time has come, on the lips of a courageous charismatic prophet shows that the old conundrum of "what happens when an unstoppable force meets an immovable object" is based on a falsehood.

In an evolving universe, there is no such thing as an immoveable object. The force may, temporarily, be halted from pursuing its most obvious trajectory, but like water it will find a way around, through, over or under until finally the "immovable object" is dissolved or demolished. Then society takes a giant step forward. For many years, however, the fractured "immovable object" will spawn guerrilla fighters who will continue to harass, snipe and attempt to derail the evolution. We are witnessing this in our times, as a global course of freedom, cooperation and compassion is being born out of the wreckage of xenophobic nationalism and fundamentalist religion.

The fully enlightened being is able to rise above the field of all games and recognize the flawed human character of what has gone before. Moreover she can come back into the marketplace of human intercourse and retain this recognition. Like the 10th ox-herding picture from Buddhism, the enlightened one can engage fully in the human drama, but never get suckered by it. Like Jesus, she can be "in the world but not of the world." Now she can challenge the other players to do the same thing, to see the same truth, but she does this with compassion not judgment. She will, however, be a constant thorn in the side of the (frequently-self-appointed) guardians of the game, who insist that every minute rule be religiously adhered to e.g., the Maggie Thatchers who insist, "The law is the law is the law!"

The strange thing is that every single teenager has spontaneously reached this place where he can critique his own values, beliefs and behavior, and that of his culture and of the world game. Society immediately tries to reel him back in under the safe umbrella of the center of the bell curve; back into nationalism and denominationalism. Society punishes all of the outliers—at one end the "criminal class" who lag behind societal norms. Their great crime is not so much that their action creates negative consequences (death, alienation of property etc.) but that their mindset and lifestyle are an assault on the sacredness of the game. If people don't respect the game, then deep within the societal psyche, the fear is touched, "perhaps the game isn't true after all?!" This is so unnerving that we cannot afford to entertain it. So we jail or execute those who question the game by their behavior.

At the other end of the bell curve lie the prophets. We also rope them in for the very same reasons. Which is the issue I want to consider in the second section.

(B) If You Don't Believe What We Believe, We're Gonna Have to Kill You.

We are much, more threatened by peoples' belief systems than we are by their actions. Actions may upset us, they may threaten our welfare, our security or even our lives, but beliefs threaten the culture, the paradigm, the cosmology, even the very fabric of the game. And that is a No! No! We can survive people who act badly but who mouth belief in the game; but we are significantly threatened by people who act lovingly but who believe in a different game. Human history is decorated with the icons of evil dictators who committed crimes against humanity but mouthed the cultural norms piously and, as a result, are canonized in our memories. Human history is littered with the vilified corpses of truly loving, compassionate prophets who we have consigned to hell, with pious incantations and the self-righteous quotation of scripture, because they challenged the game. Then (e.g., the Inquisition) and now (e.g., Guantanamo) we have tortured them and violated them all in the name of a compassionate God who suffers from periodic blackouts, during which he forgets all his own injunctions to love and, instead, insistently mandates genocide and devastation. Beginning even before the biblical "plagues of Egypt" and, no doubt, going beyond even our starving to death of 750,000 Iraqi children, this sociopathic behavior, dressed in the double-speak of the game, continues to flourish.

Let me adduce three individual examples. In 1968, Martin Luther King, Jr. was killed, not because he was a bad man, not because he was a criminal, not because he stole, or lied or took a life, but because he saw through the game of racism within our country and the game of international economic oppression on a global level. So having tried all of the other restraints first—biblical, social, psychological and physical, the game-guardians had no choice but to exterminate him.

Twenty years before that Mahatma Gandhi had to go. Having identified, challenged and risen above the game of colonialism, surviving all of the normal restraints and living to tell the tale he fell victim to his challenge of a much deeper and older game in India. Incensed by Gandhi's handling of the Muslim-backed Pakistan partition (though Gandhi was strongly against it) two Hindu radicals shot and killed him. Once again, Gandhi was not killed because he was a bad man or acted evilly, but because he promoted a different set of beliefs. And for that he had to die.

Hit the rewind button and scroll back almost 2,000 years. In a very colorful episode, Jesus has just fed 5,000 people in the Judean desert with a mere five loaves of bread and two fish. At first they want to make him king, but then he opens his mouth, preaches a very different game, and suddenly all bets are off. They take up stones to kill him. The dialogue goes more or less as follows.

> "Hold it one moment! I have done many good things for you. I have raised the dead, healed the lepers, given sight to the blind and made cripples walk. For which of those deeds do you want to kill me?"
>
> "We are not going to kill you for any of those things but because of your thinking."
>
> "What is so off about my thinking?"
>
> "You are merely a man and yet you claim to be God!"

What is the big problem about such an esoteric claim? So what if a carpenter claims to be divine? How does this hurt anybody? But it freaked them out. So he had to go. The bottom line is, you can act anyway you like, just don't think differently, or if you do, keep your ideas to yourself

(C) Travel Broadens the Mind

People travel with one of two mindsets—a narrow, closed mind that sees what is different as merely amusing or weird, and a broad mind that sees what is different as an invitation to examine one's own presuppositions and norms.

The narrow mind sees that in other cultures people dress differently and it thinks, "Will you look at those weirdoes! Our clothes are respectable and sensible." It sees that other cultures eat different foods and cook them differently, and it thinks, "Gross! How could anybody eat that stuff?" It encounters different religions and it thinks, "You gotta be kiddin' me. They really believe that?" And they read different scriptural traditions and think, "This is just folklore, these are pure myths, unlike our scriptures which are the word of God."

Such minds had a blast when Papua New Guinea was "discovered" in the 1920s. The terrain in Papua New Guinea was so difficult and inhospitable (swamps and craggy mountains) that one British expedition finally gave up its effort to penetrate into the interior after it had managed a mere seven miles in 18 months! It was presumed that apart from a few coastal tribes the interior was empty of people. But then a small plane over-flew it at night and saw fires dotted all over. Subsequently they "discovered" 700 different tribes, most of whom believed that apart from their immediate neighbors they were the only people on planet Earth. When the droves of anthropologists arrived they discovered that over ten percent of all languages on our planet are spoken by the Papuans. They were practicing every conceivable form of marriage and every imaginary form of child-raising. Seven hundred games on a not-particularly large island.

In the past, only the explorers, the colonialists and the oppressed got to experience this clash of cultures. The explorers reported it back as weird to the scientific societies and the populace e.g., the last two Tasmanian natives were shot and stuffed and sent back to the British museum; while a German report of hunting in South America noted the big game killed in one year. Under mammals it read "400 bushman females shot." The colonialists merely replicated their own game in foreign climes; and the oppressed adapted their game very slightly to the few colonial masters that lived among them.

However, in our times, there is almost nobody on Earth who is not experiencing a major clash of cultures; it can no longer be denied, ignored or hidden from.

This has led to an escalation of violence as the games meet head on. It is a very dangerous time to be alive—and a very exciting time. In 1893, at the first World Parliament of Religion, great spiritual traditions met in dialogue, the West was wowed by Eastern mysticism and the East was in awe of the insights of western psychology. Add the technological explosion to the mix and the stage is set for a global shift in consciousness that will either end with the demise of experiment homo sapiens or lead to the next great evolutionary leap.

We are all either Africans or the descendents of Africans that originated from a single mama, Mitochondrial Eve, probably in Kenya, some 200,000 years ago, and began our peregrination out of Africa about 150,000 years ago. All of us, from the isolated tribesman of Papua New Guinea to the Inuit of Alaska, the Celts of Europe and the Mayans of Central America are siblings. We have wandered away from home, forgotten our common ancestry, met accidentally, failed to recognize each other, made war and stole from each other, even wiped out entire groups, but now we are being forced to look beneath the games, the costumes and the masks of color, class and creed to our siblings-in-disguise. Moreover, we are not just being invited to recognize our common humanity but, as we climb higher up the ladder of consciousness, to also recognize the fact that we share a deep, innate kinship with *all* sentient beings, in fact with the entire manifest realm.

Now the clash becomes the embrace of a Namasté, the choreographed footwork of a new realization taking us deep into our divinity; a sacred safari into the "I Am-ness" of all that is; a lucid knowing that all violence was an autoimmune disease in which the manifest body of God was at war within itself.

(D) What Can I Do?

Here, I have six practical suggestions. Firstly, I have to examine the dark underbelly of my own individual game, the shadow side of my own self. Farmers in Africa know that weeding is much more important than fertilizing, if you want a good harvest, for fertilizer, is blind and gives accelerated growth to all it touches—weeds and grasses as well as the crop. When you live in a climate of intense heat and torrential rains, this is especially true. So, weeding the crop a few times during the growing season is vital, otherwise you are left at harvest time with the task of attempting to cull a few food items from the all-pervading jungle. Fertilizers are the people in our lives that love us unconditionally. They are great for our self-image and confidence level, but often their love nourishes our narcissism as much as it does our altruism. So we all need weeders in our lives, people who give us feedback on our selfishness. Often they exaggerate their findings and mostly they do it with glee at our discomfort, but there is always a core of truth to their statements. This, I believe, is what Jesus meant when he said, "Love your enemies." As an extraordinarily insightful psychologist and as an enlightened master he could see that shadow work is vital to mental, social and spiritual health. Various forms of shadow work, then, help me to break out of the game. Some possibilities are: psychotherapy, working with my dreams (especially the Jung-identified archetype of the shadow), invited feedback from teachers, family and friends, working with uninvited feedback from whatever source, and the introspection of full honesty in perusing my own motives in all of my relationships.

But, Carl Jung said, the shadow is 80 percent gold—by which he meant unrealized potential. From the vast possibilities we bring with us into any lifetime, family, culture and "the game" only call forth or encourage a very narrow bandwidth. If I had been born into a different family, culture or game, a different, though, probably, equally-narrow bandwidth would have been called forth. So part of my shadow work is to explore and express new possibilities. Of course, the ultimate possibility is the divine inside me. But even before I get to that realization there are many other gifts and talents I will uncover and express.

Basically, I believe, we are equipped for each incarnation with two kinds of gifts. The first kind is our talents. These were given us by God just as the post office gives letters to the mailman. These gifts belong to us no more than the letters in his bag belong to the mailman. But we cling to them, refusing to deliver them to the community on whose behalf they were entrusted to us. We are entitled to make a living from these gifts, but not a killing. Most of us inflate ourselves by hoarding these and denying the community its right and its needs.

The second kind of gift with which we come to incarnation is our issues or problems. These are our gifts to ourselves to ensure that we will never stop growing. Unfortunately, we wind up eschewing these and projecting them on others, thus denying ourselves the opportunity of evolving and, therefore, saddling society with an excess of problems not properly its own. Full shadow work involves the proper disposition of both of these kinds of gifts.

If individuals have shadows, so, too, do cultures. And that is the second suggestion I have to make. This involves recognizing and challenging the dark underbelly of my culture. Mostly, we can see very clearly this aspect of foreign cultures but not our own. When, at age 13 or so, we naturally reach this level our culture pulls us right down and focuses our attention on the rightness of our game and the weirdness or downright evil of other cultures' games.

This is a bigger job than merely wrestling with my individual shadow, for two reasons; firstly the group shadow is exponentially bigger than the individual one, and secondly there is a society-wide conspiracy to prevent me from challenging the group shadow. The disabling reluctance to face my own mess is dwarfed by the community-enforced demand, with its arsenal of restraints (scriptural, social, psychological and physical), that I unquestioningly play the game. Life moves on, but games keep groups stuck, and so eventually a gap opens up between life and the game, and the society falls into the chaotic chasm of an evolutionary dead end. This has been the track record of all the great civilizations of the past, but we believe ours will be different. It's like our attitude about death. We know that no one has ever gotten out of life alive, but we act as if somehow, we are going to prove to be the exception.

Even if I am no earth-shattering prophet, nor able, nor interested in taking my challenge public, at least I need to be able, in the silence of my own heart-mind, to see how flawed my culture's game really is.

Where others are, in fact, free to give me feedback, solicited or unsolicited, on my individual personality, the mass media, the free press and the churches at large should be performing the same function for society. Unfortunately, in our times, and even in our American culture, the "free press" has either been bought by the game-masters or threatened into silence by the politicians. And the churches mostly have sided with the status quo, being silent on the really important moral issues of our times—warfare, torture, ecological devastation, overpopulation, weapons' development, and "free trade" that demolishes real creativity in the service of a blended homogeneity that bloats the rich while emasculating the poor. Meanwhile churchmen have agreed to be diverted into making ludicrously anachronistic pronouncements, in pompous infallible rhetoric, on issues such as homosexuality, birth control, stem-cell research and women priests.

My third suggestion involves networking; joining like-minded people in our critique of our culture's game. In the absence then of a free press, and in the bought silence of largely irrelevant churches, all of us individuals who are trying to wake up and deal with our own shadow material, must also see and confront this cultural shadow. We must re-free our press, reinvigorate our churches, restore the Bill of Rights and extend it to all humans and beyond. In the past, such information could only be passed by word of mouth and opposition had to be organized into "mobs" of a few hundred people physically assembled at designated locations. Now in this age of information-technology, words and images can be globally disseminated instantly and opposition can be orchestrated into on-line challenges involving millions. The invasion of Iraq sparked protests worldwide which saw just such a response. Even though the protests failed, it was really only the training wheels for how this machine of human decency will ultimately shape the route of human destiny.

Often, it takes only a single charismatic figure or a dedicated select group to set this process in motion. They can either identify and heal the shadow of a culture e.g., Jesus, Gandhi, or identify, amplify and canonize the shadow of a culture e.g., Hitler, and the current crop of political ideologues in the United States of America.

And just as the individual shadow is 80 percent gold, so too, is the culture's shadow. There is so much potential locked in any culture's consciousness, that once it begins to be released, $E=mc^2$ will look like a mere fireworks display by comparison. So the second, and far more important, part of networking is the identifying of these possibilities and bringing them to full flowering. In fact there are, currently, hundreds of thousands of organizations addressing and promoting this evolution of human consciousness in fields as alphabetically disparate as agriculture and zoology and as scientifically disparate as physics and law.

We can all identify with a few areas in which we have interest and join the groups, in those disciplines that are promoting a spiritually-evolved version. Throughout human history all real evolutionary shifts came from the ground up. They have never been orchestrated by politicians or churchmen, since these were far too well served by the current game. So join the revolution of evolution, by that I mean the next quantum leap in human consciousness. And join the evolution of revolution, by that I mean supplementing crowd-based, placard-waving opposition with electronically mediated really-massive campaigns to identify and install alternative models from the deep reservoirs of the race soul of the human species.

My fourth suggestion is a corollary of that. Don't make anybody the enemy in the process of identifying the cultures shadow, not even the stuck, self-serving elite that is causing all of the problems. Because, unless we make it possible for them to become part of the solution, there will be two negative reactions. First, they will intensify their efforts to resist change, going to Draconian ends to ensure the survival of the game that privileged them and second, we will have slipped into a violent mindset, in which case our new game will have within it the seeds of its own undoing. Now, our game also needs to eventually be outgrown. A game which is conscious, aware and compassionately created can be seamlessly outgrown, but a game conceived and birthed in a mindset of division and anger will quickly be overthrown. Outgrow or be overthrown—develop with a soul open to feedback and input from all sides, or be caught in a maelstrom of anarchy and opposition.

My fifth suggestion is a regular practice of meditation. It seems, from the scientific research, that there is no psychological, physical or spiritual practice quite like it for moving people up the ladder of moral, cognitive and social development. That is not to say that those other practices are not beneficial, too. The ultimate purpose of all meditation, of whatever school, is to help the practitioner dis-identify sequentially with all the lesser self concepts (e.g., persona, ego, citizen of a nation, member of a church, human) and re-identify with higher and higher selves, so that "neighbor" eventually is the entire manifest realm and Self is God. With Jesus, I can then say, "Before Abraham came to be, I am."

Such a journey really does allow me to see and to know and to experience at the core of my being that all violence (mental, verbal, physical, social, international, inter-species) is an autoimmune disease and that all war is a civil war. Then the altered states lead to solidified altered traits when I come back into the market place.

My final suggestion is multi-perspectiving (taking multiple perspectives on an issue), visiting the shoe-shop of the Cosmos and trying on the moccasins of others. One of the most fascinating aspects of the near-death experience reports is the life review, in which I re-enact each event of my life, but from the felt experience of each of the participants who were impacted by it. What if I could do this with normal events? Since most of my disagreements are with intelligent, good people, there must be some merit to their positions. I am far better served learning from their viewpoint than imposing my own. This does not necessarily mean abandoning my own principles or position, or falling into the pluralist trap that all viewpoints are equally valid. The positions of Elie Weisel and Adolph Hitler on the Jews are not equally valid; nor are the viewpoints of Martin Luther King, Jr. and the Ku Klux Klan on African Americans. But even Hitler and the members of the Ku Klux Klan are articulations of spirit, albeit gravely pathological articulations, and so I need to be able to walk in their moccasins so as to understand how illusions can be so seductive as to result in such evil.

As I learn, in individual encounters, to take the perspective of another, I must not merely think myself into her position, I must try to even feel myself into her position; I must not just think and feel about her, but think and feel as she does.

I can and must learn to do this for individual others, either people with whom I have personal encounters, or public figures (historical and contemporary) I know just from literature or the mass media. And I, also, need to do it for groups, cultures or regimes. All can be grist for the mill of my growth. I am growing not just for myself but, as I expand, all are benefiting because my identity is no longer Seán (though I may use his tongue or his pen to speak from my core) but the cluster of selves now experienced as a single Christ-centered Self of which Seán is merely one expression.

By the same token an entire culture, as a culture, is called upon to be able to walk in the moccasins of an individual "foreigner" as a representative of another culture. Also, the entire culture, as a culture, must learn to walk in the moccasins of an "alien" culture. Every culture is a valid, workable version of the game of incarnation-as-a-group, and so each culture can teach our culture something valuable about the creative response to being human on planet Earth. Since all are articulations of God, then the more perspectives I can inhabit, the higher up the God-ladder I can go and the more I can widen my God-Self. Cultures that can do this shape-shifting will survive and grow; ones that can't will wither and die.

When, finally, I can inhabit the spacesuit, walk in the moccasins of, and see through the perspective of all living things from rocks to extraterrestrial beings, then I will have really come into my divinity. Then, as Eugene O'Neill said, "Seeing the secret, I become the secret."

13

Star Spark
(December 3, 2001)

A shower of yellow-red sparks exploded out of the heart of the campfire and arced parabolically across the cold autumn sky. They sizzled in the frosty air as they traced their meteoric fire-bows against the blue-green backdrop of the heavens. The camper, who had caused the spark shower by poking dreamily at the core of the fire, followed the complete trajectory of one of the sparks. And he fell into a yet deeper reverie. Or was it a vision?

The spark lived 10 billion years. As its exterior cooled, a crust formed over its furnace-center. Vegetation grew on its crust—luxuriant foliage of myriad forms. Then creatures evolved and cavorted about under the green canopy. More and more exotic animals emerged in long, complex food-chains, or in symbiotic partnerships. Some walked and some waddled; some boated and some burrowed; some swam and some squatted.

In time, a creature arose who learned to plot the history of the spark, exhume its past and predict its demise. This creature was actually writing a poem about the spark and the campfire supernova from which it was born on the very night that the spark ended its parabolic journey and crashed to extinction on the dewy grass. Even the fiery core of it sizzled into blackness.

The camper sighed, stood up and walked into the forest. In the cabin, at the edge of the clearing, the woman called to her husband, "The camper has abandoned the fire, and walked into the forest!" The husband jerked awake. He thought he had just heard his wife say to him: "The camper has abandoned the fire, and walked into the forest!" But his wife had been dead over five years. He sadly got out of bed and stumbled to the bathroom. He looked tiredly into the mirror. Nobody looked back at him. There was no image in the mirror. Then the husband realized that he was still dreaming. And he realized that he himself was only a dream.

Since there was nobody looking into the mirror, and thus, nothing to reflect on, the mirror dissolved and disappeared.

All was quiet in the non-existent cabin, at the edge of the non-existent clearing that housed the non-existent campfire, long since deserted by the non-existent camper after he had followed the arc of the non-existent spark.

And they all lived unhappily never again.

14

Change Now, 'Cause It's All Gonna Be Different

"Let him that would move the world move first himself."
Socrates

There is a saying in marriage counseling, often quoted tongue in cheek that men marry women hoping they will never change, but they do; while women marry men hoping they will change, but they don't. As a clinical psychologist I do a lot of marriage counseling; I can vouch for the impediment that is to relationships.

Children long for change, teenagers push for change, young adults create change and elders hate change—they pine for "the good ole days."

But life *is* change; you cannot step into the same river twice. The river that flows through my native city Cork in Ireland, is called the Lee. From its source in Gougane Barra to the Atlantic down by Guileen is a distance of about sixty miles. Even if its average flow is a leisurely five miles per hour then it has totally emptied itself within 12 hours. The trout-touched droplet that skips over the brown rocks of Ballingeary on Sunday morning as the bells are summoning the early risers to eight o'clock mass, is by six p.m. in time to hear the Angelus ringing out from Blackrock Church as it heads for Passage West. And by eight p.m., it is a member of the ocean community.

And so, evolution and change are the spirit of cosmic history. The difference between the sleeper and the awakened one is that the sleeper is dragged reluctantly into the future, while the enlightened one creates the future. As a first step in this waking up process, we, at least, have to embrace, work with, and be open to change.

With all of that in mind, I want to examine how Jesus woke up to embrace change and ultimately to move into Christ-consciousness.

(A) How Jesus' Understanding of Healing Changed.

When I look at the evolution of our understanding of healing, it appears to me that it progressed through four stages. First, we believed that God healed randomly. There was no system or pattern to how or who he decided to heal. Some people got healed, some got worse and some died. God comes across as an uncaring, dice-throwing, game-player. There is still lots of evidence for this behavior. Whenever I hear the few survivors of an air wreck claim that "It was God who saved me," I want to ask, "Then why didn't he save the 187 who died in the same crash?"

The second stage was when we figured out that God could be bribed, blarneyed or cajoled into healing us or granting our wishes. I want to smile when I hear a pugilist claim, after winning a big boxing match, "I prayed to Jesus and he gave me the victory!" I wasn't aware that Jesus had an interest in fisticuffs or was a fan of the Queensbury rules, or was a betting man with a financial interest in the World Boxing Association's offerings.

Stage three came when we believed that there were designated healers or channels that God preferred to use. We heard that such and such a one had "a direct line to God." Of course, it's true that in any human activity there will be specialists, talented people who have the native ability, training and interest in developing the skill set, whether that activity is athletics, mathematics, art or bridge. But all of us can walk, add, doodle and play cards. And all of us can heal; we do it all the time. Whenever you cut your hand your body knows how to coagulate the blood, form a scab, regenerate new skin and soon have you looking as good as new. You break a leg; the bones know how to knit themselves back together. You get food poisoning and your body reacts optimally to get the toxins out of your system.

And at stage four, we realize that all healing is self-healing. Both the body and the psyche are self-repairing systems. They are designed specifically to do just that. All medicine, whether allopathic or alternative, consists only of interventions to speed up these natural abilities.

You can see this progression in the gospel accounts of Jesus' healing ministry.

(B) How Jesus' Understanding of his Mission Changed.

To illustrate this huge shift in his understanding of what he came to do, I want to compare two other healing stories. In Matthew Chapter 9, Jairus, a synagogue official set out in pursuit of Jesus, to beg him to come and lay his hands upon his 12-year-old daughter who was dying. He fell at Jesus' feet and implored him to come and help. Without the slightest hesitation, Jesus agreed and the two went off together.

In Matthew Chapter 15, Jesus has decided to take a vacation. He and his disciples have been mobbed continually, getting little time to sleep or even to eat. So he invited them to leave Galilee and Israel and go into the area of the Syro-Phoenicians. As the group made its way through a little village, however, a local woman spotted him and recognized him. She called after him, "Son of David (i.e. man of Israel), have pity on me; my little daughter is dying!" Jesus ignored her. He was not going to mix business with pleasure. So the woman began to run up the dusty street, pleading all the while, "Son of David, have pity on me!" He continued to ignore her. By now people were coming to the doors of their houses wondering why their neighbor was shouting after these foreign men. Had they robbed her house? Molested her? Peter felt very awkward, so he hissed at Jesus, "Give her what she wants, everybody is staring at us. She's making a scene." Without breaking stride Jesus snidely retorted, "I was only sent to the lost sheep of the house of Israel." The woman however, was not going to give up. She caught up with the group, dashed around in front of Jesus, dropped to her knees, grabbed his ankles and begged, "Please, my little daughter is DYING!!" Crudely, sarcastically and with unbecoming racism, Jesus replied, "It is not fair to take the food from the children and throw it to the dogs." But this mother, whose dedication to her daughter far outstripped her shock at the stranger's words, was not diverted. Playing at his own game, she turned his own metaphor on its head and said, "That may be true, but, you know, sometimes scraps fall from the children's table and the little puppies are allowed to eat them. That's all I want."

This is a truly shocking story. It is shocking to Christians 2,000 years later who have to try to explain away this gross act of chauvinism; it was, no doubt, shocking to the young mother; it may even have been shocking to the hardened fishermen-disciples; but most of all it was shocking to Jesus, because, I am convinced, God hit him upside the head for this prejudicial attitude. And Jesus grew up real fast.

In both stories, the little girls benefited; in both stories, the parent benefited; in both stories, the disciples benefited; but only in the second story did Jesus benefit. And this segues nicely into the third point I want to make.

(C) How Jesus' Understanding of God Changed

In Judaism of Jesus' time, the ideal beloved of God were Jewish, male, healthy and wealthy. Each was a sign of God's benediction, and the absence of any, a sign of God's displeasure. It took Jesus a lifetime to outgrow these four biases. But he did it, event-by-event, relationship-by-relationship and encounter-by-encounter. He got the feedback-about-your-shadow piece down "real good."

So what about the "healthy" prejudice? As a long lingering legacy from the time when Judaism did not believe in life after death, it was thought that since God is one, and just, and since there is no other place to reward virtue and punish vice, it had to be done here and now. Thus "sin" was punished by illness or misfortune. But even the most dedicated adherents to the view had to admit that it couldn't explain why some people are *born* crippled. A codicil was written to the previous black and white position. Now, it was held that God would punish the sin of the parents to the third or fourth generation. This seemed to satisfy all parties. It was a parsimonious explanation satisfying the Occam's Razor test and people could now relax into a perfectly plain explanation; except for Jesus that is. He had tarnished God's reputation for justice by introducing the importance of compassion into the equation and baldly stating, "God makes his sun to shine on the good and the bad alike; he makes his rain to fall on the sinners and saints without distinction." This raised some eyebrows. This upset the neat little, "You got your just desserts!" explanation for illnesses of the adults and the neonates alike.

In John Chapter 9, there is a great story that illustrates the issue. Outside the gates of the city of Jericho sat a blind man begging. He was a standard fixture there and well known to travelers. He had been blind since birth. Once as Jesus and his disciples were leaving the city, someone asked Jesus' opinion of the matter, "Who has sinned, this man or his parents, since he was born blind?" Obviously, another consideration has been introduced here, because the man could hardly have been born blind as a punishment for his own sin unless there was a belief in some form of reincarnation and karma within Judaism of that era.

Jesus' reply, however, took the problem into a totally different direction. Enigmatically he said, "Neither has the man sinned nor his parents, rather he was born blind so that the glory of God might be manifested in him." He then went on and cured the man, which led to a much bigger controversy in which the man, his parents, the neighbors, Jesus and the Pharisees were embroiled.

Because Jesus restored the man's sight, I always presumed that the phrase, " . . . so the glory of God might be manifested in him," meant that God intended to heal him through Jesus' ministry and thus reveal his glory via a miracle, but now I have a different hit on it. I think Jesus may have said, "How can you appreciate the divine glory of sightedness if there is not occasional blindness? How can we appreciate the light if there is not occasional darkness? How can we appreciate health if there is not occasional illness? How can we appreciate goodness if there is not occasional evil?"

We already manage to miss the "ordinary miracles" that are 95 percent of our daily experiences. Shouldn't these "glitches" bring us gratefully awake to the wonders of our world? What is the value of the gift of free will if there are no choices among which to pick? And the training wheels of free will are the obviously disparate faces of light and dark, good and evil. When we have mastered this simple task, we can then exercise free will in ever-finer calibrations of good and better, until finally we are faced only with choices between nearly-perfect and fully-enlightened. This entire trajectory, this evolutionary safari, this spiritual pilgrimage is evidence of the glory of God made manifest.

The next prejudice favored the wealthy, since this, too, like health, was seen as evidence of being blessed by God, while poverty was proof, as was illness, of God's disfavor.

This, however, may have cut more deeply than the health issue, because not even the very privileged were immune to illnesses. There were groups, though, that spent entire lifetimes in luxury, so this was a much easier prejudice to maintain. Jesus saw through that one very quickly. He said, "It's more difficult for a rich man to get into heaven than for a camel to go through the eye of a needle." That put the cat among the pigeons, if you pardon the mixing of (animal) metaphors. When you upset the healthy, you are merely a weirdo, but when you upset the wealthy, you are a communist. So they called him a communist, sort of.

It's not that money or resources make us good or bad, but what our connection, use and explanation of them is. Having lived in poverty as a child in Ireland, among the poor in East Africa for 14 years and with the privileged of Silicon Valley for the last 19 years, I have first-hand evidence that among both the poor and the wealthy there are sinners and saints. The "sin" of the "sinful rich" consists of three parts. First, the tendency to view wealth as a sign of God's predilection, which leads to the notion of choseness and, hence, to pride. Second, the tendency to blame the poor for their condition and, hence become judgmental; and third, to reduce the relationships to God to a mere business agreement. Whether we call this a covenant or a testament matters not a whit. It's merely the deification of accident, making virtue out of circumstance and holiness out of luck.

So there is a story in Luke, Chapter 7, of a Roman centurion whose servant was seriously ill. He had heard about Jesus and decided to seek his help. He sent messengers to Jesus to ask for this favor. Now treating the servant of an occupying military leader is hardly your typical scenario, particularly in Galilee. Between 187 BCE and 132 CE there were 32 armed rebellions in Israel against foreign occupation (first the Greeks and then the Romans). And of these 32 rebellions, 31 had started in Galilee. So for a Roman commander to ask for help from a Galilean peasant, wouldn't seem like the smartest thing to do. However, not only the messenger but even the onlookers immediately averred that this centurion was a very good man, partial to things Jewish, and he had in fact built the local synagogue. Jesus was intrigued and so he said to the messengers, "Fine, let's go!" They were very happy, and one of them ran ahead to tell the centurion. He was shocked. He hadn't expected Jesus to actually come to his house. Since he understood Jewish Law, he realized at once that Jesus would automatically incur ritual defilement by entering a gentile household. So, in a panic, he sent the runner back with the following message, "Sir, I am not worthy to have you under my roof. Just say the word and my servant will be healed. For I myself am subject to authority, and have men under me. If I say to a servant, 'Go,' He goes. And if I say to a soldier, 'Come here!' He comes."

This knocked the wind out of Jesus, and he turned to the crowd and exclaimed, "Wow, I have never found this level of faith among the Israelites. So, I tell you, people will come from the East and from the West and sit down at the heavenly banquet with Abraham, while the natural heirs will be denied admission."

It was an eye-opener for Jesus. Now he began to see that God does not favor the Jews. He began to see; however, he was not quite there, for having abandoned the notion of "Jews-as-God's-only-chosen-people," he still can't make the complete transition. He is still stuck in an intermediary stage. He has created a two-tier citizenship; tier one consists of the "natural heirs" i.e. native Jews, while tier two consists of the adopted heirs. Saint Paul will build on this later and create a three-tier model. Tier one, Jesus as "God's only son"; tier two, the Jews as natural heirs; and tier three, the righteous gentiles as adopted heirs.

In a story recorded in John's gospel Chapter 4, he is stuck in the same place. Here he was in dialogue with another foreign woman, a Samaritan, at a well where he was resting, when she came to draw water.

Much to her amazement "for Jews do not speak to Samaritans," he initiated a conversation. She discovered in this conversation that he was a prophet, so she asked him, "Our fathers say that this mountain (Mt. Gerizim, the sacred mountain of the Samaritans) is the place to worship, while you people claim that Mt. Zion (the sacred mountain of the Jews) is the place to worship. Who's right?" Jesus said, "The days are coming when people will worship neither on this mountain nor in Jerusalem, but will worship in spirit and in truth. God is spirit, and those who worship him will worship in spirit. You Samaritans worship what you do not know, while we Jews worship what we do know, for after all salvation is from the Jews." If, indeed, he spoke the latter sentence—and its always a guess as to how much writer and editorial insertions corrupt the actual stories—then he was still badly stuck in his two-tier model.

It reminds me of Karl Rahner's pathetic solution around the time of Vatican II to the Catholic Church's teaching that only it held the keys to salvation. Rahner proposed a softened version that he called "Anonymous Christianity," whereby all people of good will could be saved, because their righteousness made them Christians at heart, even if they never heard of Jesus. Pretty pathetic! How would you feel about being called an anonymous Republican because you saved money; or an anonymous Muslim if you prayed five times a day; or an anonymous Jew if you were circumcised?

If salvation is, as Jesus claimed to the Samaritan woman, only from the Jews, I don't want any part in that God; he is far too small for me.

If salvation is, as the Roman Catholic Church taught, only for Catholics, I don't want any part in that God; he is far too small for me. If salvation is only from the Buddhist system I don't want any part in that God, he is far too small for me. If salvation is only from the Hindu system, he is far too small for me and I don't want any part in that God.

Jesus in these stories is slowly breaking out of the "Jews as God's only chosen people" and going universal in his thinking, but it is, as yet, a two-tiered universalism. Eventually he will reach full universalism. By the end of his life he will commission his disciples to "go out into the whole world" healing the sick and preaching the good news of God's unconditional love for all. In the magnificent poetry of his ecstatic moments he will widen this universalism to include all sentient beings i.e. "Look at the lilies of the field . . . not even Solomon in all his glory was arrayed like one of these" and again, "Aren't sparrows sold two for a penny in your market places, and yet, I tell you, not a single one falls from the skies without your heavenly father being aware of it!" Now he has finally got it. He has transcended the narrow theocratic nationalism of his upbringing.

So what about his male bias. The Talmud claimed that it was preferable for a father to teach his daughter harlotry than teach her Torah. Women could not be the disciples of a Rabbi. Even in modern Orthodox Judaism, there is a prayer said by the davening males, "I thank you God that you did not make me a woman."

In two of the stories I mentioned, Jesus touches or is touched by a woman, one a 12-year-old just coming into fertility and menstruation, and the other, hemorrhaging for 12 years, who is probably at the end of her fertility and perimenopausal. According to Jewish Law, both of them were unclean and anybody who came in contact with them was rendered ritually unclean. He broke through this particular prejudice rather quickly and the gospels state that there were many women (several of them mentioned by name) who followed him. In John Chapter 11, one of them, Mary of Bethany, "sat at his feet," the code phrase for being a card-carrying officially acknowledged student. This upset her own sister Martha, who was concerned both about this forbidden impropriety and also, about having to do all the household hospitality chores herself. Jesus insists that Mary had "chosen the better part, which shall not be taken away from her." Wrong! The Christian church, after a honeymoon period of deeply honoring this equalizing of male and female, soon reverted to a patriarchal, male chauvinist system that, in the Roman Catholic lineage survives right down to the present moment. For 50 or 60 glorious years after Jesus' death, his women disciples were apostles and founders and leaders of Christian communities. Mary of Magdala was his very closest companion and probably the "beloved disciple" mentioned in the gospel which, most likely, developed around her, but was later attributed, erroneously, to John, son of Zebedee. In some of the Gnostic gospels, she was the repository of the most secret teachings of Jesus' teachings which he felt could not be entrusted even to Peter, because none of the men had the same level of understanding of Jesus that the Magdalene possessed. None of them "saw" him as deeply as she.

Because, the deepest truth is that meeting God or even looking upon the face of God is not the same thing as *seeing* God, anymore than meeting Jesus or even looking upon the face of Jesus is not the same thing as seeing Jesus.

15

The Light Catchers
April 23, 2001

I'm just in time for the light show.
I have a ringside seat:
an old garden chair,
looking across the valley,
to where the sun intends to set.

Thousands of silken tendrils
are decorating the branches of the scrub oak
behind which I sit.
The spiders are having Carnival.

What is your choice?
Concentric polygons framing the sun
through the dappled branches?

Or, perhaps, the three-feet high
lone stalk of grass
with one silken thread attached,
casting it expertly
back and forth, back and forth,

like a dry-fly fisherman.
Snaring errant photons,
which bob and weave
and show their multicolored underbellies
in a frantic effort to free themselves?

Maybe you prefer to watch
the single filament of fire,
ten feet long,
which has slipped its moorings entirely
and is floating free,
undulating sensually
like a gravity-defying trapeze artist
clad in diaphanous rainbows,
and dancing above the earth
sans trapeze, sans safety net?

Three butterflies do a courtesy fly-by.
Are they simply joyriding?
Or is this the foreplay to their mating,
a mid-air ménage-a-trois?

$$F = (M_1 \times M_2) / r^2$$
begone!
Sir Isaac Newton,
Eat your heart out.

16

Let Your Dreams Shape Your Beliefs

"Let the beauty we love be what we do."
Rumi

She was a small tentative, anxious-looking woman in her late 30's. She had phoned me to arrange a counseling appointment some three weeks before. Now she was seated in my office looking furtively about her and avoiding all eye contact. Even the muffled sound of the traffic on San Antonio Road seemed to upset her.

"I need help," she said. "And I'm not even sure I should be talking to you, but a friend of mine recommended you. I don't trust men, and I have a difficult time with minorities. As male and Irish I wondered if that meant one or two strikes against me already. "I'm afraid to go out, and I suffer from panic attacks. Night sounds startle me and so I don't sleep very well." All of this came out in a gush as if she were afraid to speak more slowly lest she lose the courage to speak at all.

"Do you have any idea what the cause of this is?" I enquired, trying to disguise both my masculinity and my Irishness.

"Oh yes," she replied, "It started after I got mugged"

"I'm really sorry to hear that." I said, "What happened?"

"Well, I live in Berkeley and one evening a man ran up behind me, snatched my shoulder bag and knocked me to the ground. That's when it all started."

"And how long did the incident last?"

"I suppose 60-90 seconds."

"I am really sorry," I said. "And when did this event occur?"

"It happened 11 years ago."

So a one-and-a-half-minute incident which happened 11 years ago had become the defining event in the woman's life. It had become her identity. Of all the billions of bits of sensory input to which she was exposed in her 30 plus years, this one piece had become her signature tune. She was a victim and had grown magnificently into that role. And all of the emotional baggage and mental strait-jacketing, all of the prejudice and fear, all of the crippling belief and habits had flowed seamlessly from that sense of self.

It is a story replicated millions of times.

(A) We Are Terrorized by the Terror of Terrorism

An American president famously said, "We have nothing to fear but fear itself." Jesus said that same thing 2,000 years earlier; "Do not be afraid. Fear is useless." If what we most need to fear is fear itself, then the current political regime in this country has capitalized on it. Except it has cultivated a superlative form of fear—terror, and while inculcating it, as a policy decision, in the citizens of this country, the regime has gone out of its way to breed "terror-genies" in foreign climes. All good terror deserves terrorists, and terrorists aren't fulfilling their part of the bargain unless they can be goaded into acts of terrorism. Thus the elegant circle is complete. The politicians have the evidence wanted in order to convince the citizenry that terror lurks on every side, and then it's quite simple to offer them "security" as a trade-off for their freedoms. In short order the Bill of Rights can be gutted, the Constitution diluted, the press muzzled and torture, violence and war can now be conducted with the active support of redneck beer-drinkers and the subservient silence of liberals who fear to be branded unpatriotic.

As the only superpower, we then get to export our paranoia through aggression paid for by robbing the piggy banks of the elderly, the poor and the under-aged while we borrow one billion dollars a day from sniggering superpowers-in-the-making who are quite happy to see us slowly bleed ourselves to death. We are the dinosaurs posturing self-importantly as we guide in the meteor that will render us extinct.

It's hard to know, then, which is the cause and which is the effect. Is this cultural preoccupation with terror and foreboding the reason why so many individuals have a personal identity as victims, or is the national preoccupation with looming disaster the aggregate of all the millions of individual victims? At this stage it's a moot question because it is now an endless feedback loop, where the individuals and the nation goad and feed and complement each other's pathology.

For this essay, however, I want to focus on the situation of the individual, and to do so I will use the analogy of a necklace. Each of us wears a necklace, the beads of which consist of life events and the string of which is memory. The beads, basically, are of three kinds; firstly, "ordinary miracles;" secondly, ecstatic moments; and, thirdly; difficult or traumatic events.

The awake person is wearing a necklace that is truly representative of life: 95 percent of the beads consist of ordinary miracles, by which I mean the amazing sensorium we possess (the ability to see, hear, taste, touch and smell); the precious human bodies we inhabit (with trillions of cells in constant communication with each other, monitoring and regulating, with amazing precision, the organs, hormones and subsystems); a panoply of emotions that mine the events for feeling tone; and a perceptual mechanism that interprets the sensory input. All of these are miracles, but we have grown inured to them. Their ubiquitous presence renders them invisible—like fish in the ocean looking for water.

But the awake person *is* aware of them, and celebrates them throughout the day. Buddhists have a saying "Zen mind, beginner's mind." It means the ability to see every moment with the freshness of a young child and, as a result, be in awe of life.

Above and beyond these ordinary miracles are the ecstatic moments—a vivid sunset perhaps, a great musical experience, love-making, watching a child watching a ladybug, winning a tennis match or solving a mathematical problem. They come in many guises and they represent about three percent of all human experiences. So on the necklace of the awakened, they will be represented by the appropriate number of beads.

But the awake person will also have tough or even traumatic experiences—an illness, the death of a loved one, a mugging or a divorce. However, since in actual life, these only represent about two percent of our experiences, they too will have the appropriate number of beads on the necklace, and will be given the appropriate amount of time and energy; no more, no less.

The "sleeper," however, wears a very different necklace. Its beads are in no way representative of the actual experiences he has. The ordinary miracles fail to make the radar of his recognition. When his attention is drawn to them, he dismisses them. If, for instance, he were to be reminded of the ordinary miracle of eyesight, he would simply regard that as his due. But if something were to happen to his eyesight he would immediately focus on it. It would occupy a huge portion of his time and energy and become more proof of how unfair life is and add more data to the rightness of his claim to be a victim. While focusing on this one area that is not working he is utterly ungrateful for the myriad of things in his life that is working. If his eye problem were to be corrected, he would then quickly set about ignoring it while he cast about for the next item about which he can be upset. In his necklace, the only beads are the traumata, held together on a thick unyielding chain.

Then there are the truly deeply asleep whose necklace consists of a single huge pendant strung on the steel cable of one crucifying memory. There is no room on this hawser for the delicately fashioned emeralds of the moments of ecstasy, let alone the ordinary miracles. Often this single devastating event is not unique to them, and on an objective scale it may not even be very large. But memory and a fanatical dedication to making it the core identity ensure that it occupies 99 percent of their psychic space and waking hours. They will not be distracted from their utter commitment to enshrining this at the core of their being. No re-contextualizing data ever make it into the laboratory of their experiment with gloom. Such data are foiled at the very perimeter of their consciousness by the ever-vigilant, "Yes, but . . ."

In our dim distant past an evolutionary advantage may have been conferred on those whose antennae were always attuned to the possibility of the (much maligned) saber-toothed tiger. Not any more. This fixation is now rewarded by hyper-arousal, constant anxiety, sleeplessness, depression, gastro-intestinal problems, breakdowns in relationship, and poor work performance. The list is as painfully long as the necklace is chokingly tight.

Memory is a faculty, itself neutral, but which can be used to skewer us to the traumata of the past or let us soar on winged moments of ecstasy. Since each ecstatic moment is a déjá vu of our original soul state, we are well served by fully inhabiting such moments and then subsequently relating to life from the memory of them.

But, in truth, we wear not one but two necklaces; whereas the first consists of the beads of life events strung on the chain of memory, the second consists of the life events yet to unfold, strung on the chain of imagination. Imagination is that faculty, in itself neutral but which can be used to skewer us to the traumata yet to come or let us soar on the creative possibilities ahead.

If you think that endlessly re-living the traumata of the past is debilitating, try endlessly pre-living the traumata of the future. The sleeper manages his time equally between both, living angrily or guiltily in the past and anxiously and fearfully in the future. He manages a meal consisting totally of the worst of both worlds. The one place he never lives is in the present. The present is returned to the universe, unopened.

The one who is awake inhabits three worlds; firstly, a past, from which she learns and grows; secondly, a future, which she envisions with love, affirmation and optimism; and thirdly (and mainly) a present which is gratefully unpacked moment by moment for the precious gift that it is.

Both the sleeper and the awakened one create an entire way of life—that of self-inflicted torture or that of liberation for the life-long embrace of our true nature.

(B) Christianity—a religion for the past or spirituality for the future?

Just as individuals can fixate on a single event and create an entire identity from it, so too can entire religions. And, in fact, they have tended to do that. Judaism's founding myth is the Exodus, the escape of slaves from Egypt in 1250 BC. And it has led to a not very healthy fixation with the notion of victim-hood, a notion which strongly defines Judaism even today. There are two versions of this. Firstly, "Why do bad things only happen to us?" and secondly, "God chose us to suffer vicariously for the sins of the world." Either way suffering is wrapped up with identity.

Islam has frequently fixated on the notion of Jihad, the "holy war," and while this may be interpreted as an inner confrontation with intra-psychic shadow material, in reality it primarily has been acted out in the global arena as physical, military violence. Islam, which in the period of 1,000-1,500 AD was a leading light in the pursuit of literature, philosophy, mathematics, architecture and science, has since then fallen into a decline in which Jihad is advocated against the perceived de-sacralizing influence of the sciences.

And Christianity has made the agonizing crucifixion of Jesus, its founding myth, and, in turn, proposed that the world is a "vale of tears;" we are here to suffer; the rewards will come in heaven. In this fixation, the death of Jesus is the whole point of his life, a death that finally assuaged the utterly justifiable ire of God and was the agreed upon price Satan needed to be paid to hand us back to our "Father." Some father! Some story! Some sickness!

In truth, Jesus' ministry would have been no less effective if he had lived into his 80's and dandled his great-granddaughter on his knee, because his mission was not about dying but about living in the fullest alignment with love and light. It was his Christ consciousness, not his crucifixion that was his gift to planet Earth.

But western Christianity, in particular, has concentrated on the last three days of Jesus' life while ignoring the invitation to Christ-consciousness. It has been attending a "survivor group" for well nigh 2,000 years and saying, "Hi, my name is Jesus, and I'm a victim of crucifixion."

When Paul, that sometime ecstatic, but frequent articulator of partisan theology claims, "God chose us before the world began . . . he predestined us to be his adopted sons so that in Christ and through his blood we have been redeemed and our sins forgiven," he was doing the best he could for his times. But this teaching of Paul is long since passé. For one thing there are no chosen ones, not individuals, cultures, ethnic groups, nations, nor yet particular religions. All that is, is of God and all is equally beloved. The problem is that not all individuals or groups have learned to love equally.

And there is no predestination. God did not sit down before the big bang and cruelly choose those she would save and those she would damn. There are neither damned nor saved but simply souls on safari, spirits in spacesuits, beings en route to enlightenment.

Nor are there adopted sons. The universe does not grant a three-tiered citizenship: Jesus, the only-begotten son; Jews the natural heirs; and Christians, the adopted heirs. There is only God, transcendent and utterly ineffable, who is, also, immanent and lovingly present in all his emanations.

As for salvation in Christ's blood; Christ does not have blood. Christ is a state of consciousness, a state of soul. A full-blooded human may put on Christ-consciousness, but this consciousness does not have blood. As for redeeming us; what a weird notion! To redeem means literally to "buy back." The notion of God buying back souls from Satan through spilling Jesus' blood is best buried in the antiquity of the childhood of Christianity. It is a meaningless and grotesque image for the 21st century. For if God bought us back he must first have sold us. A father who sells his own children into slavery is hardly one to be admired, let alone worshipped.

When Jesus originally commissioned the 12 for local ministry, his mandate was twofold, preach good news and heal sickness. At the end of his life when he re-commissioned them for a global ministry he gave them the same mandate, preach good news and heal sickness. Nowhere does he exhort them to go out and tell people how I suffered. Tell them, in lurid detail, how they captured, tried and crucified me. Tell them that is how I want to be remembered, a bloodied, exhausted body hanging grotesquely on a tree!" He did not send them to be long-faced reciters of the trials and tribulations of the master.

And what is the good news? It is that God is not a distant demanding deity; he is not a law enforcement officer; he doesn't punish the bad or reward the good. Rather, Jesus said, the kingdom of God is "en mesoi," a Greek term meaning both "within you" and "among you." The kingdom of God is not a yet-to-be-earned afterlife, but a now-to-be-experienced reality that lies within the Self (as Christ-consciousness), and lives among us (as compassion). It is not a future place but a present state of mind and a state of community.

And of what does healing consist? It is firstly sealing the divisions within myself, the bringing of my own shadow into the light of my own soul's luminosity, so that I am not at war within my own psyche. And, secondly, it is realizing that all sentient beings are my neighbor, who I am meant to love in the same way I love myself, because they *are* my Self—my real Self, my God Self.

Healing will involve a politic that goes beyond nationalism, beyond a fixation with terrorism (which is the ultimate form of reliving the future endlessly) and beyond a mentality of wars-as-the-solution-to-war. Healing will involve going beyond a religion which believes literally in myths, to an understanding that myths are profound but metaphorical articulations of eternal truths.

Even the greatest teachers were forced to articulate their insights in a way that moved their audiences forward, but not in such a way that was totally beyond the audience's comprehension. Thus no articulation of truth, even by an enlightened master, can be the *final* articulation of the truth. A final articulation awaits an audience of fully enlightened beings. To everybody short of full enlightenment, a final articulation would be incomprehensible and therefore useless.

Imagine I were asked by a group of my friends in Palo Alto to lead them in a bike tour of Ireland, since I grew up there and know the terrain. If I cycle so fast that when the group gets to the first intersection, I am out of sight and they don't know whether I have gone straight ahead or to the left or to the right, then I'm not much of a leader. However, if I hang out in the middle of the group, so that every time the front riders reach a crossroads they have to stop and let me catch up in order to ask directions of me, once again I am not providing leadership. The true leader, even if he be a Lance Armstrong will be ahead of the pack, but not out of sight.

So it has been with all the great teachers. They either articulated their truths in a way that was intelligible but challenging to believers of the current paradigm, or else they used stories, metaphors, parables, analogies so that no matter at what stage a member of the audience was, he could see in it what he was capable of seeing. Moreover, the same story can be mined by the same listener at greater depths as he makes spiritual progress. Even hundreds of years later these same stories can be revisited and panned for the gold which was present from the beginning (if the images aren't by then too foreign to us e.g., sheep and goats, wheat and cockle.) This was a favorite medium of Jesus.

Gratefully, each interpretation contains the seeds of its own undoing, just as each solution to a human problem bears the seeds of its own undoing.

I say, gratefully, because spirit is never going to allow us to stop evolving this side of enlightenment.

(C) Shall We Dream?

I want to suggest practical ways in which we can move towards Christ-consciousness. This involves both aspects of the space-time continuum; I suggest that, as individuals and as groups, we need to create sacred spaces and sacred times.

Can you find a special place (forest, mountains, river, lake, ocean, church, mosque, temple) where you feel the presence of the numinous? Visit it often, alone, then reproduce it, on a small scale, in your own home. Dedicate a room or a corner of a room and make it a sanctuary. Honor its sacredness by creating a special ambience there through icons, flowers, incense, a water feature. Visit it often, alone. Then you can begin creating sacred times. An ideal to aim at is:

1. One hour each day
2. A half a day each week
3. A weekend each month
4. A week each year

Most of us could create all of that time simply by reducing our TV, radio, or newspaper time. It actually is not that difficult to achieve, and the results are immediate and amazing.

So what will you do in that space and at the time? Why, dream your dream, of course! Dreams come in many guises through many kinds of exercises. They come through fantasizing, through active imagination, through silence, through meditation, through gardening, through creative writing. If your dream is too small, scrap it. The energy that fashioned our universe (and, according to quantum mechanic theory, innumerable others) loves a challenge. Your wildest imaginings won't put the slightest dent in its abilities. A source that gave us William Butler Yeats and daffodils, hippopotami and supernovae is not going to scratch its head in frustration at your modest request. But your dream has to be in alignment with your beliefs. If your beliefs tell you that your dreams can't come true, then the universe can only give you back your ambivalence. If dreams don't shape your beliefs, then certainly beliefs will shape your dreams.

Everything of value in our world has been contributed by those whose dreams modulated their beliefs. Jesus called this dream-belief, "faith" and assured us that the energy which *made* mountains could *shift* mountains when this faith was applied.

All frustration in the world is the outcome of the gap between dream and belief. There is no more wretched person on the planet than one who doesn't have the courage to set out in pursuit of the dream. And this courage only comes when beliefs and dreams are aligned.

So how to "follow your bliss?" First, you've got to " . . . leave your father's house." This was Jesus' teaching about the first stage of marriage. It means you have to step outside the box which has defined you up to now, whether that is a body image, a sense of self, a cloying relationship, or a dead-end job. It means listening to love not to fear. And it means having a plan to translate the dream into real life e.g., what mentor do I need? What timeline have I in mind? What will be my very first action?

And as you set out, remember not to selfishly trample on other people's dreams in the pursuit of your own. Of course, there will be people who choose to be upset and even alarmed at the changes you're making. They will attempt to force you, persuade you or guilt trip you back into the old box. That, however, is their stuff. As long as you are sensitive to their real rights and your real responsibilities, you can ignore the outraged protests of "I liked you better before," or "I'm glad your poor ole mother isn't around to see you now!" As Brendan Behan, the Irish playwright said, "F . . . the begrudgers!"

Finally you must dream a dream for Gaia. The truly great dreams are ones that come through us for her. As, in the past, the shaman dreamed for the tribe, today we dream for the planet. For far too long Gaia has been living in a nightmare dreamed by small fearful minds. If you want to dream the greatest dream of your life, dream a dream of a quantum leap in planetary consciousness.

Victims define themselves by their personal nightmares; visionaries define themselves by their cosmic dreams.

17

The Journey of the Black-backed Beetle
(May 22, 2007)

Left-right, left-right, left-right. I almost stepped on him. Sorry! Après vous, monsieur. He is lumbering across my path, as we both make our way along the madrona-ornamented, redwood-dominated mountain slope. But left-right, left-right, left-right is much more complicated when you are a six-legged black-backed beetle. So I sit on my haunches to see how he does it. Even though he moves so slowly, it's hard for my eyes to visually track the chronology of the leg movements, because with six legs there are 720 possible permutations.

It's like rowing a six-oar boat, except that there is no coxswain keeping them all in synch; rather each oarsman is doing his own thing. But there definitely is a plan to which they have all agreed, because not once did any leg get entangled with any other.

I watched and crawled after him for 20 minutes. I wished I had had a video camera, so I could view it later in slow motion. Here, however, is my best guess:

> Left-front-leg stretch forward and pull,
> Right-front-leg stretch forward and pull,
> Left-middle-leg stretch forward and pull,

Right-middle-leg stretch forward and pull,
Left-rear-leg stretch forward and pull,
Right-rear-leg stretch forward and pull.

As a result there is a definite lurch to his walk; it's not the smooth flow of the boat, nor the fluent gallop of a horse, nor even the silent slither of a snake. But he's getting there nonetheless; except I have no idea where "there" is, and I wonder does *he* have any idea where "there" is. When he left home today, did he tell his roommate, "I'm headed for Meditation Rock; I'll be back by sundown."

I estimate that his eyes are about a quarter inch off the ground; that makes my eyes about 275 times further off the ground than his. So the fallen six-inch in diameter branch that he is now climbing over is actually 137 feet high, and Meditation Rock, which is 7 feet high for me, is a towering 1,925 feet for him. Pena Creek, 530 feet below us is a ravine that plummets to 145,750 feet for him; the equivalent of five Mount Everest's stacked atop each other.

So, how does he navigate? His line of sight is constantly interrupted by massive fallen twigs, humungous pebbles and gigantic grasses. Is he on a random amble? And, if so, how is he ever going to find his way home? Maybe he doesn't have a housemate or even a house. Perhaps, he's a perpetual nomad, the archetype of our hunter-gatherer forebears.

Or, maybe, he has conscious access to his etheric body. Maybe this astral self of his hovers like a helicopter high in the sky, mapping the terrain meticulously and acting like an automobile's GPS system," In 1.6 inches turn left!" But, I suspect, it's much more poetic and organic than that, "In one body-length turn towards the morning sun, where the honeybee is sitting upon the California poppy."

Black-backed beetle of the six legs, however you do it and wherever you are going, may God go with you.

18

Real Men Play in Parallel Universes

"Man has something divine in him, and he can prove this by
his endurance in the path of love."
Hazrat Inayat Khan

One of the most fascinating aspects of working with dreams is that they speak simultaneously at several different levels. A single dream can speak to you about:

1. Intra-psychic issues peculiar to just you,
2. Interpersonal issues involving relationships you're in,
3. The business of an entire group or community where you are a member (part of the function of the shaman, for instance, was to dream on behalf of the tribe)
4. An issue facing the global family.

It's the same with a great story or a piece of art, or the scriptures. For example, there is the story in Genesis 22 of Abraham setting out at God's command to sacrifice his son Isaac. Initially they go with two servants, but at one stage of the journey Abraham bids them to stay put while he and his son continue. The little boy feels very important and is delighted to be with his dad. He skips along merrily beside him, chatting up a storm while his father broods silently. Isaac points out, "Father we have the wood, fire and knife for the sacrifice, but where is the sacrifice itself?" Abraham swallows hard and replies, "God himself will provide the sacrifice, son." Isaac is happy with this response. What he doesn't realize is that he himself is to be the sacrifice on God's orders. Child-sacrifice to the gods was a common feature of both patriarchal and earlier matriarchal cultures who believed fertility demanded satisfying the gods with, particularly, the first fruits of the harvest, whether the harvest was grain, grapes, goats or children.

At the first level then, this was a story of an internal, intra-psychic struggle in which Abraham wrestled with the promises and demands of his God; between his natural love for his son and his supernatural fear of the deity masquerading as obedience.

At a second level, it's a story of an interpersonal issue. He was going to have to look blankly into the shocked face of his son when he grabbed him, trussed him up, laid him on the crude rock-altar and raised the knife to slit his throat. He was going to have to look defiantly into the enquiring faces of his two servants when he returned without Isaac. And most anxiety-provoking and guilt-inspiring of all he was going to have to deal with the insane screaming of his wife, Sarah, when she discovered that he had killed her only son, the miracle child God gave her in her old age; an obviously psychopathic god who intervened to grant her wish to become a mother though she was barren and post menopausal, only to snatch her baby 12 years later in a sick, cruel sacrifice.

At a third level this story addresses a community issue. It epitomizes the belief that a particular god chose a particular man, and through him a particular progeny, to be his special patrimony, on whom he would bestow a promised piece of Middle Eastern property in perpetuity in return for foreskins and fidelity. And this willingness, on the part of the man, to kill his son was the final test before the covenant was ratified.

And at a fourth level this child killing was a worldwide issue. And it wasn't that this god finally grew up and said, "No more killing," simply that he was satisfied with Abraham's submission and didn't need today's blood fix. It would be many more years before human communities would outgrow this practice.

As an after thought, this god saved face by supplying a wild ram caught in a thicket in the place of the traumatized child. But this god wasn't quite so lucky himself 1,850 years later when Satan demanded *his* "only son" as a sacrifice in an even bloodier ordeal. Satan proved to be an implacable negotiator.

In truth, both the Abraham story and the theory that Jesus was sacrificed to pay back a debt are equally disgusting. They represent, not the plan of God, but fear-filled fantasies of very immature human thinking. However, for now, I simply want to focus on the multi-faceted levels of interpretation whether the matter be scriptures, art or stories. Enlightened teachers always speak to us in multi-tiered messages, which is why they mostly use parables, analogies and metaphors. At the end of any such teaching, the master will typically say, "He who has ears to hear, let him hear! He, who has eyes to see, let him see!" The same story will be understood very differently by different members of the audience, depending on their own developmental stage. And the same person may revisit the story years later and see a whole new depth of meaning in it, because he has grown spiritually in the interim.

That, I believe, is the meaning of the enigmatic story in one of the Gnostic gospels. The disciples complained to Jesus that he is giving Mary Magdalene preferential treatment and ask him," Why do you kiss her on the lips? Jesus replies, "Two men are in a very dark room; one of them is blind, while the other is sighted. But because of the dark neither of them can see. But if they come into the presence of the light, the sighted one will now see, while the other will still be blind. That is why I kiss Mary on the lips."

My hit on this vignette is that, in the absence of the light of Christ-consciousness, all of us are in the dark. But when this light appears the sighted will see and comprehend the Christ-consciousness and its message, while the blind will still flounder in their ignorance and react merely to the surface level meanings of their encounters.

(A) Jeremiah—His Times and His Teaching

Jeremiah flourished around 600 BCE. He was a prophet during one of the most turbulent periods of Jewish history. As of 721 BCE the ten northern tribes had been exiled by the great Assyrian Empire. Now in 600 BCE, the last two remaining tribes were under siege by the Babylonian Empire. The Babylonians finally captured Jerusalem, flattened the city, razed the temple and deported the people. Only a few vinedressers were left, together with Jeremiah, who had been predicting this for years and warning the rulers about their straying from the "Law of God."

Now his worst fears were realized and he inveighed mightily against the incompetent shepherds of Israel who brought this on themselves and on the people because of their mismanagement. Another prophet-priest, Ezekiel, who was one of the deportees, took up this shepherd image, as did Jesus some 600 years later.

Jeremiah was correct when he claimed that their situation was their own fault, but he was terribly wrong when he blamed God for it. God is not the one who punishes or rewards or forgives. There is a far better explanation; it is called, Karma. Karma is the first principle of life, of science and of evolution, namely every cause leads to an effect and for every result there is a precipitating reason. God doesn't punish you for jumping out of a third story window by breaking your leg; gravity is *how* that happens, and karma is *why* that happens.

Every thought, word or action has a consequence. We live in this very elegant feedback system that tells us what, previously, had been the results of similar thoughts, words and actions. This feedback system we call history—our own personal history, that of a group and that of the species. Sages have been at pains to collate data in this system and have offered us rules of thumb to help us avoid unpleasant consequences and attract pleasant ones. For the main part, we ignore their wisdom and continue to engage in our individual, group and global efforts to do the same dumb things while expecting radically new happy outcomes.

This is the meaning of Jesus' statements, "You shall be held accountable for every idle word" and "What you whisper in secret, will be shouted from the housetops." He is not warning us about a God who is an unforgiving cosmic certified public accountant, nor yet advising us that God is the ultimate gossip, scandalously spreading our secret sins for the voyeuristic delight of bored housewives.

A thought is a very powerful creator of subsequent reality. When you give repeated, focused intentionality to a thought, you will eventually manifest it, because the universe, at core, is pure energy and it resonates and responds to any energy redirected within it by any component of itself e.g., a human mind. And so that thought becomes reality in one of three ways. First, as an experience later in this life; or second, as a theme in another incarnation; or third, right now as a parallel universe. But how can we be living in parallel universes and not be aware of them? You *are* aware of them at the soul level, but not at the level of individual ego-centered incarnations. Let me use an analogy. Sean Penn is one of my favorite actors. Suppose I were to arrange a Sean Penn movie festival in which the theaters of the Bay Area agreed that on a designated day each of them would show one of his movies. So, depending on which city you were in, you could take in one of his movies. Now Sean Penn, the man, is aware and remembers all of the roles he played in all of his movies, but the character Sam, the retarded man in "I am Sam," is not aware as Sam, of the character Matthew who is the murderer awaiting execution in "Dead Man Walking." Similarly, while my soul is aware of all the roles I am playing in the parallel universes right now as the ego in any one of these universes, I am totally unaware of all of the other egos of mine in all the other contemporaneous universes. Nonetheless I am dealing with each and every one of them with the consequences of my choices—a little bit like having stocks in several different companies. My net worth varies with the fortunes of the combined investments. So my soul's evolution is the aggregate of all the learning, failings, successes and "sins" in all of my incarnations. Real men play in parallel universes.

In this respect we mimic our meta-mother, the matrix of all manifestation, which, when faced with a choice between A and B chooses both; and when the choice A results in C and D, she again chooses both; and when the choice of B results in E and F she opts for both avenues again. She creates parallel universes and then peoples all of them with the results of her choices.

This is the beauty of life and this is the evil of the mass media's fascination with terror, war and violence. They are not, as they claim, pointing out the inevitable; rather they are creating the un-wantable. We need to stop polluting our minds and our sitting rooms with their darkness and, instead, harness our energy for light-making and life-promoting.

In Jeremiah's cosmology, a cosmology that embraces the notion of "corporate singularity," the tribe was a single entity, so that when a member of the tribe sinned, all members needed to be punished. So God used other tribe's kings to punish his "own" people and their kings. Unfortunately, this notion did not die with Jeremiah; it is alive and killing in our times. We, however, have added a further element. As the world's only superpower we have a penchant for seducing foreign leaders into sin. We arm them with weapons of mass destruction and with intelligence data on their and our (current) enemies; we train both their spies and their torture-masters; and, then when they have outlived their usefulness to us we turn on them and on their innocent subjects and wipe them out. This is an engineered corporate singularity.

In Jeremiah's time, it may have made sense. It doesn't any more—for two reasons. First, it is based on an anthropomorphic God; and second it hasn't, doesn't and won't work to bring peace among peoples.

(B) God and His Very Large Shadow

Though we have always claimed that we are built in God's image and likeness, in fact, we have consistently created gods in our own image and likeness. More than any other companion on this Earth safari we have anthropomorphized our gods. We have been unable to imagine anything more advanced than personhood, so we have ascribed it even to the deities we have invented. We have taken human virtues, magnified them and ascribed them to God; and we have taken human vices, magnified them and ascribed them, too, to God. And so the God of Islam justifies Jihad; the God of Christianity blesses crusades and inquisitions; and the God of Judaism in the Torah, enjoins genocide on his military leaders. Every single moral injunction these gods revealed to us, they themselves have broken. Their anger at our immoral behavior is only surpassed by their own immoral behavior. In truth, of course, all of it is *our* immoral behavior, acted out first hand in our dealings with others, and then projected onto the imagined actions of our gods. The greatest sickness of all, is that we have believed our own lies, been fooled by our own fantasies and been terrified by the monsters we have hidden under our own beds.

We've had minor breakthroughs in this anthropomorphic game of ours. Some religions teach us not to give God a name, since no name can describe him. It's a step in the right direction. Some religions proscribe any images of God, since his essence cannot be depicted. It, too, is a small step in the right direction. With these two steps we have spotted the misdemeanors, but these self same religions have missed the felony. While realizing that neither names nor icons can capture God, we then went on, in paroxysm of theological somersaulting, to describe in lurid detail the mind of God, his daily routine, his likes and dislikes and his plan for his chosen people—who are always us.

Only the mystics have it right—no names, no images, and no theologies. In Taoism, "those who know don't say and those who say don't know;" in Buddhism, "If you meet the Buddha on the road, kill him"; and in Christianity, "I pray daily to God to rid me of God."

For a few moments, then, let me outline a model which I think describes the evolution of our God-thinking; and then show the shadow side of each stage. It appears to me that at the beginning of this process, we began to speak ABOUT God; the second stage was when we started to speak TO God; the third stage was when we claimed to speak on BEHALF of God; and the fourth stage was when we learned to speak AS God.

Stage one, speaking ABOUT God, represented the infancy of religion, and it is the era of the theologians. It was transcended (and remember "transcend" means to "move beyond while including") by the second stage, speaking TO God. This was the era of the priests. It, too, has been surpassed and included by stage three, speaking on BEHALF of God. This is the era of the prophets. The final stage, which transcends the other three, is speaking AS God. This is the era of the mystics.

Each of these stages was an appropriate response given the level of development of humanity in general, and of religion in particular. But each had a dark underbelly, which in time became obvious and proved a huge hindrance; until it became the grit in the oyster for the next phrase of pearl making.

So stage one, which began as a genuine effort at cosmological thinking, and making sense of the mysterious world in which we lived, in time became an endless maze of pedantic ruminations. Nearly 2,600 years ago,

Gautama Siddhartha, took issue with the interminable speculation of the Brahmins of his native India, and advocated religious empiricism. "Be a lamp unto yourself," he said. "Don't believe anybody until you have tested the practice for yourself."

Within scholasticism, Christian theologians argued about how many angels could dance on the head of a pin. Of course it depended on the size of the pin, the size of the angels and the kind of dancing they were doing. Your average pin could accommodate many more average-sized angels doing line dancing than it would if they were heavy-weights doing break dancing.

And the 17th century Jewish mystic, Baal Shem Tov, eschewed books and study in favor of ecstatic experiences in nature.

Stage two, speaking TO god, started as an overwhelmingly grateful response to the source of life. It resulted in psalms, hymns, canticles and Upanishads. In time, however, it became primarily a venue for petitions, and eventually, for arm-twisting and bargaining. In a gymnastic coup-de-grace, we learned to beat our breasts with one hand while twisting God's arm with the other. And we figured out all kinds of tricks and techniques to get our way, fully convinced that we had cracked the code to the god's treasure trove.

But the shadow of stages one and two are very minor in comparison to that of stage three. Stage three shadow has two main expressions. Firstly, there are individuals who claim that within a particular religious tradition, only they speak on BEHALF of God. All other members of that faith can only access God through these designated (or largely self-appointed) spokesmen. Roman Catholicism, for instance, with over one billion members, took 1,871 years to figure out that the pope is infallible when he speaks "ex cathedra" on matters of faith and morals for the edification of the entire community. Strange that though for the longest time they claimed to be Christ's vicar on planet Earth, they never purported to be infallible.

Moses, too, for most of his career had the same kind of megalomania. He carried it off so well that the people pleaded with him to go talk to their God, while they kept a respectful distance from the base of the mountain which had been designated as the venue for the encounter. They were convinced that only Moses could look on God's face and survive. To enhance this reputation he took to wearing a veil over his face because even the reflected shine on his "punam" would have been dangerous for the Israelites to behold. In fairness to Moses, eventually under the promptings of his gentile father-in-law, Jethro, a priest of the Midianites, he agreed to share God's spirit with 72 other elders.

From 1,100 BCE to 400 BCE each of a whole slew of Hebrew prophets claimed he alone was God's mouthpiece, as he ridiculed the false prophets who flattered the rulers with their oracles. By 400 BCE, Judaism had finally outgrown this dogmatic assertion, and Joel, speaking on BEHALF of God would ecstatically proclaim, "In the days to come I will pour out my spirit on *all* human kind; your young men will see visions and your old men will dream dreams."

The second branch of this third stage shadow is when an entire culture claims that it alone is God's chosen group. This is the social equivalent of a four-year-old who boasts that his daddy is the strongest daddy in the world. But you'd be surprised how many cultures held this view. And you'd be even more surprised by how many groups still believe it.

The Japanese have a foundation myth that says they are descendents of the Sun goddess, Amaterasu Omikami, who made Japan the center of the world. The sun appears on the national flag. The Emperor is descended from her and, in fact, the same dynasty has ruled Japan continuously for 2,000 years. And this sense of superiority was part of the reason why Japan had never suffered defeat in war, until 1945.

Judaism has a foundation myth that claims a god chose Abraham, around 1850 BCE, from the home of his idol-maker father, in Ur of the Chaldees (modern day Iraq) and promised him his own land, a territory centered in modern day Israel whose boundaries changed significantly throughout biblical history. This God, who initially was simply one among legions of gods, eventually proved to be top God and, finally, the only God. He made a covenant with Abraham that in return for worship of him and the sacrifice of their foreskins they would be his special patrimony. It's as ludicrous a myth as that of Shintoism. A modified version of this says that gentiles will be saved by association with Judaism, and Jews suffer vicariously for the sins of the world.

The Maasai of Kenya/Tanzania have a foundation myth that says God created all of the cattle of the world for them, and it is their God-given duty to repatriate them. So cattle-raiding is a tribal imperative for them. As ludicrous as this may appear, it is in fact the least silly of all the "chosen people" claims, since genetic research has firmly established that modern humans originated in East Africa around 200,000 years ago. We are all either Africans or descendants of Africans. Most of us are the progeny of those who emigrated out of Africa. The Maasai are the progeny of those who stayed.

Roman Catholicism has a foundation myth that says God rejected Judaism when Judaism rejected his only son, Jesus. In their place, he chose Christians. Eventually this shift of God's allegiance was articulated in the theological dogma of "Extra ecclesiam nulla est salus" i.e., "Outside the (Catholic) Church there is no salvation." People went to hell in droves because they were not in communion with Rome. Eventually Catholicism, too, attempted to soften the blow by creating a new category of "Anonymous

Christians" which meant that God-fearing folk, even if they weren't the full shilling, could be saved because their piety gave them a second-class citizenship that allowed them into the lesser seats in heaven. Can you believe this mishugas?

At the hand of right-winged politicians and fundamentalist preachers, the United State of America is deliberately re-doing its own foundation myth, so that it is now the Promised Land with the God-given right to conquer and rule the world by economic hegemony, or, if necessary, military might. This claim is literally part of a document crafted by a coterie of fanatics who are part of the government as I write this, in August 2006. And this is coming from a regime which is borrowing one billion dollars a day to sustain a campaign which has emptied the coffers of healthcare, childcare and eldercare. The inmates are definitely running the insane asylum.

If we don't quickly wake up to this large-looming shadow of stage three, it will destroy the entire species.

So it is time to embrace stage four, where we learn to speak AS God. This may seem like opting for even greater megalomania. It is, only if I think the I who speaks as God is the ego. But it is *not* the ego; rather it is the divine spark at the core of all manifest things. Even though every cell of my body has consciousness and contains the entire DNA to reproduce all of me, yet each one is subservient to the full organism that is the totality of my spacesuit. In the same way as Seán, who contains the fullness of God, but is not the full expression of God, I must be subservient to God's transcendent fullness. So when I speak as God, I am dis-identified with ego and re-identified with my divine nature. This is the same divine nature that is present in you and in rocks, trees, cows and galaxies. So when I am identified at that level there can be no separation and therefore no violence between us. The fact that the DNA in every cell of my right eye is identical with the DNA in every cell in my left kneecap makes it impossible for my right eye and left kneecap to make war on each other. This is the mystical realization; and mysticism does not mean flaky esotericism, rather it means essential, empirical, practical reality. Accessing this next stage is the only way to extricate ourselves from the mess we are in. More importantly it is the very reason we are on the planet in 2006.

In summary, our world is being beggared by leaders who have promoted themselves or cheated their way into power. They are making violent decisions that punish both the perceived enemy abroad and the citizens at home who allegedly elected them. They claim divine authority and guidance for their megalomaniacal and old-boy-network decisions, suppressing all evidence that clearly shows the inanity of their policies. They use media-malleable outlets to feed us their version of the glorious victories being achieved, victories, however which are never so decisive and final that we can afford to relax our vigilance or end our war-mongering.

Perhaps these political, military, economic and religious responses to the vicissitudes of life on planet Earth were, at one stage, age-appropriate behaviors. We expect 18-month-old children to soil their diapers, but it is very worrisome when five-year-olds do it. So the time is long since past when these same political, military, economic and religious responses are appropriate. They are, at least, 2,600 years out of date. The great avatars have all pointed out the unworkability of the old violent responses and focused us on global and mystical stages. We can no longer afford to unpack religious experiences along tribalistic lines that give allegiance to partisan gods. The time has come when all religious experiences need to be unpacked along global lines that give allegiance to a cosmic God.

(C) So What Can You Do?

Slowly but surely a critical mass of "ordinary" people is coming awake to this mystical awareness of the next phase of human evolution. So what about you? What will you commit to doing? Here are a few suggested "do's" and "don't's."

Do not continue to pollute your mind and your sitting room with negative, terror-fixated images from radio, TV and newspapers. These are not truly representative of what is happening on the planet; moreover they are doctored and spun to create a specific reaction and to co-opt your fear in the service of a violent agenda. Instead, fill your mind and your sitting room with ideas, journals, books and radio and TV programs that show the full range of human compassion and creativity. In every walk of life and in every profession there are heroes walking among us doing great things for humanity. Find out who they are, and join them in their efforts. There are even mega-groups (e.g., the Bioneers and the Institute of Noetic Sciences—check out their websites) that collate information from thousands of single-focus organizations. This will do two things for you. Firstly, it will warm the cockles of your heart to know that so much good is being done; and, secondly, you will easily find some groups who are working at an issue particularity dear to your heart.

Another plea I make is this; do not vote for war-mongering, terrorist-fixated, lobbyist-controlled politicians in this next or any election. Instead support candidates who think as citizens of the planet and will legislate now while keeping in mind the world they want to bequeath to our great-grandchildren.

Thirdly, examine and let go of any dogma or any religious belief that separates you now or in the afterlife from any other human being. Such a God is far too small for you. Discover the God whose currency is not dogma but mystery; a God who does not ask that you believe blindly but that you live lovingly.

Fourthly, do not make war, in your mind or in your heart, against your spouse, your child, your parent or your neighbor. For if *you* can't be at peace in your own soul, how can you expect the world to be at peace in the global soul? Rather, cultivate thoughts of healing, and learn practical ways to resolve your personal disputes, so that both parties can win. Do a weekend seminar on communications, or join a class in non-violent communication.

Conclusion

The prelude to the feeding-of-the-5,000-with-the-five-barley-loaves story was that the crowds had seen him getting into a boat to go off for a break. They figured out where he was headed and set off on foot in pursuit. They finally caught up with him, though they were exhausted and hungry by then. After the miracle he was afraid they'd try to take him by force and make him king, so he fled alone into the mountains. I'm sure they waited for his return hoping to change his mind. He failed to disappear fully on that occasion. When he did manage to disappear, after his resurrection, the apostles were convinced he would return imminently to usher in the kingdom. For 2,000 years eschatological rapturists have been predicting, and even attempting to force, his return, all the while behaving in a manner antithetical to his teaching of love, compassion and inclusivity.

The joke is that he has already come back. Many times! And each time we failed to recognize him. So we crucified him again. Christ is here right now; are we done crucifying him yet?

Are we ready yet for Christ-consciousness? Because he is not here now as a Galilean carpenter; he is here in the consciousness of ecological interconnectedness; he is here in the concern for justice, compassion and peace; he is here in the realization that all the children of Gaia are children of God.

Open your eyes wider. He *is* here. He is YOU. If that doesn't scare you, then you don't understand Christ-consciousness. And if that doesn't fill you with passion for your mission, then you don't understand yourself.

19

For Whom, Pray?
(July 8, 2002)

Busy little human,
measuring tape in hand,
eyes intently fixed on the path,
I stride purposefully ahead
to measure the evaporation rate of the pond.

Suddenly I am speared
by a shaft of setting-sunlight;
startled, and stopped in my tracks;
knocked from my course
as was Paul from his horse.
The sun
—Chepkelyon Sogol (the Nine-Legged One),
as the Kalenjin call him—
has found a gap
between two groves of redwoods.

Mystical, unseen faery hands
(I wonder how many faeries
and how many hands)
are expertly juggling
a troupe of one thousands gnats;
bouncing them aloft
in vertical, elliptical orbits;
none of them colliding
and none of them slipping through the faery fingers.

The sun-shaft has spotlighted the performance.
The entire audience, and I
are too awestruck to applaud.
We simply stop, and time does, too.

And all of this, for whom, pray?
If I think it is for me, Seán,
I am hopelessly inflated.
If I do not realize it is for ME,
I am spiritually a neophyte.

Wherein lies the Truth?
This is the Truth:
I have been watching
God en-Sunned
Spotlighting God en-Gnatted
Borne aloft by God en-Faeried,
In a God en-Redwooded space,
For a God en-Humaned witness.

I see YOU!

20

The Rainbow Body—Jesus in Tibet?

"My religion is very simple. My religion is kindness."
The Dalai Lama

None of them was ever the same again. Seeing planet Earth from a quarter of a million miles away changed them all irrecoverably. For each one of them it was a life-altering experience. It was a life-altering experience for Neil Armstrong, the first man to walk on the moon and for Edger Mitchell, the sixth man to walk on the moon. So profound an experience, in fact, for Mitchell, that shortly thereafter he founded the "Institute of Noetic Sciences" (IONS) currently based in Petaluma, California. "Noetic" is another derivative of the Greek word, Gnosis, from which we also get, "knowledge," except that "noetic" has more a sense of esoteric or deeper knowledge. Mitchell's idea was to set up an organization to research what consciousness is all about. It now has about 60,000 members worldwide and is a clearinghouse and supporter of consciousness-raising activities in all disciplines from the legal profession to physics, from psychology to ecology, and from leadership models to mysticism.

A few years ago they commissioned two well-known Catholic priest-scholars, Brother David Steindl-Rast and Father Francis Tiso, to do field work and research on the tradition within Tibetan Buddhism of the "Rainbow Body." I recently listened to Father Francis' report to an IONS audience. According to this tradition, there are esoteric, meditative practices which, when fully mastered, enable the practitioner at death, to dematerialize the physical body to pure light. Witnesses report that nothing remains except light in rainbow colors in various configurations. Other accounts claim that, occasionally, hair and nails may be left. Father Francis, who has a PhD from Colombia in Tibetan studies, personally interviewed some of these witnesses, and is utterly convinced of the authenticity of this phenomenon. He went on, in his lecture, to draw parallels between the rainbow body and the resurrection of Jesus in Christian tradition.

(A) Transfiguration As a Theological Device

Today's gospel from Mark is an account of the transfiguration, a story which is repeated, almost verbatim in Matthew's gospel and in Luke's gospel. Some few weeks before his death, Jesus chose three of his 12 disciples (Peter, James and John) and led them up to the top of Mount Tabor. There he had a deep mystical experience which was so profound that his inner vision manifested externally, enabling the three disciples to also see and to hear it. Jesus' face glowed brilliantly and even his garments shone much more brightly. Moses, who flourished about 1,250 years before Jesus, and Elijah who flourished about 800 years before Jesus, appeared to him and they were in dialogue. Peter exclaimed, "Lord it is good for us to be here. Let's build three huts here, one for you, one for Moses and one for Elijah." Then there was a loud thunderclap and they heard the voice of God say, "This is my son, the beloved. Listen to him!" The three got really scared so they fell to the ground and hid their heads. Things got very quiet. When, eventually, they had the courage to look again, they saw no one but Jesus.

On the way down the mountain Jesus adjured them not to speak of this event to anybody until he had risen from the dead. So they then began to discuss among themselves what "risen from the dead" might mean.

Neither Moses nor Elijah was a stranger to transfiguration. They both, in their own ways, had such experiences. After his encounter with God on Mount Sinai, Moses' face shone so brightly that, subsequently, he had to wear a veil over it so as not to blind the Israelites. And Elijah was physically assumed into the heavens in a fiery chariot, an event witnessed by his protégée Elisha. Moses and Elijah are the two key figures in Biblical Judaism, for the following reason. When the Jewish canon of scripture was formally defined it was divided into three sections represented by the acronym TaNaKh. The "T" stands for Torah, the first five books of the bible (Genesis, Exodus, Leviticus, Numbers, Deuteronomy) whose author was believed to be Moses. It is sometimes simply called "The Law" and is somewhat akin to the notion of "Dharma" in Buddhism. The "N" stands for

"Neviim" (the Hebrew word for "Prophets") and it consists of the teachings and actions of the major and minor prophets of Israel and Judah from about 800 BCE to about 400 BCE. The first, and greatest of these is Elijah. He gave himself this name. In Hebrew it is "Eli-yahu" which translates as "Yahweh is my God." By this name he was challenging his countrymen to give up following the god, Baal, and come back to Yahweh, the god who took them out of Egypt 450 years before.

The "K" stands for "Kituvim," the Hebrew for "writings" (very close to "Kitab" the Arabic for "book" and the Swahili "Kitabu" which also means "book" and is borrowed from Arabic because Kiswahili is a cross-fertilization of the language of the Arab traders to East Africa and the Bantu languages of East Africa). These "writings" were the existential musings and wisdom reflections of the Hebrews who survived the Babylonian exile (597 BCE to 529 BCE) during which time they were hugely influenced by Zoroastrianism, the great religion of Persia. There may well be an etymological connection: the Persians were called "Parsis," whose language was known as "Farsi" and this is very similar to Pharisee. Now the Pharisees (lay theologians) unlike the Sadducees (the priestly caste) fully accepted the Zoroastrian notions of:

1. Life after death
2. Angels and demons and spirits
3. Resurrection.

This division between the two camps persisted down to the time of Jesus (500 years later) and, in fact, was very cleverly used by Saint Paul during his own trial before the Sanhedrin. He was being tried because of his allegiance to the Jesus movement, and knowing that some of his accusers were Sadducees and some Pharisees, he claimed to have been arrested simply because he was preaching resurrection. This set the Sadducees and the Pharisees at each other's throats and took the focus off Paul.

So the designation "Pharisee" was very probably an acknowledgement of how this group and their thinking had been influenced by the Parsis. Today, their language (Farsi) is still the mother tongue of the Parsis, a large number of whom live in India and still practice Zoroastrianism. Many Iranians who now live in the United States of America continue to use the Farsi language.

When it came then to creating the Hebrew Canon, the Pharisees accepted the "Kituvim" but the Sadducees did not. But everybody accepted the Torah and the prophetic books as divinely revealed. So, Moses and Elijah represented "the Law" and "the prophets" and thus, the undisputed core of the Hebrew Bible.

In placing Jesus on Mount Tabor, in dialogue with Moses and Elijah, the gospel masters are showing that Jesus, too, gets transfigured, that he is in the lineage of the Torah and the Prophets, and that he is, in fact, the culmination of the *Old Testament* and the bringer of the *New Testament*, the final agreement between God and us.

This use of transfiguration as a theological device was installed into the liturgy of the Christian movement by the Syrian Church in the fifth century. In Rome, in the year 1457, on August 6, Pope Callistus III publicly announced the decisive victory of the Christian armies over the Muslim Turkish forces in Belgrade. To mark this "great intervention by God on the side of right," the pope inserted the Feast of Transfiguration into the liturgical calendar of the Roman Catholic Church. It's been celebrated ever since on that date.

Moreover, as icing on the cake, this feast comes exactly 40 days before the feast of "The Triumph of the Holy Cross" which is celebrated each year on September 14. And, as we all know, 40 is a very sacred number. It was the number of years the Israelites wandered in the desert; it was the number of days Moses spent atop Mount Sinai in dialogue with God, and it was the number of days, Jesus spent in the desert after his own baptism by John, as he wrestled with Satan and his own mission. And, of course, liturgically it is also the duration of Lent, that period of ascetic practice, each year, when we prepare for the death and resurrection of Jesus at Easter.

Some of this manipulation is very elegant, and some of it is God-awful. But, then, churches and religions have continually used the mystical experiences of their founders and visionaries to advance narrow political and dogmatic agendas. Many of these agendas are 180 degrees in opposition to the teachings of the founders and visionaries. All minds are attracted to big ideas. Great minds are attracted in order to embrace them and thus transcend, while small minds are attracted in order to harness them for personal or cultural power trips.

(B) Transfiguration as a Scientific Event

I believe that, for Jesus, the transfiguration experience was a kind of a "test run" for the resurrection. His body, obviously, sent off some powerful energy; so powerful that even his clothes were affected. Now, in actual fact, at core, we all have light-bodies. We are composed, of about 10^{14} cells, each of which contains about 10^{14} atoms, each of which contains a photon of light. If there were some known way of instantly releasing this light, one human body could illuminate a baseball stadium at one million watts for three hours. You'd only need seven sacrificial lambs for the World Series.

Imagine what that kind of energy could do to your tuxedo; or your Christian Dior evening gown; or even your burial shroud. Well, in the case of the burial duds, you don't even have to guess, because, apparently it *has* been done. The Shroud of Turin, which is supposed to be the cloth in which Jesus was buried and in which he resurrected, is an utterly unique artifact by any standard. Carbon 14 dating that claimed that it only dated to the 13th century because a tiny section removed from the outer edge showed 13th century sweat is pathetically inadequate. This cloth, which on occasion has been put on display throughout its history, was always handled at its edges by the Canons who had charge of it. Of course, a sample from the edges is going to register the perspiration of these handlers. None of the fabric which contains the actual marking was used, for obvious reasons. However, the type of whip that was used was indeed the dumb-bell shaped tips of the flagellum used in Roman floggings from the time of Christ. It had long since ceased to be used by the 1200s. The crucifixion marks showed that the nails had been driven through the wrists (which is how it was done in Jesus' time) and not through the palms despite the fact that that is how Christian iconography always depicts it. The "scorching" that appears on the cloth is much more pronounced where the cloth touched the body e.g., forehead, chest, and much lighter where the cloth was away from the body e.g., neck and sides. This ability to represent perspective was unknown to art at that time. Moreover, there is no paint on the cloth, but there is blood and albumin. However the final kicker is that the original is actually a *negative* image. Only when it was first photographed did the true image emerge. If it is a forgery, it was done by a very talented artist who had also perfected time travel.

Since Einstein, we all know that ultimately matter reduces to energy. And energy is "neither good nor bad, but thinking makes it so," as Shakespeare said.

Jesus, it seems, knew how to harness this energy. He did so regularly in his healing ministry; he did so dramatically in his transfiguration; and he did so very dramatically in his resurrection. The Tibetan lamas, it seems, also know how to harness this energy. They do it regularly in their siddhi practices; and some of them do it rather dramatically at death, leaving rainbows as the final manifestation of physicality. It certainly cuts down on funeral expenses.

Others, too, have learned to harness this energy. American scientists were the first to use it to develop weapons of mass destruction. And on August 6, 1945 the American military was the first to drop a bomb full of it on a civilian population, grotesquely extinguishing the lives of 100,000 human beings. What a great gift for a Christian nation to give the world on the Feast of the Transfiguration of Jesus. He practiced resurrection so his followers could perfect annihilation?

To understand resurrection, transfiguration and energy more deeply we have to look at the notion of body in more detail. In Western medical science we have an utterly impoverished notion of body. Most other cultures and eras had far more complex models, ranging from two levels of bodies (Egypt, Persia) through three levels of body (Greek i.e. sarx, soma and pneuma), to seven in the case of Hinduism. Most, however, agree that we need to acknowledge at least three levels or kinds of body. These levels are often called the gross, the subtle and the causal body. The gross is what Western medicine accepts. It can be seen, touched, measured, palpated, cut, radiated and medicated. It has weight and occupies space.

However, the gross body is just the "hard copy" of a more subtle program, an information matrix, a blueprint. This blueprint takes in carbon, hydrogen, oxygen and nitrogen from air, sunlight and food to actually create the gross body. So this blueprint is called the subtle body. Not only does it build the gross body, it constantly refreshes the gross body, just as your computer screen refreshes any image you keep on display. But, above and beyond even the subtle body, lies the causal body, which is the ultimate origin of both the gross printout and the subtle contractor. Let me use an analogy. Imagine a brilliant engineer. He designs a computer, including the chip, the display unit, the printer cables and plugs etc. Then he designs a software program that allows him to type on screen, and to send commands to the printer. Finally, he prints out an actual document; let's say a love letter to his wife. Now, by analogy, the engineer would represent the causal body or original source; the hardware (CPU, monitor, printer, cables etc.) would represent the subtle body; and the love letter would represent the gross body. Every living thing from humans to daffodils and from dinosaurs to mountains is a love letter from the transcendence of God (the ineffable ground of being) to the immanence of God (the manifest, created realms).

Now these distinctions are not merely the product of esoteric, self-engrossed navel-gazing, rather they have very significant consequences for theology and for medicine. Without an understanding of subtle body, for instance, transfiguration and resurrection are on the same order of reality as Santa Claus and the Tooth Fairy. For hundreds of millions of believers, however, whose cosmologies do not include these discriminations, transfiguration and resurrection are articles of faith that they cannot defend in any coherent or intelligent fashion. They can only reply with "I believe it to be true, because the scriptures tell me so."

(C) Transfiguration as a Mystical Reality

Resurrection and transfiguration are manifestations of the subtle body, but there are many other manifestations also. All of them are invitations to begin a journey of returning to the causal body. Now, anyone can have mystical experiences, and, indeed, we all do. However, we can only unpack them, and therefore, benefit from them, at the psychological and spiritual level we have reached. Deep experiences do not necessarily mean we are advanced spiritually. And just like $E = mc^2$ in the hands of militarists can be a global disaster, so mystical experiences in the theology of fundamentalists can too. Both Moses and Elijah, undoubtedly had profound mystical experiences, but they were men of their time and men of their place, so Moses translated these experiences into a document that, on God's orders, enjoined genocide as the spiritual response to the mission of the Israelites. Elijah, too, was a very violent character. His "zeal for the Lord" allowed him to personally supervise the throat-slashing of 450 prophets of the God, Baal.

Near contemporaries of Elijah, who lived further East, Lao Tzu (200 years later) and Gautama Siddharta (250 years later) were much more advanced spiritually and were able to translate their mystical experiences into much more profound documents and dharma. They preached alignment with source, and compassion for all sentient beings (not just humans.) This is a far cry from the bloodthirsty, partisan God who preceded them, and, unfortunately, still survives to robustly bless genocide some 2,600 years after their ministries.

It's bad enough when leaders and religions follow the dictates of violent founders, but it is extremely upsetting when leaders and churches brutalize the teachings of enlightened founders, turning compassion into crusades, and turning spiritual questing into torturous inquisition. This, unfortunately, has been the legacy of Jesus' teaching.

The self-same mystical experience in the hands of different people will come out looking and being explained very differently. A terrorist may interpret it as an injunction to become a suicide bomber; a reductionistic scientist may explain it as merely a petit mal seizure; a Christian fundamentalist will be convinced that it proves beyond a shadow of a doubt that "Jesus is the only way"; a Hassid will be convinced that the Jews are, indeed, God's chosen people; while the true mystic will see in it the reality that there is only God and all beings are manifestations of God and deserve to be loved and treated with uttermost respect.

This distinction between mystical experience and stages of spiritual development is so important that I want to spread myself on it, by way of an analogy. In the analogy, I am trying to show several things; first, the trajectory of the evolution of spirit; and, second, the difference between *stages* or levels of spiritual and psychological development on the one hand, and *states* of mystical experiences on the other. I will speak of this trajectory and mention some types of experiences we may have at any level.

Imagine a skyscraper. Let's keep it simple, let's imagine it has only six floors or levels, and that it has only eight rooms on each floor. It is built in a circular cylindrical shape. Up through the core/center of the skyscraper runs the elevator and when you exit the elevator, on any floor, you find yourself in a circular corridor. All the rooms on each level open off this corridor. Since the building itself is built as a circle, each of the rooms will be wedge shaped: the wall with the door in it will curve *into* the room and the opposite wall will curve *away* from the room. It's as if you cut up a bagel into eight equal pieces. On the "back" wall of each room is a section of a great mural. To see the full mural, you have to visit *all* the rooms at that level.

Now, if you have only reached level one in the psychological/spiritual journey, you might still visit each room on that level and see the sections of the mural. You will then be convinced that that is the total mural; and indeed it is, but only for *that* level. Thus, previous eras of human culture were sure that they had the full picture, one that allowed for genocide or suggested literalist interpretations of Moses' parting the Red Sea or Jesus being born of a virgin. Indeed, these were adequate interpretations for their times. But once intrepid explorers took the elevator to the next floor and saw the mural up there, they came to an astonishing realization. The mural on the second floor included all of the first floor mural but added a whole lot more. It's as if you had seen a black and white stick figure drawing and been impressed by it, only to come across another depiction of the same scene in which the artist used real figures and lots of colors.

However, you cannot stop even at the second floor. Typically, cultures do stop at a second floor, get really impressed with the new discovery and smugly decry the infantile thinking of the first floor. But Spirit is committed to a journey all the way to the penthouse suite, and human evolution and spiritual development will be truly satisfied by nothing less. The mural on each level will fully incorporate all newly-emergent elements not contained in the earlier murals. Only when we, as individuals or as a species, have reached the top level will the full mural be revealed. Then, and only then, will religion have matured into non-dual mysticism. Then the altered states will have solidified into altered traits, we will have grown into the full realization of our own divinity, and recognized the divinity of all others also. At earlier levels we mistook the range of states, at that level for evidence that that was ultimate reality. We settled for *states* of consciousness rather than evolution through *stages* of consciousness; we mistook tee-ball for major league baseball; mistook the doodlings of a four-year-old for the masterpieces of Michelangelo; misread the creative differences within the manifest realms as evidence of God's partisan nature; and misinterpreted the metaphoric musings of the mystics in fundamentalist, literalist and dogmatic decrees.

When Peter blurted out, "Lord it is good for us to be here!" he was situating himself somewhere along the spectrum of this elevator side. Some, who met the Christ-consciousness of Jesus, regarded his words and actions as mere entertainment; those who were ready got his message; those who were more ready got who he is; and those who were fully ready got who they themselves are.

But the voice of God was the real clincher, "This is my beloved son, listen to him." Those at level one of the skyscraper, merely heard thunder; those at level two got scared; those at level three convinced themselves that it was only their imagination; those at level four said that this proved Jesus was God's only son; those who got to the penultimate level realized that God speaks those same words to all of Her creatures; and those who have gone all the way know that God was speaking to Himself, His transcendence in dialogue with Her immanence. For, in truth, there is only God.

When you have reached this level, you have seen planet Earth from one-quarter of a million miles away; when you have reached this level, you have seen the Milky Way Galaxy from a billion light years away; when you have reached this level, you have seen the entire cosmos from a God-year away.

Life-altering experiences don't come any bigger than that.

21

A Tale of Hide and Go Seek
(6/11/2002)

Part I—The Meeting

It was a work of art—but it wasn't meant for display. In fact, it was specifically crafted not to show. And that was a pity, in many ways, for it deserved to be seen: concentric polygons of the flimsiest silk, yet strong enough to survive the beating wings of the expected "guest." A guest whose hundreds of eyes and lightning-fast reflexes were no match for the artwork's radar-dodging design.

So there you have it; that is the conundrum; a work of art designed not to be visible to the hoped-for guest.

But this particular artist had a problem; one might say a "glaring problem!" The artist in question was Miss Spiderwoman, and her masterpiece an intricate web spun between the lowest branch of a scrub-oak and the tallest grasses of the meadow. Its stealthy nature had been the source of several lovely meals; but last night's heavy dew had bejeweled the entire structure with glistening water droplets, like a multi-ringed necklace of color-catching diamonds. Now it was even prettier to behold—unless, of course, you were Miss Spiderwoman. Then it merely presaged a day of fasting.

She danced daintily into the center, and putting a leg on each of the main "guy lines" (as she was wont to do when trying to locate the position of a trapped and struggling morsel), she shook the entire web as vigorously as she could. The diamonds jiggled, splitting the morning sunlight into thousands of rainbows, but they all held on for dear life to their places on the necklace.

She tried many times, for after all, as king Robert Bruce of Scotland once observed, spiders are not quitters. Alas, the necklace shed not a single one of its tears.

Just then Mr. Hummingbird darted by. He was thirsty, so flapping his little wings hundreds of beats per minute, he suspended himself a few inches from the web, speared a water droplet with his curved bill and sucked it aboard. He repeated the maneuver a few more times, and was just about to be on his busy way, when Miss Spiderwoman coughed politely to get his attention and observed "Beautiful morning, sir, don't you think?" "Why yes, it most certainly is" replied the hummingbird, a little taken aback at being engaged in conversation by a spider. Spiders and hummingbirds, you must realize, don't normally acknowledge each other. "I have noticed you fly by, on many occasions and if you'll pardon my being so presumptuous as to offer a personal comment, I am in awe of both your dexterity of flight and of your multicolored feather jacket." She blushed. So did the hummingbird. "That, that is fri-fri-fri-ghtfully kind of you," stuttered the hummingbird, "in truth, I have oft remarked to myself, for I am given to such musings, on the highly intricate engineering of your delightfully constructed domicile!" They both blushed again.

"Alas, I fear, it may no longer serve its purpose," said the spider wistfully. "I am sorry to hear that. May I be so forward as to inquire into the reason for it's becoming obsolete?" "The cause of the problem is simple, really," said the spider, "but the solution resists my boldest efforts." She sighed (a little self-pityingly, were the truth to be told) and went on. "It's not easy being a Black Widow. No man about to do the chores. You may have noticed that these water droplets are advertising the existence of my web. I fear, therefore, that today may be a hungry one for me." She dropped her eyes modestly, and wrung her legs—all eight of them.

The hummingbird was finding it taxing to remain so long in the same position, so he said, "Can you excuse me a minute?" and darted off to release the tension in his wings. Moments later he was back and asked, "Is there any way I can be of assistance?"

"Well, I don't like to presume upon your generosity, nor do I wish it to appear as if I have been prying into your personal affairs, but I did notice you drinking several water droplets from my web . . ." "I am so sorry," interrupted the hummingbird, "I should, of course, have asked permission, or drunk, instead, from the cup of that tulip over there." "No, no, no, I am not at all objecting to your choosing to have a drink at my place" said the spider reassuringly. "In fact, that is precisely how you may be of assistance to me. You see the water droplets are calling attention to the presence of my web and, I fear I shall not manage to trap a meal at all today! I'd be ever so grateful to you, were you to drink up all of the droplets with your elegant curved bill." The hummingbird was quite relieved that he wasn't being accused of bad manners, and happy at being asked for help. "I should be delighted to do exactly as you request," and suiting the action to the word, he began to vacuum the entire web. In less than no time the web was dry enough to deceive even the 2,700 eyes of a dragonfly. Truth be told, the hummingbird's interior was sloshing about a bit, and he was having to beat his wings even more rapidly to bear the extra weight aloft. But he felt really proud of his good deed, and the spider lavished praise and gratitude on him. "Do call again," she coyly intoned. "Thank you kindly for the invitation," responded the hummingbird and, dipping his wings in salute, he flew off.

Spiderwoman took up her position once more, in the nexus of the web and settled back confidently to wait. She was feeling really good. She'd made a new friend, the sun was shining, and lots of flying insects were buzzing about their business.

Part II—The Dying

Fly-by-day was quite young, but he had learned his trade well, had excellent flying skills, better than average eyesight, and first-rate reflexes. He had just come from teasing a horse; walking all over its back and neck and sides; inserting his long proboscis and extracting drinks of nice, warm blood. The horse would flinch, skin quivering like ripples on a pond, stamp a foot agitatedly on the ground, and flick his long tail like a whip at the site of the surgery. But no matter how fast the tail came, Fly-by-day was always too fast for it. Seconds later, he was back for more. He smiled now as he remembered. After nine or ten "treatments" the horse had galloped off, furiously trying to dislodge his uninvited guest. Fly-by-day laughed aloud. Now don't get me wrong, Fly-by-day is not an evil person; not sadistic or mean-spirited; nor was he wont to gloat over the discomfort of a fellow creature. It was simply that he needed food, and he very much admired his ability to look out for his own needs; most of the time! But just at that moment, with tears in his many eyes from laughter and the morning sun shining straight at him, he hit an invisible, elasticized obstruction. It didn't hurt at all but it did surprise him. It oscillated backwards and forwards a few times. Now he could see it clearly; it looked like flimsy, silken strands; shouldn't be a big deal. One wing and two feet were stuck to the silky stuff. He pushed down with two more feet to free himself and the other feet also stuck fast. He shook himself vigorously (much like the horse had done) but only managed to jam the second wing. He panicked and pushed his last two free feet against the silk—and they, also, stuck fast.

In her control center, the spider quickly figured out where her first meal of the day had lodged. The uninvited guest of the horse, was now the unintended but very welcome guest of Spiderwoman. She arrived at the site, expertly assessed the size of the fly, and instantly set about tying him up in a ball of sticky web stuff. Fly-by-day was now too scared to move and was unable to, even if he had wanted. Then, suddenly, an injection (much like he had done to the horse) and he began to feel woozy. "Count backwards from eight," admonished the spider. He only got as far as six, and he passed out.

Within minutes, Spiderwoman liquefied his interior and sucked him out of his spacesuit, leaving only a desiccated shell. The substance-sucking spider on the hummingbird-sucked-dry web completed the cycle on the horse-blood-sucking Fly-by-day.

She was well into her meal when she heard the ground reverberate. The horse, now being teased by a brother of Fly-by-day, galloped wildly in her direction. Before she had time to wipe her mouth, the huge brute had crashed through her web, which stuck to his heaving flank, together with the remains of her meal and her frightened self. Then the horse flicked his mighty tail—and the lights went out. The hummingbird saw it all happen. His little heart exploded in grief for his newfound friend; he fell from the heavens, landed with a thud on the sun-scorched earth, rolled onto his back, stuck his two little legs in the air, and expired.

Part III—The Beginning

Three invisible, immaterial, mystical umbilical cords undulated into the fifth dimension, acting as conduits for the three newly released souls. The soul of Fly-by-day was the first to arrive—a brilliant white light with fuzzy edges and an orange core. Next came the soul of Spiderwoman—a yellow aura with pink interior. Finally, came the soul of Mr. Hummingbird—purple fringe with blue center.

The three souls coalesced and, if you could see it, you would have witnessed the most extraordinary dance—a merging and parting, a uniting and a separating of three soul mates. Laughter filled the air until the ecstasy of their release was complete. Finally, the laughter subsided, and then I heard them speak.

White-orange said "Wow! That felt so real. I'm sorry I teased that horse, and I really felt fear when you were trussing me up." "I know" said yellow-pink "I quite enjoyed that piece, and liberating you from your spacesuit.

But I think I felt the same as you, when the horsetail smacked me." "How about you?" they both asked of purple-blue. Purple-blue said "Isn't it amazing how every time we incarnate, we totally forget the drama we've pre-planned together. Each time, as we are about to go back, I promise myself, this time I will definitely remember, but I don't. I had no idea who you were when I met you as Spiderwoman, even though that was precisely the spacesuit we had agreed upon for you." "I know, I know" chipped in white-orange excitedly. "I tried the same thing, but when I actually found myself in the Fly-by-day spacesuit, I really believed that that is who I was!" "You know," said yellow-pink to purple-blue "when I first saw you sipping the droplets from my web, I had a kind of deja-vu experience. For a split second, I remembered that we had rehearsed it before we descended. But it was instantly gone again. Don't you hate when that happens."

"I can't wait until green-violet arrives," said white-orange. "I wonder what it was like being in that huge body? I'm kinda glad I prodded him a few times."

"Well, that's our math lesson over for today" said purple-blue "I'm sure Teacher will be very pleased with us—hummingbird has two legs, horse has four, fly-by-day has six and Spiderwoman has eight. How about next time we do an alphabet?"

The three auras merged once more and formed a beautiful, all-seeing eye. With absolute love and total compassion they watched and encouraged the horse as he lived out the rest of his incarnation and approached his designated exit.

Still trying to escape the torturing fly, the horse galloped heedlessly towards a cliff. Fifty feet below, the river patiently awaited his spacesuit. At an infinite distance of nearness, the eye awaited his soul.

22

When God Felt Compassion—for Herself

*"There is no better way of living in this world and yet living the
inner life than being one's self, outwardly and inwardly.*
Hazrat Inayat Khan

Last Thursday morning, I snuck up on a mother playing with her baby
in the woods along the banks of Pena Creek. In my 12 years living here I
have almost never encountered another in this place; yet here they were.
The mother looked like an original native of the area, and the infant was
plump and well fed. Because, over a decade of trekking alone in these
woods, I have learned to go very quietly and so wasn't noticed. I came upon
them and watched maybe 15 minutes before I revealed myself.

I was fascinated by their game. The mother had found a natural slide
and would place the baby on it. She was wearing a voluminous old-fashioned
apron and she held it like a trampoline. The child would hold tenaciously
onto the sides of the slide mustering up the courage to let go. Eventually it
would and for a joyous moment it was totally free to dance with gravity and
tumble into the apron-trampoline. Then the mother would heave it back
up into the air three or four feet and the dance would enter the second
movement; the child once more would fall squealing into the apron only
to be catapulted upwards, perhaps two or three feet. This oscillation was
repeated two more times, and each time the mother would toss it aloft, but
not as high as the time before, because it obviously took a lot of energy.

So, on the fourth or fifth fall, the mother would enfold the child in her apron and they would both squeal with delight.

When I did make known my presence they were not upset, so we fell to talking. I asked their names. The baby's name was "Droplet" and the mother's name was "Tranquil Waters." And who were they?

The night dew had left little pools of water on the broad leaves of the trees that overhung the creek. Every so often, a drop of water would detach itself from a pool and trickle towards the lowest part of the leaf. There it would shimmer in all its ontologically discrete individuality, refracting the morning sunlight while trying to muster up the courage to let go and fall into the still pond below. As it hung on the very tip it would become pearl-shaped, but as soon as it let go it would rearrange itself into a perfect sphere. A drop of water looks like a tiny object, and it is, yet if one could peel off its millions of layers—because it is built like an onion in concentric spheres—and lay them beside each other, each drop would cover half an acre.

But as it hung perfectly in mid air it was only aware of this game. As soon as it landed, the pond made an apron of itself, undulating like a plate that had been transmogrified into a bowl. Then it would reconfigure itself once more as a plate bouncing the droplet aloft. My vision sped up so that I could see the whole act in slow motion. The droplet would jump back up off the trampoline of the pond-apron, though not as far as the leaf-slide. Each bounce a little less vigorous than the one that preceded it, until after four or five bounces the pond would absorb it fully into herself, while the droplet willingly surrendered the surface tension which gave it its sense of cohesion and identity.

As soon as mother had unconditionally accepted the baby back fully into her own essence, another droplet would detach itself from the little pool on the leaf and the game would begin all over again. Hundreds of pool-leaves were playing the same game with many other ponds of tranquil water.

Evolutionarily speaking, humans are water which has learned how to think. So as a thinking 150-pound cluster of water droplets, I want to write today about compassion which is the merging of the droplets of individual lives with the tranquil pond of the ineffable God.

(A) Defining Compassion

For purposes of making an important point I distinguish between sympathy and compassion. Sympathy is seeing somebody stuck in a pit, feeling bad about their predicament and jumping down into the hole with him, so that you both become stuck. It is powerless solidarity. Compassion is seeing somebody stuck in a pit and finding a way to pull him to freedom, so that you both become liberated.

And compassion has nothing to do with pessimism even in the face of dire global circumstances. Pessimism in such a situation is simply an expanded version of personal victimization; it is a wrongful identification of experiment homo sapiens with world history.

Why is it that history books are all about battles and wars and conquests? This is the same kind of conflation of psychology (literally, "the study of the soul") with psychopathology. But history is *not* about "man's inhumanity to man" rather it is a record of the evolutionary trajectory of Spirit-as-human.

(B) The Levels of Compassion

Being a mathematician, I'll number these from one upwards; being Irish, I'll deal with the first one last.

Level one compassion is physiological. I believe we are literally wired for that virtue, and modern neuroscience has just caught up with me. There is a newly discovered class of neurons, appropriately called "mirror neurons." These neurons fire in the brain of somebody who is watching another person suffer, and they fire in the same area of the brain, as do the neurons of the sufferer. On a much more mundane level, have you ever found yourself wanting to cough on behalf of somebody who is talking to you, and has a "frog in his throat?" Your body is uncomfortable with the same vicarious sensations as the speaker's.

Or what about men who get morning sickness when their wives are pregnant? Or even the phantom limb pain where one can feel physiological compassion for a no-longer-existing part of oneself?

Level two compassion then is the normal full-blown feelings one has for one's *own* real-time pain—physical, emotional, mental or spiritual. This, however, is never to be confused with victimization, a sense of self-as-victim. This always results from mixing up an event with an identity.

Level three is where one feels compassion for the non-self. This can develop in concentric circles from mother, to family, to clan, to tribe, to nation. "Scientistic" thinking in socio-biology and psycho-biology has attempted to reduce this to the "selfish gene" theory, which would have us believe that there is no such thing as human freedom or free will. Rather we are simply taxis that genes use to promote their agenda. Or that apparently altruistic behavior is merely a group-orchestrated response to sacrifice the individual in order to enhance and protect the welfare of the tribe. This kind of reductionism seems to have no problem about crediting tiny components of a system (e.g., a gene) with a degree of intelligence that it denies to the sum of the parts (e.g., a full person.)

I believe, however, that this expansion of compassion is Spirit's way of helping us along the inward core of the journey back into the God who was its origin.

Level number four adds a whole new dimension to compassion. It is compassion allied to a meta-cosmology, a cosmology which completely re-contextualizes one's own pain or the pain of another or even global pain. It involves the zoom-lens approach, looking at any event or situation from four, increasingly wider perspectives. First, I look at it in close up, this event, in this period of this lifetime. Second, I zoom out a little and experience the same event in the context of my entire life (or the other's lifetime or the globe's entire lifetime.) Thirdly, I go much further out and see this event in the context of multiple lifetimes in multiple re-incarnations. Again, this is true for another person or the planet itself. Fourthly, I zoom out to the widest possible lens and view the event or situation from the eternal perspective, "before" there was time or "me," or "other" or "globe"; before there was either birth or death and, therefore, before suffering was possible.

Compassion operating from this level four allied to such a cosmology can never be reduced into pessimism by any life event of any magnitude. From this place of "I-AM-ness," all vicissitude ceases, all pain, which is the price of admission into incarnation, and all suffering, which is the result of inadequate interpretations, dissolve into the embrace of God as we thoroughly enjoy the end of the illusion of separation.

And now having dealt with compassion level four, let me deal with compassion level zero. God IS, God KNOWS fully who she is, and God LOVES who he finds himself to be. But, in order to EXPERIENCE herself, God needs to CREATE. So the very first kind of compassion was that which God felt for himself. You thought you knew love, when you loved your mother, until you "fell in love" and then love-for-parent seemed but a pale imitation of the "real thing." Then you had your first child and you couldn't believe that such love as you felt for your baby was possible. You thought your heart would burst. You would watch over your sleeping infant for hours in earnest, unequivocal adoration. For perhaps, the first time in your life you knew that you would be prepared to give your own life or take the life of an attacker to protect your offspring. And so it is with God. She had no idea how much love she was capable of until she began to birth creation. You became ecstatic when you just birthed a spacesuit. Imagine what it must be like to birth a soul. Part of your overwhelming joy was that you thought you had conceived, carried and birthed the whole package, spacesuit *and* soul. But God had cuckolded you. You conceived, carried and birthed his child! You fashioned a spacesuit and, he fashioned the soul. You are a land-trapped hen raising an eagle that will soar.

(C) And Who is My Neighbor?

I need to revisit compassion level three for a moment. I said it was compassion-for-the-non-self. That, actually, is not quite accurate. It is only true when "self" is reduced to "skin-encapsulated ego." As we begin to move higher and higher up the ladder of spiritual development, we realize that compassion is always for the self, even when it reaches level zero and becomes, again, God having compassion for God.

So, when "neighbor" and compassion expand in tandem, then we are integrated. However, "integration" means very different things at different stages of development. In 1973, I was the Head Master of Kipchimchim Harambee High School in western Kenya. I taught physics, math and religion, and would try to cross-fertilize among these topics. At one stage in physics class, I introduced balloons to kids who had never in their lives seen one, while I was also teaching about the divinity of Christ and Saint Luke's enigmatic statement in Chapter 2 of his gospel, that the child Jesus "grew in wisdom and age and grace before God and man." Everybody could agree that Jesus was once a month old and probably measured 21 inches; that he was later 14 years old and measured 60 inches. They had some problem accepting that he could have grown in *wisdom*. After all, he was God, so he must have been born knowing fluent Kipsigis and advanced calculus. But where they really, really baulked was at the notion of his "growing in grace." So I grabbed one of the balloons, blew into it and pinched the mouth closed. I held it up and asked, "Is this balloon full of air?" "Yes," they replied. "Is there any space within this balloon that does not have air in it?" I asked. "No," they chorused. So I blew into it some more until it was about twice the size it had been. "Okay," I said, "Is the balloon full of air now?" "Yes," they said, puzzled. "Is there any space within this balloon which does not have air in it?" I asked again. "No," came the perplexed response. I repeated the procedure again, blowing and asking the same questions and getting the same responses. "Fine," I said, "is the balloon the same size now that it was after I blew into it the first time?" "No," they said, "It's much bigger now than it was then." "So," I said, "that's how it was with Jesus and grace. At each stage of his life he was filled with the grace of God. There was never a space in him where God's life did not reside. But as Spirit continued to breathe into him, his capacity to receive Spirit increased and so he was wiser and more grace-filled in later stages than in earlier stages of his life. Never did he lack God's indwelling presence, but as his journey unfolded his capacity and therefore the "amount" of grace in his being increased."

And that is what integration looks like also. There are levels, degrees and stages of integration and each stage incorporates but transcends all of the previous stages. So, compassion allied to neighbor-as-tribe is a higher form of integration than compassion allied to neighbor-as-family; compassion allied to neighbor-as-species is a still higher form; compassion allied to neighbor-as-all-sentient-beings is a yet higher form; and compassion allied to neighbor-as-God is the highest form of all. It is complete integration and full enlightenment. It is the path from, "Oh God, that could have been me!" to "Oh God, that *is* me!" With John Donne we can then proclaim, of the sad-sounding funeral gong, "Ask not for whom the bell tolls. It tolls for thee."

The problem is that what constituted integration, in previous stages, no longer qualifies as integration in subsequent stages. Let me use an analogy. An integrated 18-month-old child is able to walk but can't yet speak fluently. However, the same child is not integrated, if at age five years, she still can't speak well. Similarly, there was a time in human history when you really would be an integrated person if you exercised compassion for neighbor-as-clan. Being at such a stage, however, would no longer earn the title "integrated" for you today.

We are strung out along the spectrum of these levels and lenses. The sociopath is stuck at the stage of "only this period of this life is real or matters," allied to a definition of neighbor as his own skin-encapsulated ego. The enlightened being, the one with a facility for non-dual mysticism, can zoom effortlessly and appropriately among the perspectives and neighbor is understood as God herself. Most of the rest of us tend to fixate on this period of this life and neighbor means family and close friends.

Unfortunately, today 70 percent of the world's population thinks that integration consists of compassion allied to neighbor-as-my-nation. This is *not* integration. This thinking has led, in the last 200 years, to genocide, world wars and weapons of mass destruction. It was integration, perhaps, in 1800, but not today. Today it is retardation. It's a spiritual intelligence quotient that brands us global idiots, and yet the major religious, political, economic and military leaders continue to promote it as the ultimate stage of human development.

In truth, nothing less than compassion allied to neighbor-as-all-life-forms will save us from nuclear or ecological disaster. But that is the wrong reason for wanting to expand neighbor. It is a fear-based reason. The real reason to strive for compassion allied to neighbor-as-all-life-forms is because that is our origin, our birthright, our mission-on-planet-Earth and our final destination.

It's the difference between the stick approach and the carrot approach; between the fear of God and the love of God; between depressing dread and ecstatic expectation.

So, go into the pristine forest of your own soul and watch your mother bouncing all of her children in her apron, and then enfolding them squealing with delight into her very self.

23

Jet Plane
(April 24, 2001)

It speeds silently
across the evening sky,
glowing pink,
like the belly of a salamander.
Later I will hear its purring power.
It is a silver jet, seven miles above me,
catching the red rays
of the setting sun
on its shiny, metallic undercarriage.
Two white trails of vapor
mark its progress,
like the silky tracks of two heavenly snails,
shellmates on safari.

May you go safely.
May you go happily.
May there be excited friends
to greet your arrival.
May all the jets of the world
bring friends together.
May there be no more enemy jets,
theirs or ours.
May there be peace on Earth.
May the red bellies of the jets
be the throbbing hearts
of friends coming home.

24

Love of Leadership or Leadership of Love?

"By the accident of fortune a man may rule the world for a time,
but by virtue of love and kindness he may rule the world forever."
Lao Tse

In a country that doesn't have the ability to live fully in the present and plan creatively for the future, the only recourse is to cling tenaciously to a mythologized, romanticized, and antiquated past, which soon becomes a fixation, stultified identity and the primary cause of its inability to evolve.

That was a large factor of Irish life for nearly 300 years. It is the defining truth of the "troubles" in Northern Ireland that is only now barely beginning to dissolve under the relentless advances of the Celtic Tiger and a genuine economic explosion.

Beginning with the Plantation of Ulster, in 1609, when the local, Catholic, population of the north eastern part of Ireland was disenfranchised and its land given to Scottish Presbyterians, brought in by the colonizing British Empire, the two communities have ghettoized themselves and dialogued only in stereotypes.

For the Protestant community, the defining myth is the Battle of the Boyne, which was fought in 1690. Two foreign monarchs exported their personal war to Ireland and seduced Irishmen, Protestant and Catholic, to take up arms on their behalf and fight their vendetta for them, and determine which of them should be king of England.

The Catholics backed the Englishman James II who had converted to Catholicism in 1672. He was a man given to panic in crisis situations and a poor military strategist. The Protestants backed his nephew and son-in-law, William of Orange, a Dutch Protestant. And the prize was the kingship of Ireland, England, Scotland and Wales. Incidentally, this is why militant northern Irish Protestants still call themselves, "Orangemen."

At the end of the day, significantly outnumbered (36,000 to 25,000 troops), James thought discretion the better part of valor and fled to Dublin, and quickly thereafter to France. He might well have quoted Shakespeare's Richard III, "A horse, a horse, my kingdom for a horse!" He, who had no compunction about dragging another country and colonized subjects into his personal ambitions, now abandoned his troops and his crown and opted instead to save his hide. When they learned of his cowardly run, a shout went up from the Catholic troops, "Change leaders and we'll fight again!"

(A) Who is a Leader?

I believe that on a spectrum of leadership, there are six main levels. Firstly, there is the leader who, on acquiring power, simply uses it for self-aggrandizement. History is replete with such people—Caligula, Idi Amin, Hitler, Stalin etc. The second level is the leader who exercises his power to reward his backers and implement their agenda. These can be found even in democratic regimes, and so the concept of, "one person, one vote," soon becomes, "one dollar, one vote," as Senator Feingold so aptly put it. On the third level is the leader who seeks to reward only the part of the constituency that voted for him—sending a strong message to those who didn't, in order to educate them about how they need to vote next time around. It is very upsetting to find that leadership in many allegedly democratic regimes is largely at levels two and three, and occasionally even verges on level one.

Level four is that leader who attempts to address equally, the needs and concerns of the entire electorate, those who voted for him and those who voted for his opponents. Only at level four do we have "good" leadership, but it is still not "great leadership." Level five may earn the title "very good" leadership. It is the person who thinks of the welfare of the entire country, not just the person, county or state that he represents. And for the person elected to national office, level five leadership means thinking of the good of the whole country in the long-term and not just of its immediate needs. But even this leader is not yet "great." That title is reserved for people, at any level of office, who think, long-term for the good of the entire planet. It is far too late to elect leaders in America who only think as Americans for America and of America. If America is to survive we need leaders who think as global citizens for Gaia.

For it is not just about the survival of America, it is about the survival of humanity; it is about the survival of "all our relations" as the native peoples of this continent named the 10 million other species of life on this planet; it is about integrity, not just survival, about doing the right thing because it is the right thing to do; it is about being a karmic yogi, to use a Hindu description of such self-less behavior; it is about true love. It is not about the love of leadership but the leadership of love.

(B) Revisioning American Domestic Policy

As an American citizen, I watch in horror as our Bill of Rights is being eviscerated; as our constitution is being molested; as our environment is polluted and up for bids; as attempts are made to give over Medicare to the wolves of the private sector. I watch in horror as children, the sick and the elderly are economically choked so that the Chevrons, Reynolds, Monsantos and Exxon Mobil companies can post profits of five billion dollars a quarter; and as we spend one billion dollars a day invading sovereign lands, on fabricated charges, and then kill hundreds of thousands of its citizens and offer the Halliburtons of the world their heads on a silver platter as we "spread democracy."

If America is to stop its slide in despotism it must, I believe, undertake immediately the following changes. First, there must be accountability and transparency in the voting process. There is little point in voting for the candidate of your choice, if the voting machine is free to alter your vote. During my 14 years in Kenya, all too often I saw elections stolen by the very simple act of replacing boxes of real votes with pre-prepared alternative boxes, at the behest of one of the candidates. There is grave suspicion over the trustworthiness of some of the voting machines employed here in the 2004 elections; and it doesn't help that suggested legislation that would create a paper trail is being so vigorously opposed by some government leaders.

Second, there must be serious and radical campaign finance reform. The power of lobbyists, operating on behalf of big business, to impose a very disproportionate effect on national policy, is the antithesis of government of the people, by the people and for the people. When some of these extremely partisan lobbyists are appointed to sensitive areas of policy making within the government, then you have the fox in charge of the hen house. This little "you scratch my back and I'll scratch yours" game has been so blatant in recent American policy-making that it makes an utter farce of participatory democracy. That we then have the chutzpah to admonish foreign governments about their need to embrace democratic reform is hypocritical in the extreme. As it stands, overwhelmingly it is only those people with huge egos who have backers with huge wallets that have any chance of election to national office. When megalomania goes to bed with cornucopia, truth, justice and integrity all get jailed.

Third, the content of campaign ads, whether in newspapers, radio or TV must be first passed by some decency-in-campaign-ads non-affiliated body. The viciousness of some of these is probably a good indicator of the type of representation we can expect from the politician whose cause they promote. Is this level of debate okay because after all everything is permissible in love, war and politics? Borrowing from ice hockey, maybe such an ad should earn the candidate time in a "sin bin," where he/she is not allowed to make either a personal appearance or run an ad for a specified number of days. Or perhaps, borrowing from soccer, one infringement might earn a yellow card, and for a second infringement a red card—"You're out of this election race!" Perhaps, over the course of a public political career, one should, at least, be subject to the "Three strikes and you're out," rule.

Fourth, we have to re-liberate the press. On August 1, 1982, when a small group of Air Force personnel attempted a coup in Kenya, their first item of business was to capture the Voice of Kenya (VOK), the national broadcasting service. They had learned their lesson well. Controlling the airwaves is worth a few regiments and a whole bunch of guns. We have watched the consolidation of the press in this country with growing alarm. A few moguls, whose intentions are less than virtuous, want to tell us, what's really happening, where, why, who's to blame and what we need to do about it. Why waste time having to think for ourselves? Sit back enjoy the movie, order a pizza and big brother will solve all our problems for us.

Fifthly, we need a real separation. I am not in favor of the separation of politics and spirituality. A truly spiritual person has to be politically active otherwise he/she is merely a dropout masquerading as a mystic. But I am in favor of the separation of church and state. However, that is only a tiny part of the necessary separating that needs to happen. And let me hasten to add, separation is not the same thing as non-cooperation or non-complementarity. Our constitution provided for the separation of the executive, legislative and judicial branches of government, but this separation is leaking significantly at the seams. A president who nominates a supreme court that subsequently selects a president is not separation. A legislative branch that cedes almost limitless war powers to the executive branch is not separation.

Moreover, the following institutions need to be separate from, though in cooperation with, each other and government: the media, industry, science, academia, religion, peace officers and the military. At the moment we appear to have a congress elected by and owned by industrialists, on whose behalf the legislative and executive branches employ and control the media, science, academia, religion, peace officers, and the military in order to enrich and protect the industrialists, who, in turn, guarantee to keep re-electing these representatives. It's the nearest thing to perpetual motion to come along in decades.

So how should things be? The function of both science and religion should be to discover truth, exoteric and esoteric, respectively; the function of academia and the press should be to fearlessly and fairly teach and report these truths; the function of congress should be to enact legislation that reflects these truths; the function of the judiciary should be to interpret the constitution in the light of such legislation; the function of the police and military should be to protect these truths; and the function of the executive branch should be to oversee this entire process on behalf of all citizens.

(C) Revisioning American Foreign Policy

It is sickening that we would even discuss, in our august national congress, the degree of torture permissible. It is sickening that men, who were themselves tortured in foreign wars, would participate in such debates and accede to such decisions. And it is sickening that men, who repeatedly dodged the draft and vigorously resisted all efforts to have them wear their country's uniform in foreign wars, are the chicken hawks pushing this legislation. There are few bullies as vicious as bullies who are themselves cowards.

America has been acting in America so as to make America the personal plaything of a few such Americans; and America has been acting in the world so as to make the world its plaything. It is time that ordinary Americans take back America from this uncaring oligarchy; and it is time that America cease to be the biggest bully on the global block. Yes, it is time for America, with its extraordinary resources and its multi-cultural talent, to become the prototype of where an enlightened culture can lead our planet—beyond war, beyond poverty, beyond prejudice, beyond plague and beyond pestilence.

We must truly become the leaders in addressing global issues like the greenhouse effect, the hole in the ozone layer, deforestation, pollution of our air, land and water, pandemics, war, terrorism and poverty. And we have to lead by example, being willing to make the kind of sacrifices that others make because they have no choice. We have to sign the international accords on ecology, war crimes, nuclear disarmament and decommissioning of weaponry. We have to research, develop and promote alternative energies and make it less profitable for industries that deface our world and poison our people.

We have to ask not what the world can do for America, but what America can do for the world.

(D) Maturing from Religion to Spirituality

It is time that we differentiate between spiritual values and sectarian, religious fundamentalism masquerading as "the American Way." Fundamentalism's orienting response is to reduce spirituality to religion, to reduce religion to morality, and to reduce morality to sex. Sure, sexuality needs to be expressed in an ethical fashion, but there is far more to morality than sexual ethics. And, sure, morality is an important navigational tool in regulating human society, but there is far more to religion than moral issues. And, definitely, religion is the great carrier of human wisdom, but spirituality is far deeper than mere religion. When we wrest religion out of this nested context, we inevitably boil down an ineffable, mystical core to mere simplistic edicts which attempt vainly, and often hypocritically, to deny our own sexual shadow. Then the demagogues get incensed over artificial contraception, masturbation, homosexuality, women's rights about abortion, and stem-cell research, while ignoring the issues of war, violence, torture and poverty. How many fundamentalists who bomb abortion clinics do you find bombing chemical weapons depots or demonstrating against Guantanamo Bay or Abu Ghraib? Fundamentalist pressure persuaded the congress to rush back from vacation to attempt legislation to save Terry Schiavo's life. Where was the fundamentalist pressure to force congress to abandon its torture manual preparation?

One of the great issues facing our world today is terrorism. Isn't it time we responded to terrorism with truly Christian values, like forgiveness, feeding the hungry, clothing the naked, sheltering the homeless, repatriating refugees, healing the sick and liberating the unjustly incarcerated? Among other causes, American arrogance and the absence of Christian principles from our military, economic and ecological policy are significant contributors to the meteoric rise of terrorism. It will not be solved by brutality abroad, nor by curtailed civil rights at home, but by a truly global dialogue in which each nation has an equal voice.

(E) A New Anthem for a New Millennium

> God bless the 20 great religious traditions of the planet
> God bless the 200 nations of the planet
> God bless the 5000 cultures of the planet

God bless the six and a half billion people of the planet
God bless the myriad of other life forms of the planet
God bless the planet herself
God bless the solar system that birthed our planet
God bless the Milky Way Galaxy that birthed the solar system
God bless the Universe that birthed the Milky Way Galaxy
God bless the mind of God that has created this universe and
    countless others of which we know nothing

May there be not merely peace in our time but also enlightenment.

25

The Dance Master
(July 9, 2002)

I've waited eight minutes for you,
and it was worth every second.
What an exhibition you have just put on!
I once saw a movie
where the combatants
ran up vertical walls
and jumped incredible distances
from rooftop to rooftop.
I thought it so hokey!

But now, here you are
outperforming them.
I watch you balance on a single, fragile willow leaf
and then leap onto another,
without once losing your footing.
I see you dancing on the water
without once losing your faith,
unlike Peter.

I intentionally disturb the water,
creating ripples and waves.
You take it all in your stride,
not missing a step,
in perfect harmony with the music.

I've waited eight minutes for you.
What a journey you took:
93 million miles of star space.
And, at the end of it all, you landed,
not with a crash,
nor even with a thump,
but lithely and lightly.

Was Jesus punning when he said:
My burden is light ?
Perhaps, he didn't mean the weight of the burden,
But rather its composition?
What if the burden of mission
Is to recognize and become Light?

I've waited eight minutes for you.
I've waited five billion years for you.
I've waited because
I bought the illusion of time.
Now I don't have to wait anymore.

Teach me to walk on the waves.
Teach me to dance on a leaf.
En-Lighten me.

26

God 101—Things You Always Knew But Didn't Have Time To Think

"Belief resides within the shadow of doubt. It only functions effectively in direct proportion to the suppression of doubt that it seeks to override."
Tony Parsons

In July and August of 1963, I set out to collect as many Irish proverbs as possible. The Irish word for proverbs is, "sean-fhocail," which literally translates as, "ancient words." So I spent two months in the village of Cúil Aodh in the West Cork Gaeltacht (a Gaeltacht is a region in which Gaelic is still the mother tongue for most of the population.) In the course of two months, I collected 432 of them. I visited with old men and women and asked if they would share their wisdom with me. When they gave me a proverb, I would ask them to explain its meaning and the kinds of contexts in which it would be used. Occasionally, I asked for a "second opinion" on a proverb I had learned from somebody else in the village.

On one occasion, I did just that, only to be answered with a derisive snort. What I didn't realize at the time was that there was an old acrimonious rivalry between those two particular old men. So he laughed dismissively and said, "Sin sean-fhocal a dhein sé féin dó féin" ("That is a proverb he made up himself for himself!")

I'm going to open myself up today, to the same kind of accusation, because I am going to rewrite the first three chapters of the bible, the stories of creation and of the fall as recorded in the book of Genesis. Tír na nÓg (a very famous Irish mythological version of Atlantis) is the name of my home in Healdsburg. So I have given this "scripture he made up himself for himself" the title "A reading from Tír na nÓg." And here it is:

A Reading from Tír na nÓg

In a probable beginning, Ha Shem built a cosmos-creating bonfire. It was such a great fire that it produced 10^{27} brand-new universes every second for every cubic centimeter of 11-dimensional mathematical space. Most of these were quickly quenched by the moist night air, but lots survived to trace arcs of light across the darkness of the nothingness. The history of each one of these spark-universes is on record—somewhere.

I was invited to look at one such record. It was entitled, *"God 101—Things You Always Knew, but Didn't Have Time To Think."* This record describes the life and times of one spark-cosmos, which is now 13.5 billion years of age (as humans calculate time.) This spark-cosmos is the womb for 150 billion galaxies, each of which is, itself, a womb for 150 billion stars, who, themselves, have wombs full of planets, whose wombs birth a myriad of species, whose wombs birth babies, in whom Ha Shem delights. I was given eight hours to delve into that record in order that I might write a simple account for those children, so they could trace their ancestry and know their cousins.

This reading, and the homily which follows it, *is* that simple account. It is only as true as my memory is accurate and only as deep as your soul is awake. So, here is the story within my story:

"In another probable beginning, there was only God; a God who was pure, blissful love. But God was lonely; lonely to love another. But there was no other to love; only Himself. So God said, 'Let there be air!' And Einstein asked, '$E = ma^2$?' And there was evening and there was morning the first day. So God said, 'Let there be breath!' And Einstein asked, '$E = mb^2$?' And there was evening and there was morning the second day. So God said, 'Let there be light!' And Einstein exclaimed, 'Aha! $E = mc^2$!' And there was evening and there was morning the third day. And God saw that it was all very good.

Then the serpent, whose modern name is National Security, tempted the man and the woman and they created the A-Bomb, which is the abbreviated form of its full name: the A-Bom-ination. And God saw that it was very bad. And there was Hiroshima and there was Nagasaki the last day.

And so God really needed to rest. And when She was well rested She began to send avatars, highly advanced souls, to love us so deeply that we, also, would learn how to love. These avatars were so advanced that they had the ability, soon after Nagasaki, to retroactively insert themselves into world history, long before Hiroshima. So we find accounts of them under exotic personal names, in disparate foreign places, at alluring ancient times, as Lao Tzu and Confucius in China; as Mahavira and Gautama Siddharta in India; as Zoroaster in Persia; as Jeremiah and Ezekiel in Israel; as Socrates, Plato and Aristotle in Greece; all between 2,600 and 2,300 years ago; and as a very powerful being called Jesus of Nazareth around 2,000 years ago.

And God realized that She would have to work long after the customary retirement age if She was to help fragile earthlings develop into cosmic creatures. And She was willing.

(A) Preamble

The problem with God is that He is a genius, and like all geniuses He gets carried away; He gets involved in a new idea and loses all track of time; the thoughts spill out like water from a burst dam and, before you know it, His entire workshop is littered with all kinds of inventions. So, in a beginning, there was only God; a God who was pure, bliss-filled love. But God was lonely; lonely to love another, but there was no other to love; only Himself. So God decided to *create* another; and another; and another; and another; and another. And pretty soon His workshop was littered with baby universes; 10^{27} of them, every second, in every cubic centimeter of His 11-dimensional mathematical brain.

I awoke on Tuesday morning last in an altered state of consciousness and it lasted for several days. During that time, I got to hang out in His workshop. He asked me, "What do you want?" I pointed to one of those universes lying there on the floor and I said, "I want that one!" "I'll tell you what." He replied, "You can play with it for a few hours but I want it back." So I did, and because I'm a boy, I tried to take it apart, so I could see how it worked. He looked over the rim of his glasses and said, "Make sure you put that back the way you got it." I want to tell you a few things I learned as I was playing with it.

(B) How things got to be you

This little cosmos that I spent hours playing with started with a big bang, which was the sound of God laughing when He first got the idea for it. Thereafter it spread like wildfire, creating gasses that expanded into the void which was created to accommodate them. In time, through a law, which is known as gravity, and which is also built into the model, clusters of these gasses began to group and the galaxies came into being. When the force of attraction became even more intense, these gasses became stars; lots of them! In much the same way that coal under intense pressure becomes diamonds, so ordinary, everyday gasses under intense pressure became stars. As a side bar here, you can never become a star unless you can handle intense pressure elegantly.

In some cases, this attraction, which formed stars, was so very intense that their hearts burst with love in supernova explosions which started a whole new cycle which resulted in the birth of planets.

Our own little planet was born of such heartbreak 4.5 billion years ago. At first it was a fiery mass of gasses, that became a molten orb, which in time cooled a little so that it developed a thin crust of rock (like the skin atop a cooling pot of boiled milk). This skin we call "the physiosphere." After 800 million years, when it was just cool enough, the first life forms came into being—bacteria and protozoa, which still live, and in fact, reign supreme even today. This new layer of the planet is called, "the biosphere." Surrounding the molten core, the physiosphere and the biosphere is an insulating layer called, "the atmosphere," a clever device to protect life from gene-altering radiation that comes from deep space. And surrounding all of those spheres is another layer, which the great Jesuit paleoanthropologist Pierre Teilhard de Chardin called, "the noosphere." It is the consciousness sheath, our localized version of cosmic consciousness.

In another chapter, I suggested that both humans and the planet have seven levels of body—the gross, etheric, astral, mental, causal, atma and Brahma. So the physiosphere and the biosphere constitute the gross body, with all of its physical sub-parts: water systems (rivers, lakes, oceans, rain and snow), earth systems (mountains, soil and minerals), air systems (wind, oxygen and hydrogen) and fire systems (the molten mass and lightning). The etheric body is the morphogenetic field which produces bacteria, plants and animals. The atmosphere is the astral body. It is both the conduit and the buffer zone between, on the one hand, the gross and, on the other hand, etheric and the "higher" bodies. As dreams and emotions both buffer and channel information from Brahma, from atma, from causal and from mental down to etheric and gross, in the case of individual humans, so too does the atmosphere act on behalf of the planet.

The mental body is the noosphere, a hologram of cosmic consciousness (or Brahma.) It is from this level that Gaia gets her great ideas about how to proceed creatively with the evolution of life on Earth.

The causal body of the planet is light itself. As the causal body of a *person* is the first truly transpersonal level of the individual, manifesting as it does psychic gifts which indicate we are "entangled" parts of a field of consciousness, so also does light connect us not just to the sun, but to the supernova which produced many suns and countless planets.

And the Atma of the planet is love, the first born of Brahma, who is the unborn.

At first Gaia was tentative in her creating; having dabbled in bacteria, she waited almost three billion years before mustering the courage to be daring. But when she finally got the hang of things she became utterly outrageous. Beginning about 700 million years ago she fashioned the sea creatures. Three hundred million years later came the first dry land creatures, who were descended from the "retired navy beings." This led to reptiles and mammals. Some of the mammals decided to go back to the ocean permanently, millions of years later. In fact the biggest creature of all time—the blue whale—came into being then and still leaves "tsunamis" in its wake with one splash of its enormous tail. The blue whale, a warm-blooded mammal, is the largest creature ever to have lived on the planet, knocking even T-rex off his throne. A female weighing 168 tons and a male measuring 110 feet have been found.

While the sea-blubbers were frolicking in the deep, the land-lubbers were having their own kind of fun. But a particularly violent assault on the atmosphere resulted in the extinction of the dinosaur, and now the mammals, who up to now were tiny (no bigger than field mice) found the candy store owner missing and had a ball. The African elephant at seven and a half tons, while no match for mama blue whale, is the largest land animal alive today, outweighing 100 average men.

Gaia's extravagance led to another line, the primates, some of whom, the chimps, share 98.6 percent of our DNA. About five million years ago, the hominids made their appearance but it was only about 200,000 years ago that anatomically modern humans developed on the plains of East Africa, all descended from a single female, whom scientists have dubbed "mitochondrial Eve." In time these intrepid explorers migrated to all the landmasses of the planet. In the process they evolved art and religion, about 50,000 years ago; horticulture (the digging stick) about 12,000 years ago; agriculture (the ox-drawn plow), and science, mathematics, orthography, literature and philosophy about 5,000 years ago; industry about 300 years ago; and computers and information technology in the last 50 years.

Which brings me to *you*. You are a direct descendent of that Eve. Moreover, speaking statistically and reckoning on inter-cultural contact over the last 5,000 years, you are a direct descendent of everyone who lived on this planet before 1,000 CE and who had children. Which also means that every human alive today is literally related to you, not just in the sense of being a fellow human, but in the real, genetic sense of being family. And, even more interestingly, if you have or will have children, you are a direct ancestor of every human being who will live on this planet (or elsewhere) in 600 years time. If the average generation is 30 years then only 20 generations separate you from them. So you are the great-great (18 times) grandparent of every human being alive in the year 2,600 CE.

Do you want to be a deadbeat dad or will you acknowledge and provide for all of your children, no matter what skin color, beliefs, culture or language they have? Don't you want to leave every single one of them a legacy of love?

(C) Where is it now?

This exciting evolution is throwing up species all over the universe, in different dimensions with different missions and different resources. In what many scientists regard as the second most important formula of the 20th century, Francis Drake, a radio astronomer, created the following equation in 1961. It was his logarithm for the number of civilizations, in the Milky Way Galaxy, which had evolved technology that would allow them to communicate with others outside their own solar system. It says:

$N = R^* f_p N_e f_l f_i f_c L$ where
- N is the number of such civilizations
- R^* is the rate of formation of suitable stars (like our sun)
- f_p is the fraction of those stars that have planets in attendance
- N_e is the number of those planets that are Earth-like i.e. rocky and temperate
- f_l is the fraction of those planets that have thrown up life
- f_i is the fraction of those that have thrown up intelligent life
- f_c is the fraction of those that have developed communication technologies
- L is the longevity of such a civilization

And longevity, as we are finding out, is a crucial concern, because any species that develops such a level of technology also develops the ability to wipe itself out in a nuclear holocaust.

On feeding the data into each of these parameters, Drake estimated the statistical probability is that about 10,000 such civilizations exist. And that is in just one galaxy among hundreds of billions of galaxies.

A rule of thumb among these "players" is that no species is allowed to leave its own solar system until it has figured out how to think and act as a united, peace-filled planet. Cosmic exploration, like charity, begins at home.

These super-species, these ultra civilizations will not sit idly by if we attempt to visit our species-specific psychopathology on a galactic stage.

Two-year-olds are entitled to throw tantrums in the tolerant safety of their own homes, or occasionally even in a supermarket, but parents and child will be quickly escorted outside if the hissy-fit happens in a concert hall during a symphony. The canticle of the cosmos has no parts for spoiled brats.

(D) What we can learn from nature

Nature has three great cards in her hand; an elegant parsimony, compassionate patience and extravagant creativity—all at the same time. Parsimony is the ability to produce a result with the simplest possible moves. Western science speaks of "Occam's razor," a rule-of-thumb that says, "The simplest explanation for any given set of data is the best explanation." Well, nature invented Occam, and his razor.

Side by side with her parsimony however is her compassionate patience. She will spend millions and millions of years perfecting a species, until she gets it "just right," and then more years modifying sub-groups who wandered into different climate zones.

And the third card in her hand, paradoxically (and nature gets high on paradoxes), is her utterly extravagant creativity. She does stuff just for the sheer heck of it. Watch an aquarium full of fish, whose shapes even Euclid couldn't define and whose colors barely fit into the electro-magnetic spectrum. Sometimes it doesn't quite come off—like a rockfish or a hippo, but mostly she gets an A+.

If a two-year-old has anger-management problems, flies into a rage and physically pounds on his mother, she can smile and take it, but if a 19-year-old has the same issue and cannot control it, he can do serious damage to her; enough, perhaps, to cause him to be taken out of circulation.

If we compare pre-industrial peoples (2-year-olds) to modern humans (19-year-olds), we find that most of them weren't much different from us; they merely lacked the technology to do lasting damage to their environment (with a few exceptions, like the Easter Islanders whose de-forestation led to their extinction.)

In the past, nature could easily assimilate both our personal waste (feces, urine, CO_2, sweat), which it recycled within days, and society's waste ("left-overs," trash, "throw-aways") which took a little longer. Now, however, it's going to take nature 10,000 years or more to assimilate some of our recent waste. This may not be fast enough to prevent us poisoning ourselves with it—but nature will ultimately recycle it. She will respond with patience, parsimony and creativity. Nothing we can throw at her will kill her, but if we keep escalating the damage, then her patience, parsimony and creativity will probably lead to mutations that provide an environment in which humans will no longer be players, because we will have rendered our home uninhabitable—to us—but not to the new species birthed from these mutations caused by our violent behavior. Her parsimony may demand solutions that make conditions unlivable for homo sapiens; her compassion may demand that she protect her other children from us; and her creativity may demand a brand new species, a far superior one to us, that will take the baton we have dropped and become the life form that finally allows Gaia to realize her goal of creating a species capable of recognizing its own divinity and the divinity of all other creatures. The irony might well be that we invent this new species (e.g., artificial intelligence) before we commit the societal suicide.

In a twist of fate the "greens" and the "industrialists" are both focused on anthropocentric issues. The "greens" who swear they want to save nature are, in reality, concerned primarily about human survival, for nature definitely *will* survive and be ever-more extravagant as it experiments with new possibilities. The "greens" are, of course, rightfully saddened at the human-orchestrated extinction of so many other species. But nature will replace all of these in time; which of course is poor consolation to a compassionate "green" right now. It's rather like telling a bereaved child not to cry because mammy can make a new baby to replace his lost sibling.

The "industrialists," too, are focused on humans. They either don't think about nature, don't care about nature, regard nature as the enemy or believe nature can look after itself. In this latter regard they are absolutely right; nature *can* take care of herself.

The difference between the "greens" and the industrialists is that while the "greens" are thinking about the survival of the entire human species and its needs, the "industrialist" is thinking about the survival of just this one human being and his greed.

The truly great pity, from nature's point of view, is that in homo sapiens, she has produced the most advanced life form on the planet; one which can appreciate the entire evolutionary trajectory and join consciously in its future development. She has put a lot of work into us. Like a gardener who has devoted countless years to breeding the perfect rose, only to have that rose set about destroying all of the other breeds of roses in the garden, as well as the potatoes and the apple trees and grass. At some stage the gardener is going to have to call off the experiment.

And let's remember that it wasn't always the dominant species that birthed the next dominant species that replaced it. There have been many cul-de-sacs, for example, the dinosaurs. Only with the extinction of that awesome dominator species, were mammals, the largest of whom was then only the size of a field mouse, free to grow and evolve and throw up whales, dolphins, elephants and apes—and, eventually, humans.

E) What part do you not understand?

At one stage, as I was continuing my examination of the universe, before I had to give it back to Father-God, someone came up behind me, bent down and kissed me on my crown chakra. It was Mother-God. She then moved a few universes gently to the side and sat cross-legged in front of me. "I want you to bring back a message for me." I said I would, and I listened very carefully to what she told me. The rest of this chapter is my recollection of that, in her words.

"When I said, 'Do not kill, rather love your neighbor as yourself' what part of that do you not understand? When I said, 'Don't your traders sell sparrows two for a penny in your market places, and yet not a single one falls from the sky without your heavenly father being aware of it?' Do you think that was an invitation to destroy their habitat and have them fall from the heavens by the thousands? When I said, 'Look at the lilies of the field; they do not spin nor weave nor gather into barns, and yet, I tell you, not even Solomon in all his royal finery looked as good as one of them', do you think this was an invitation to spray then with pesticides?

"When I said, 'Look, I have carved your name in the palm of my hand', what part of that love do you not understand? I will not destroy you, no matter how many of my other children you will kill. I do not believe in the death penalty, but you may well kill yourselves. Others of my children have done that in the past. Then I will whisper your name in the silence of the cosmic night. No mother should have to bury her own child.

"Do you really think that you, humanity, are my only children? Or even the brightest of the bunch? Have you never looked up at the night sky? Do it now, and then tell me if you are the only one. There are children of mine all over this universe with which you were playing; some of them were in post-doctoral programs before I ever conceived you. I have lost some. Not that any soul is finally lost, just that particular experiments with some species didn't ultimately work out. Each of the souls, however, got other chances to grow in other places at other times. But it always pains me when a particular experiment fails because of arrogance. Free will is one of my favorite creations, but it is the one that has caused the most 'failures.' Of course, there are no final failures.

"Now let me talk to you about Jesus. You know him only as the Christ, but he is known to other communities in this universe you hold, and in other groups on your little planet by different names, because that being whom you call, 'Jesus of Nazareth,' has been among you many, many times, in many different locations and many different guises. He was always far enough ahead of the culture to inspire but not so far as to be unintelligible. Unfortunately, when you inspire some you inevitably enrage others and pay a heavy price.

"But let me just focus on the incarnation by which you know him, the 'Jesus of Nazareth' one. It is ironic that those who claim copyright on his teaching are those who have understood him the least—from claims of infallibility to claims of being 'the vicar of Christ on Earth' to life-eviscerating fundamentalism that would reduce deep mysticism to partisan literalism. How could spiritual infants like you copyright the teachings of an ascended master? It is bad enough that you are doing that with my simple gifts—air, water, seeds and soil. I gave these to you freely for everyone, and you have polluted them, then grabbed them, attempted to copyright them and now you want to sell them! All that is really bad, but then to pretend you can copyright the mystic transmission of an ascended master! What part of 'chutzpah' do you not understand?

"When you heard him pray, 'Father, I thank you that of all those you gave me, none has been lost except the one who was destined to be lost,' do you think he was talking about Judas? No! Judas is fine. Judas has grown. He was talking about all of the times he volunteered to intervene at critical times in the evolution of other planets and other dimension; times such as you are now entering. And he was grateful that only once did he 'fail.' And by 'destined' he did not mean that we had previously determined one civilization should be lost. Do you not have a saying in the Hindu tradition,

> Sow a thought and reap an act.
> Sow an act and reap a habit.
> Sow a habit and reap a character.
> Sow a character and reap a destiny.

> The trajectory of your species shows that if you
> Sow thoughts of anger, you reap acts of violence.
> and when you sow acts of violence, you reap a habit of warfare;
> and when you sow a habit of warfare you reap a character of
>   genocide;
> and when you sow a character of genocide, you will reap a destiny
>   of self-extermination as a species.

"That is what he meant by 'destiny.' He came back to that theme on other occasions, because it was a 'loss' that ravaged his compassionate heart. Once after he had miraculously fed the multitude in the desert and then invited them to eat 'real food,' his own body, by which he meant his level of consciousness, the crowds turned in disgust saying, 'How can this man give us himself as food? This is disgusting teaching' and they turned, full-bellied, and walked no more with him. He looked at his twelve closest friends and asked, 'Will you also go away?' Do you really think this was the petulant reaction of a rejected teacher? No! Rather, it was an appeal directed to all of humanity, that you not blow it and become another 'lost child.'

"And when, at last, he said, 'Father, forgive them because they do not know what they are doing,' do you think he was appealing to an angry divinity to stay His hand and not repay them with an Armageddon? Not at all! He was declaring his unequivocal intention of coming back to Earth to try again. And he has kept that promise, many times since.

"And do you understand the end game he modeled? He symbolized two possible end game scenarios. One gospel account says he died crying 'My God, my God, why have you abandoned me?' Was this really the despairing wail of an ascended-master-in-the-flesh? It was not. He was repeating the cry of that other child, at the last moment when having pushed its technology beyond its ability to use it wisely, it now wanted to blame God for its own suicide. That is a possible end game for Homo sapiens. Another gospel account says, 'He ended the Jesus-of-Nazareth incarnation with the words, 'I and the father are one. It is completed.' And that is how experiment homo sapiens is meant to end. Gaia will have completed her mission, and then Earthlings will be ready to become cosmic creatures.

"When this experiment first started, and the newly-born, wet, shivering infant-humanity lay in a pool of my blood, it reached out tiny fingers in panic. And I raised it to my breast and sang,

> 'Can a mother forget her baby
> Or a woman the child within her womb?
> Yet even if these forget
> Yes even if these forget
> I will never forget my own.'

What part of that lullaby do you not understand?"

27

The Leaf Folk of Pena Creek
(November 30, 1999)

Families of fallen leaves are gathering;
clustering together, in the shallow parts of Pena Creek;
and hanging on
to the sides of little stones
that peep through the surface of the water
from their gravel bed some inches below.

Two recent arrivals are spooning
like sleeping lovers in a bed.
The busy, rain-swollen creek
continues to deliver newcomers,
each seeking out its own clan.
Darker clouds are racing from the West;
it will rain some more.
Then the little creek will puff its chest
and force all of the leaf families
to emigrate to the lowlands.

I hope no one gets lost.

28

Bad Games, Good Games

"Let him that would move the world move first himself."
Socrates

They call themselves the Bioneers—Biological Pioneers. For almost 20 years they have been holding their annual meeting in San Rafael, California under a motto that states, "Wisdom from the heart of nature." It is an umbrella group for thousands of different organizations and projects in disciplines that span anthropology to zoology. They are interested in raising human awareness, of moving towards, what I would call, Christ consciousness or Buddha nature. So, for instance, law, medicine, agriculture, education, urban planning, architecture, politics, and religion are inspired by how nature solves its problems.

In an era and in a culture dominated by the depressing "news" fed us by the fear-mongering media moguls, they offer us lots of other places and sites into which we can plug to learn the real news, to be educated and enthralled and enthused by the hundreds of millions of people who are walking a new talk for homo sapiens. I will call this chapter, "Games People Play."

(A) Bad Games

To put it simplistically, we play two kinds of games: bad games and good games. And each of these two categories breaks down into three sub-games.

The good games are, the soul game, the Gaia game and the neighbor game. The bad games are the power game, the money game and the fear game. Let me speak first of these bad games. There will be many articulations and versions, but all misunderstand the soul game, fight against the Gaia game and seek to reverse any advances made in the neighbor game, by restricting "neighbor" to fellow citizen and then by spying on these fellow citizens in the interests of national security. Then three sub-groups will emerge. Firstly, the "unthinking masses" whose motto is, "eat, drink and be merry, for tomorrow we die" fueled by an oligarchy-serving media that promises bread and circuses—or pizza and TV. Secondly, those who "escape" into esoteric religion, based on the admonition to "be holy, don't be political, politics is a dirty, secular affair, best left to the irreligious." Since the "unthinking masses" have no interest in or time for politics (mostly, they don't even vote), and the "religious escapees" think politics is dirty, then that only leaves the third group to do battle with the oligarchy. And that third group operates under the opposite admonition "be political, religion sucks; it's an infantile vestige from our remote origins." Thus, their very platform, the raison d'etre of their political involvement is eviscerated, from the beginning, of the only true, authentic and adequate tool to make positive changes; in other words, a supra-human perspective.

A recent form of these bad games is an updated version of the Immortality Project. Since humanity began to play with the notion of "life after death," this idea has gone through many iterations. Firstly, it was felt that survival was only guaranteed by having children; lots of them. As long as somebody remembered me, I still lived on. So a combination of having many offspring, calling them by the names of their ancestors and by passing on stories about them (famous escapades, feats, battles, buildings etc.), they could be guaranteed to "live" for several generations into the future.

Judaism took this so seriously that it enacted the Levirate Law mandating a surviving man to marry the childless widow of his dead brother in order to raise progeny to his departed sibling, thus giving him his shot at immortality.

And among the Kalenjin, if a woman proved to be barren, she would use part of her dowry to marry another woman whom she then presented to her husband. The first child of the union belonged legally to the barren woman. So she, too, might live on.

The second phase came when it was felt that there was actually an after life place, but it was reserved for dead kings and pharaohs, who, after all, were semi-divine to begin with. So great expense went into embalming them, surrounding them with the necessities of the journey (money, food, weapons, transport and even servants who were sacrificed to accompany them). The third phase was, perhaps, the first great notion of human rights, a belief that not only kings and pharaohs, but perhaps even ordinary people like us could inherit eternal life. The one sine qua non was that we be "righteous" as the pertinent religious dogma defined it. For the "unrighteous" it was extinction-as-usual by dissolution into nothingness. Soon however, a fourth phase arrived which said that all humans would survive bodily death. In this version the righteous would go to heaven (sometimes with purifying way-stations like purgatory or re-incarnation). The "neutral" (e.g., unbaptized babies) lived on in places of natural happiness (e.g., limbo) without ever having the opportunity of the beatific vision (seeing God); and the "unrighteous" would go to hell, to burn for all time. In one very enlightened and compassionate Christian version, the righteous got to look upon the spectacle, as they ate popcorn and chucked empty coke cans at suffering ones down below in Hades. This fourth version survived in various forms until Nietzsche arrived to breathlessly announce God's unexpected demise. Since nature hates a vacuum, a fifth version of the immortality project rushed in. While humanity was mourning God's untimely death, science was developing its own very reductionistic and materialistic version of the ineffable mystery of life. Not to be outdone by its more famous brother, physics, biology wanted to prove its newfound patriotism, too, by telling us that we (individual humans) were merely taxicabs for genes. This, allegedly, was the new "Good News." I'm not sure if biology was miffed that homo sapiens didn't cheer and dance at this wonderfully liberating pronouncement. If only we had taken it to heart, I'm sure it would have been the end of all depression, anxiety, violence, internal warfare, fear of death and annoyance at having to pay taxes. But we are an ungrateful bunch, and we have continued to engage in all of the above activities without any sense of gratitude to the biologists.

On the contrary, since misery loves company, we decided, instead, to confer personhood on organizations. We christened them, "corporations" and we gave them all the rights of individual humans up to and including the right to be taxicabs. But since corporations are mega-people, they deserve to be carriers not of mere genes, but of memes or ideologies. Now the selfish meme has augmented the selfish gene. Just as the individual cells in a human being die and are replaced on an hourly basis, so too, individual human beings (even the CEO's) are merely cells in the corporate body and they die and are replaced equally frequently. "Here's your hat, what's your hurry!" What survives now is the corporation, the meme or the ideology—until future generations of the corporation ask, "communism who?" or "gasoline who?" or "yahoo who?" Most dead memes don't even make it to the obituary pages of "Who's Who on planet Earth."

When Jesus said, to the utter shock of his audience, "The Sabbath was made for man, not man for the Sabbath," he was knocking the pre-eminent meme of his time on the head. In effect he was saying, "memes were made for humanity, not humanity for memes." That is the good phylogenetic news, and the ontogenetic news is equally good, "genes were made for individual humans, not individual humans for genes.

(B) Good Games

Now that I have the "bad games" out of the way, let me focus on the "good games." The first of these is "the soul game." Each of us has indeed, volunteered to assist Gaia in her task, but before that and after that we committed to the game of becoming bodhisattvas. So the apex of a soul's mission is to reach enlightenment, while making Earth a Garden of Eden en route. This meta-mission, once it is remembered, allows us to navigate tranquilly through the troubled waters of incarnation, because we have a much longer timeline than a single human life span and a far greater perspective than that of our individual egoic agenda. Walking with a non-dual awareness we realize we have to be both holy and political. We have to walk our talk, but first our talk has to come from truly cosmic thoughts. And cosmic thoughts only come from regular voyages into altered states of consciousness. There are many avenues that have proved adequate in that regard, throughout human history. The Shamanic illness or even ordinary illnesses, especially those involving fevers or near death experiences, have allowed countless millions the opportunity to enter those realms. So have the initiation ceremonies of pre-industrial cultures which flooded the initiates with real or symbolic experiences of death and rebirth. Music, dancing, fasting, self-inflicted pain (especially if it involved significant blood loss) also do the same thing. Controlled psychedelic sessions with appropriate mind-set (that it be a spiritual not just a recreational experience) and setting (a sacred place with a priest/shaman/facilitator) have proven to be very powerful avenues to these transpersonal realms. And, of course, that includes a daily meditation practice.

Many modern spiritual leaders are beginning to develop and teach practices that bring the physical, emotional, intellectual, social and spiritual aspects of life into a unified program. e.g., Murphy and Leonard's, "Integral Transformation Practice" and Wilber's "Integral Life Practice." This movement is, finally, bringing the best of pre-industrial shamanistic cultures, Eastern mysticism and Western psychology into a powerful new tool for the soul game.

The Gaia Game is four and a half billion years old and began when a Mahatma volunteered to vitalize the third rock from the sun and evolve it until it produced a species that was fully awake to divinity. In the last chapter I wrote about how lesser souls signed up to help out even during the pre-mammalian life of planet Earth; how they kept returning, and were joined by a great increase of volunteers after Gaia had produced homo sapiens; how some of these were advanced and hit the deck running, while others were far "younger" and more susceptible to the "bad games." And here *you* are, remembering how you volunteered to help Gaia. As a resource you have two great yogic traditions, Jnana yoga and Karmic yoga.

Jnana yoga, or the path of mind, is your ability to think, read, talk and discuss great ideas. It gives you the ability to set in place your own "personal cosmology"—an explanation for life that can accommodate all of your unique experiences and keep you centered in love, compassion and serenity. It will be a cosmology that you will continue to tweak, and occasionally radically overhaul as life gives you more experiences, and as the soul game bleeds more profusely into your Earth psyche. Jnana yoga will enable you to set the mass media free to do its job of disseminating real information about non-trivial events and ideas; and it will help you develop sciences that probe the mystery with a truly open heart.

Karmic yoga is the path of right action. It will take the insights of Jnana yoga and translate them into behavior, individual and group. As its outlets it will use ecology, systems theory, social justice, economics, politics and human rights. It will vilify none of those; rather it will sanctify all of them. And it will do so one person at a time, one event at a time. Nothing will be too lowly for its undivided attention. And it will act without regard for recognition, gratitude or even results.

And the third good game is "The Neighbor Game." It is double-pronged. Firstly, it will greatly and continually widen the definition of neighbor; and secondly, it will reframe the notion of morality.

Let's look at neighbor. Initially, it was a non-starter. Like a newborn infant today; the species arrived in the grip of total narcissism, only to find out very quickly that as a survival mechanism, narcissism wouldn't even get us to first base. If we just use a single criterion (and not even the most important one), that of life expectancy, we can quickly see that expanding the definition of neighbor pays immediate dividends. Your narcissistic first human who attempted to hide what he had "scored" (whether it was a deer he killed or a banana-grove he discovered) so as to be able to gorge himself eternally, quickly discovered tomorrow that either the hyenas or the chimps had polished off his leftovers. He might have to wait a hungry week for lady luck to smile on him again. However, if he shared his find with the little band (average size about 100,000 years ago was 15 to 40 people) then everybody had enough, and tomorrow somebody else might luck out. And the life expectancy was a princely 18 years.

Then the idea of neighbor was widened to tribe, and the techno-economic model changed to horticulture (the digging stick). Now sharing was more widespread and we could expect to live to the ripe old age of 25, an increase of 39 percent! With the invention of agriculture (the ox-drawn plow) and the expansion of neighbor to nation, longevity jumped to the 50s, a more than 100 percent increase. Then came the first efforts at a global village. The industrial revolution got underway and life span reached the high 70s, if you were female, and the low 70s if you were male. This represented a further 50 percent increase.

With the onset of the information technology revolution, we began to think seriously about our non-human relatives, the 10 to12-million other species with whom we (hopefully) share the planet. And now, predictions are for a life span in excess of 120 years—another increase of 60 percent. This trajectory is interesting. Of course, longevity is not the most important parameter, and it is not causally related to a widening of neighbor, but it certainly is a most interesting correlate. I believe that when we finally begin to think as cosmic beings, the life span will dramatically increase. But, much more importantly, the quality of life and of relationships will hugely improve. Then, truly, there will be paradise on Earth.

And somewhere along that path from neighbor-as-self to neighbor-as-cosmos, somewhere, hidden in the sacred burning bush of mystical teaching, came the injunction to think of the "enemy" as neighbor. This piece has continued to cause indigestion in the processing of the evolution of relationship. But it is a vitally important part of the path. When, either as individuals or as groups, we realize that we "have seen the enemy and the enemy is us," then for the first time humanity will be truly free to embrace its destiny. And cosmic humor will have had the final belly laugh: a cartoonist will have discovered and articulated the truth before the theologians or the scientists.

So, let's look at morality. Builders and ethicists and pyromaniacs were the first three Earth groups to steal from the gods. Prometheus stole fire; he was punished, but we kept the "gift." The builders began to construct ziggurats and pyramids, in an effort to keep up with the Joneses and with the goddesses. And the ethicists, in the best tradition of French court etiquette, sought to live as the gods lived. What an unruly mob the gods must have been if our slavish imitation is in any way accurate. Obviously, when having laughed themselves silly, they tired of our pathetic charade; they decided to dictate how *they* wanted us to live. So we got the code of Hamurabi (for the Mesopotamians) and the Torah (for the Hebrews), the Brehon Laws (for the Celts) and "People" Magazine, for those who never heard of the other three. However, the trajectory of ethical evolution must move from a fear-filled obedience to allegedly revealed commandments (however important these may still be) to a commitment to ending suffering for neighbor, in its fullest expanded sense. Jesus fired a significant volley in this development when he offered the beatitudes as a more growth-promoting idea than the Decalogue.

The United States Constitution (before it began to be molested), the Bill of Rights (when it was still honored), the United Nations Charter (if it ever gets to be followed), the Kyoto Accords protocol (1997), the Landmines Agreement, The Earth Charter (2000), the Rio Declaration on the Environment and Development (1992)—all of these are modern articulations of what true morality should look like. So long as we keep reducing morality to sexual ethics (for all their real importance) we will miss the much bigger picture and not recognize the much greater invitation. Nero fiddled as Rome burned, the band played on as the Titanic sank, and humanity heatedly fixates on the morality of premarital sex as experiment homo sapiens threatens to extinguish its light.

So, let's look at some modalities for a better ethics. None of these is new; but the way to use them must be new. First, there is religion, an extraordinary insight that helped us plug into the cosmic source. In its evolution however, the parts have worn thin, rust has built up, resistance has sapped power; and so the appliances which should be in receipt of the full power of universal love are barely getting by with a trickle of life as it attempts to seep past culturally grown prejudices and individually grown biases. Religion badly needs to clear the pipes, replace worn parts and change the oil. If a million megawatt generator can't light an average house, something ain't right.

For years to come many people will continue to look to their religions as the chief source of inspiration and the ultimate origin of ethics. Religious leaders have a solemn obligation to teach love and to translate what this means as we relate to all of our neighbors.

The next mode I want to consider is economics. As a starting premise, any future economic model must ensure that all my neighbors, human and non-human get to sit at the table; that each have the basic requirements for incarnation: space, light, earth, water, education, housing, medical attention, security, freedom, and food. These new economic models must immediately begin to shrink the utterly immoral discrepancies in lifestyle, resource-consumption and income *between* communities (e.g. "developed" world and "third" world) and *within* communities (e.g. class structure, management levels within companies). The following is a quote from "Executive Excess 2005" compiled by the Institute for Policy Studies and by a group called, United for a Fair Economy, "The ratio of average CEO pay (now $11.8 million) to worker pay (now $27,460) spiked up from 301-to-1 in 2003 to 431-to-1 in 2004. If the minimum wage had risen as fast as CEO pay since 1990, the lowest paid workers in the United States would be earning $23.03 an hour today, instead of $5.15 an hour."

The third mode is politics. Neighborly morality in government will be an evolution from big daddy to big brother to big boy. Big daddy was the first phase of governing communities. It was government by a distant demanding daddy who was both unpredictable and uncontrollable. He didn't tell us what the rules were but he punished us for breaking them. We finally dismantled him. Then along came big brother. This was/is government by self-serving oligarchs who intrude on people's privacy, trample human rights, invite them to spy on each other and are, themselves, above the law. The tiny carrot that justifies all of these sticks is "security in the fight against terrorism." Well, we have seen the terrorists and it is the oligarchy. So evolution of government cannot stop there, it must proceed to big boy, a system in which every citizen of planet Earth is precious and is free and motivated to participate in true democracy; not the smoke and mirrors illusion of democracy but the real thing: government of the people, by the people, and for the people.

The fourth mode is science. Its portfolio is to show us how the physical cosmos works, and especially planet Earth, so that we can become caring stewards of the spaceship which is at once our home and our transport. It must remain true to its purposes, which is truth-finding, and avoid three forms of harlotry. First, selling itself to the highest bidder, "we will tailor the data to your agenda." Second, closing its mind to new areas of study or new theories about old areas, simply because they rock the current paradigm. And, third, allowing possibility to outpace decency. By this I mean that science must monitor itself. Just because something can be invented, prototyped and developed doesn't mean it should; take nuclear bombs for instance, or genetically modified foods.

The fifth mode is the mass media. Its privilege and responsibility is to share the truths of science and of spirituality in a truly representative fashion without fear or favor. The days of the "court historian" have long since outlived their usefulness. This cannot happen, however, if the news outlets are owned by a few. This is the area perhaps where centralization and privatization are most dangerous and have impaled democracy on the sword of "free trade." Free trade has traded freedom for a slavish lapping up of the pitifully infantile offerings of this big brother outlet. Lose your media, lose your freedom.

And the final modality I want to mention is Peace Officers. There are two main branches: police officers to ensure that there is no anti-social behavior *within* a community, and the military to ensure that there is no inhuman behavior *between* communities. Many countries of the world have unarmed policemen (Ireland for instance) but the uniform, the moral authority of the office, and the agreement of the community is enough to lend real clout to their presence and interventions. If weapons' manufacturers, with the blessings of government, weren't supplying arms to both sides in all conflicts, then even a lightly armed military peacekeeping force would be adequate to the task. They would truly be a moral presence between communities who don't see eye-to-eye, but in the past have operated on and eye-for-an-eyes basis.

(C) Rights and Responsibilities

Let me end this chapter by briefly discussing rights and responsibilities. Like all things great and small, rights have an evolutionary history. At first the only right was the right of the gods to abuse us at will. They were the gods, we were the humans, they had the power, and we didn't even have the right to complain. C'est la-vie. In time, rulers began to claim this privilege; it was known as "the divine right of kings." Since they, alone, were God's anointed they had all His prerogatives. This right extended even to the "jus primae noctis" (The right of the first night.) This was the sovereign's right to test the virginal status of a bride on her wedding night, by himself deflowering her. The "celibate" clergy eventually got into this act, when bishops became major landholders and "princes" of the church. Later we had the infallible right of the Pope (1871). Before that there were the democratic rights of freemen in ancient Greece. In time, slaves were freed and extended previously withheld rights; then came women's rights and recently the rights of children. In many cultures animals and the entire eco-system have advocates fighting to grant them rights. No less a genius then Mikhail Gorbachev is the luminary behind the Earth Charter of the year 2000.

This entire journey chronicles the development of both the notion of neighbor and the refinement of morality. And it has a flip side which is the idea of responsibilities. In dysfunctional systems the masses have few responsibilities and fewer rights, while the leaders have lots of rights and merely those responsibilities that ensure the masses don't get angry and wake up to the game. In true evolutionary fashion, however, each expansion of neighbor and each sensitization of morality and each accumulation of rights brings corresponding responsibilities. The price of each right is the responsibility to be even more aware and even more involved.

In the game of neighbor, you are fully enlightened when you see all manifestation as emanating from your Self. When you have become the quaternity: you are "Father" which is the "I am-ness" of all that is; you are the "Son" who is God's total self-knowledge; you are the "Spirit" which is the bliss-filled love that God has for Herself; and you are the "Mother" who needed to create in order to more totally experience such love.

Quite a game, huh?

29

Jacob's Ladder
(2/10/2008)

"God the biologist,
We honor you.
You who whirl ecstatically around your own image,
In the double helix of life making,
We honor you."

That is a verse from the Eucharistic Prayer of the Cosmos, which I composed in May 2007. Today, nine months later, I had another vision about it. I saw the spiraling ladder of Watson and Crick's double helix of DNA, whirling around itself. And I saw that the two curving, spiraling "shafts" of the ladder were God-love and God-light, and that the result was Earth-life. It is an alive ladder, not just an inert artifact fashioned once and then abandoned to lean against some cosmic wall, in an unvisited corner of God's backyard, to rot slowly in accordance with the second law of thermodynamics, together with a collection of God's old bikes and several buckets of decaying paint from when He put the finishing touches to sunsets and flower petals. No, it is very much an *alive* ladder. It is the Jacob's ladder of Genesis, touching Earth at a "Caol Áit" that acts as a portal between the mystical and the mundane. And Jacob understood the significance and it gave him the courage to go into combat with the divine. For his audacity he was rewarded with a new name—Israel, which literally means, "the man who wrestled with God."

What does it mean to wrestle with God? It means to wrestle prejudices and theologies and tribalism to the ground, in order to discover the mysterious origin from which all forms come. It is to fight the spiritual battle of seeing beyond all separation, behind all ontological, discrete differences to the heart of the Oneness. It is the single cell realizing it is part of an organ which is part of organism which is part of a family which is part of a species which part of all sentient beings which is only a single face of the Faceless Source.

This wrestling match is the mission of everyone on Earth who is coming awake. Like a consummate chess master, God is aching to play simultaneous matches with all of us—if you don't mind me mixing my games' metaphors. Getting thrown out of the Garden of Eden was the first round in that wrestling match. We were not banished because of a sin, we were liberated from the prison of mere instinct, because of our courage, to venture into the luxuriant forest of free will, onto the golden wave-washed beach of moral capacity, and up the serene mountainside of self-reflection.

And now, in the next phase of that journey-back-into-our-divinity, we are ready to challenge God to another bout.

The rungs on that ladder-of-life are myriad, but I will mention just a few major steps on a safari that began with the Physiosphere, the third rock from the sun, which a Great Soul agreed to animate in order to accelerate the return home. And the antepenultimate rung on the ladder-of-life is Christ Consciousness. When we stand on tippy toes on that rung we can see into the womb of no-self, no-thing and risk dissolving into the mystery, leaving not a trace behind. "Poor soul" those who are on the lower rungs will say, "He's gone!" Instead, I who loved to watch sunsets and spiders, listen to the wind and the waves, stroke the velvet, mossy lichen on the oak trees and the shaggy red coat of my dog, Kayla—now, I who used to DO all that, AM all that. For now, once again, there is no me, there is only God, looking at and feeling into Her creation.

But I have gotten a little ahead of myself with the story. So let me talk about these rungs that connect those spiraling arms, at once giving them stability and the freedom to dance. These rungs are not made uniformly to the same exact dimensions nor even of the same stuff. Each rung is a single-issue limited edition of a new masterpiece.

The ladder sits atop the physiosphere, the allegedly inert stuff that physics likes to study and figure out. Already, this apparently simple "dead" matter is highly intelligent and extremely complex. While it is, indeed, the very ground that holds up the ladder, it is, simultaneously, the first rung of the ladder. For this is an organic ladder; the two legs of it grow, and as they grow, they send out connectors to each other. With the precision of two space stations docking as they hurtle along at thousands of miles per hour, so too these spiraling arms never fail to connect with each other. Not a single rung dangles abandoned in mid air, vainly searching to make contact with its partner. Rather, with unerring accuracy, the partners dance and connect and never miss a beat.

The next level to emerge is the Biosphere, the "Life Sheath." On Earth this began with the lowly, long-lived bacteria, those selfless shareware seekers who first colonized the planet, learning to extract hydrogen (a very good choice since hydrogen is the most plentiful "food" in the cosmos) from sunlight, rocks and water. This sheath has been evolving for four billion years, and it has created ever more sophisticated rungs as it journeys from single-celled creatures to multi-celled organisms of extraordinary complexity, in which sub-communities with billions of members accept pivotal specialties like respiration, elimination, digestion, sensation, perception . . . This sphere, which contains very many rungs, embraces all life forms from the tiny trilobite, that invented the eye, to the jellyfish, that invented muscles, to the worm, that invented the brain, to reptiles, dinosaurs, mammals and hominids.

Teilhard de Chardin posited a new sheath surrounding the biosphere. He called it the "Noosphere"; "Noos" being another form of the Greek word for knowledge. So, it is a sheath of consciousness. The "world wide web" and the "global brain" are modern examples of what he was speaking about. It is a field of information and wisdom; it is the very ocean of data in which we swim; from which we download all of our ideas; and back into which we upload all of our personal musings and words. It is rather like a reservoir from which we draw all of our water. We have to be very careful that we do not, in turn, dump our waste and toxins into it, for then it will merely feed us back our own garbage. It treats us so well, but if we abuse it in return, it can only subsequently repay us with our own poison. It is environmental karma at the level of mind. And this dance of the noosphere's rungs and legs will lead to either great evolutionary shifts or to horrible mind-boggling mutations.

The next sphere I call the "Animasphere," the Soul Sheath. To remember this level and to attain it as a species, we have to discover, or more precisely, to re-discover the unity underlying all manifestation. This is a way-station beyond all war, a place without prejudice, a state of no separation. From this perspective violence is an autoimmune disease, selfishness is insanity, and greed is unfathomable.

Next comes what I call the "Pneumasphere" or Spirit Sheath. Here even the notion of separate souls drops away and there is simply, Unity—there are no more waves who regard themselves as anything except expressions of one ocean; there are no more drops desperately attempting to achieve independence from the wave. Now there is true Christ Consciousness.

But the spiral keeps dancing, all of the way into the Causal Void, the infinitively creative womb, the Formlessness of No-thing-ness which births all that is, all that has been, and all that will ever be.

And, finally, the Godhead Itself, the ultimate I AM, about which we can say nothing. It is that That that is That beyond any that That that is Who.

> "God the biologist,
> We honor you.
> You who whirl ecstatically around your own image,
> In the double helix of life making,
> We honor you."

30

The Meaning of Life

"The risks of entering a spiritual journey may be quite formidable,
but the risks of not entering it are unquestionably frightful."
Paul Brunton

If you think life is weird, you don't know the half of it. If you think mystics are weird you don't know the quarter of it. The reason mystics are weird is that they really *see* life, while the rest of us see what appears to be, what we expect to find or what we're told is there. And since life itself is weird to begin with, "ipso facto," mystics who see it clearly are weird. Take Muddy as an example. "Muddy" was the name I gave to my paternal great-grandmother, who lived until I was almost ten years old. Since I was her first great-grandchild, she loved me dearly, so I spent lots of quality time with her. She was the first mystic I ever met, the first adult who refused to forget what all young children know—what lies on the other side of the veil. But she wasn't the poster girl for mysticism. If you're imagining a slim, Hollywood-beautiful, mild-mannered, inoffensive, esoteric flake, imagine again. She was wider than she was tall, resembling a squishy ball clad in black, supported on two inadequate legs and topped with a grey head, in which one eye was totally blind. Add to that a no-nonsense personality with scant regard for silly societal conventions or sensitive egos. But her heart was filled with compassion for all who suffered, and she spent her very meager resources attempting to lessen others' burdens. She did it in a matter-of-fact way that neither called attention to their ill fortune nor to her own loving action. But the ocean in which this "karmic yogini" swam was the "bhakti yoga" of extraordinary devotion to Jesus, and an even greater relationship to his mother, Mary. Most of her day was spent in dialogue with that pair. Often you could hear this dialogue, for while "old people" talk out loud to themselves, mystics tend to talk out loud to the transcendent.

When I knew her she lived on the top floor of a three-story, creaky tenement building. She would asthmatically wheeze her way up and down the stairs several times a day as she went to mass, contemplation, grocery shopping or visiting her daughter (my grandmother) and her eight grandchildren, who lived in a new housing estate in Gurranabraher (try pronouncing that!) Before she visited her daughter (whom I called "big mammy") she would go to the "English Market" in the city center, and buy some shavings of ham and some soon-to-be-discarded fruit. Her favorite fruit was apples, which she would peel with a small penknife before eating. Mostly these apples had big brown rotten-spots, that had to be surgically removed before even a hungry child would find it tempting.

Armed with her "mála cogaidh" ("war bag") she would trundle off to Patrick Street stopping off at the Franciscan Church, the Augustinian Church and Saint Peter and Paul's parish church en route to catch the Number 2 bus to Gurranabraher. I got to accompany her on many of these safaris. Each double-decker green-colored city bus had a platform and a vertical shiny pole to help you board and a staircase to the upper deck, while a quick left, off the platform, took you into the down-stairs compartment, which was bifurcated by a passage-way up the center between rows of forward-facing seats. The first seat on each side was a three-seater, as distinct from the rest which were two-seaters. It was quite a struggle for her to climb aboard the platform, and then another struggle to climb the step into the lower compartment, so there was no way she could spare the effort to walk through this section looking for an empty seat as the bus lurched into motion. Mostly a kindly gentleman, child or able-bodied woman would offer her one of these back seats; but if they didn't she'd simply order them, "Out! That's my seat." It wasn't a request, simply a declaration of intent and the promulgation of a self-evident truth. I never remember anybody ever refusing or even debating the issue with her. So, she'd plop into the back seat and say, "Sea, más sea! This is practically untranslatable from the Gaelic. Literally it simply means, "Yes, if yes!" but it really meant, "Great job, well done, mission accomplished, it is consummated."

Mostly the bus conductors knew her, for she traveled daily and, moreover, her grandson, my Uncle Jack, was a bus conductor. Occasionally however, a new recruit would attempt to exact the fare from her. She'd smile dismissively and say, "Go 'way child an' don't be annoyin' me." And he'd "go away."

Then she'd start exploring the contents of her "mála cogaidh" with her left hand, as she held a good grip on it with the right. In its deep recesses could be found, among others, the following items: her rosary beads, prayer-book, ham trimmings, black pudding, white pudding, sausages, rashers, melting chocolate—and a dozen or so brown-spotted apples. She'd fish one out, hold it aloft and proclaim, "John" (which is what she called me) come here until I give ye an apple!" I'd be farther up the bus and, of course, as a small boy, I'd blush to the roots of my very-unkempt hair at being made "the cynosure of neighboring eyes." I'd drag my embarrassed ass to the back of the bus. Then she'd dig her right thumb expertly under one of the big brown rotten spots, gouge it out and fling it off into space with abandon. Some poor bastard in the third or fourth row would get spattered in the nape of the neck or on a bald shining pate, reach instinctively for the "bullet," examine it in disgust, identify it by look and by smell and wheel around to confront the sniper. By then, of course, I'd be the one holding the apple.

As I said, mystics are weird. Muddy was easily the biggest influence on my early childhood, and her lived-cosmology has hugely impacted my view of life. From Muddy and Monty Python, I learned "the meaning of life."

There are eight different categories into which theories of the meaning of life fall. I'll deal briefly with the first four and then spread myself a bit more on the final four. Here, is the list, so you can salivate in anticipation:

Theory

    A. Life begins at birth and ends at death.
    B. Life begins at conception and ends at death.
    C. Life begins at conception but continues infinitely after death.
    D. Life begins *before* conception and continues infinitely after death.
    E. Life recycles many times—reincarnation
    F. You are your own grandpa!
    G. Parallel lives.
    H. Simultaneous lives.

(A) Life begins at birth and ends at death

This is the simple, black and white credo of materialistic, reductionistic scientism. It's very neat, and very silly. It holds that nothing exists which does not consist of "stuff"—tangible, concrete material that can be sensed directly by our eyes, ears, tongue, nose or finger tips or, by extension, through our instruments. Consciousness does not exist; it's merely the epiphenomenal side effect of the bioelectrical activity of the brain. God is a pitiful holdover from the infancy of the species, and rightly deserved to go the way of the tooth fairy, Santa Claus and the Easter Bunny. You, my dear friend, are merely the number two bus for clever (much cleverer than you) genes which use you to hitch a ride to gene-Gurranabraher. They fashioned you, at birth, and when their ride is over, they'll abandon you to death. And, unlike Muddy, you also have to pay for the ride in the form of work, anxiety, illness and despair. Isn't that good news!

Of course, these geniuses have shot themselves in both legs and then stuffed a bloodied foot in their mouth because since only material things are real, then all of mathematics, statistics, and logic (without which no scientific research can be conducted) must also go the way of fairies and goblins. As for non-material stuff like truth or love or a sense of humor, these dour-faced practitioners of scientism create a machine-like robotic life if we take them seriously.

(B) Life begins at conception and ends at death.

Materialistic medicine has daringly gone where materialistic scientism feared to tread, and given us graphic accounts and photos of the "in utero" leg of the journey of life. Apart from that, and a passionate addiction to stave off death at whatever cost, the two sets of materialists are hard to distinguish between. The medics swear to "first do no harm," yet iatrogenesis was the leading killer of Americans last year, out performing cancer, strokes and heart disease. So something isn't adding up.

Could it be that the model itself, not to mention the attendant technologies and treatment procedures, is grossly inadequate? What if we are not merely gross bodies? What if the Chinese, the Indians, the Persians, the Egyptians and the weirdoes who speak of energy medicine are even a little bit right? Maybe we could actually have a medicine based on a science of wellness rather than on a science of disease. And perhaps at the "end" there could be death with dignity instead of monitors, strangers, noise, IV's, "life-support" machines and HMO-decreed interventions. Maybe we could exit the incarnation phase of life surrounded by family, friends and soothing sounds, as we meet the welcoming committee on the other side.

(C) Life begins at conception but continues infinitely after death.

This is the theory of Roman Catholicism, and much of Christianity. When a sperm meets an egg, it gets an "I've been waiting for you" smile and implants itself. God, ever vigilant, spots a brand new zygote and pushes the "make a new soul" button. He then gives detailed directions to this entity and sends it on its way to planet Earth. A high percentage (about 30 percent) result in spontaneous abortions. Perhaps a zygote developed as far as the embryo, or maybe even the fetus but didn't have a resident soul—and so gave up and left via a miscarriage. Or maybe the soul changed its mind, didn't appreciate the cramped conditions in a body that was not very sophisticated and opted for the "later perhaps" exit. Either way, this is a one-sided-infinity model: there was a beginning but there is no end. Good news if you wind up in heaven; bummer if you get the thumbs down.

(D) Life begins before conception and continues infinitely after death.

This is the two-sided-infinity model: there was no beginning and there will be no end. If you're in it for the long haul, this is really good news; if you're the kind of guy who gets bored easily, this could be hard to take. In this model, since eternity is not merely "a long time" but rather is literally, timelessness, then there is no such thing as time—so you have always been; not as Jack or Jill or Brian or Brenda, of course, but as a divine creative thought. Since, even for us as humans, thoughts create reality and create experience, then God created us in no-time. This is the view of what I would call, "conservative New Ageism." Once "you" decided to savor incarnation, you got catapulted into time and may even have experimented with the experience of being a rock, a flower, and a mouse before you tried homo sapiens. The only limit is your imagination. Esoteric literature will call this, "the Transmigration of Souls." Mystics can experience that entire trajectory—now.

(E) Life recycles many times—reincarnation

This, for me, is when things really begin to look up. If you are lucky enough or advanced enough to try out for "Team Human," you don't get to start as the quarterback, you have to earn your stripes. You work your way up from addiction to sensuality, through addiction to power, through the illusion of compassionate service as love-of-other, to the realization that all are one and You are All. I will really spread myself on this latter point in model number eight.

Reincarnation, of course, is merely a weird New-Age-wanna-be-Eastern thing, right? I'm afraid not. It's been a staple of many cultures and wisdom traditions throughout most of human history e.g., the Celts, the Kalenjin of East Africa, Hindus, Buddhists, as well as the mystical wings of Judaism, Christianity and Islam. Oh, and did I mention that Jesus, too, seemed to teach it? Let me pick out just two of the more glaring examples. In Matthew's gospel, Chapter 17, Jesus is on Mount Tabor with three of his apostles, Peter, James and John. He has a vision which is so powerful that they, too, witness it. He is transfigured and both his face and his garments become dazzlingly white. He is in dialogue with Moses, who died about 1200 years before Jesus' birth, and with Elijah who died about 800 years before his birth. When the vision ends and they are on their way down the mountain, someone asked, "Why do the scriptures say that Elijah must come again, before the messiah can return?" Here, he alluded to a prophecy from Malachi in the year 455 BCE. Jesus responds, "Elijah has already come, but they did not recognize him." And chapter 17 adds, "Here, he was talking about John the Baptist." So, it appears, Jesus was claiming that the Baptist was Elijah reincarnated.

In John's gospel, Chapter 9, Jesus and a group of his disciples are leaving the city of Jericho when they see a well-recognized beggar, who was born blind. Somebody asked, "Why was this man born blind? Was it because of his *parent's* sin or his *own* sin?" According to Moses, God would punish a sin to the third or fourth generation. How could a newborn infant be punished for his own sin, unless they believed in a reincarnation and karma from a past life? The simple answer is that Judaism accepted reincarnation and certainly mystical Judaism, e.g., the Kabbalah, taught it.

On a purely rational, ethical and "fairness" level, reincarnation answers many questions that models number 1-4 can't explain. For example, if a three-month-old baby is killed in a drive-by shooting, what becomes of it? Does God say, "Okay, baby that was your total experience as a human. Come in your number is up!" If the child is "lucky enough" to have been baptized, then, according to Christian theology, he goes straight to heaven, without ever having to be tested in the crucible of life to see if he actually *merits* heaven. The usual pathetic response to this is, "God knows all things, and knew this child's heart; He knows if the child would prove worthy or not." Then God is one sick bastard to create beings who He knows will wind up in hell. I'm sure that, as a little boy Himself, this God pulled the legs off spiders and poured petrol on cat's tails and set them alight, before He graduated to frying humans in hell.

And what of the man who is an occasional drinker and mostly leads a good life? He is honest, hardworking, religious and ethical, but he gets drunk one night, crashes his car and dies. Since, according to Roman Catholicism, drunkenness is a mortal sin, then he is consigned to eternal punishment. Is *this* fair?

And what of the multitude of Hindu and Taoist saints who lead exemplary spiritual lives but are never baptized "in the name of the Lord Jesus." According to fundamentalist Christianity, none of these can get to heaven either. Is this fair?

The theory of reincarnation provides very elegant solutions to all these thorny questions. Let's say that you, fallible mortal though you are, could create two systems. In one, all of your children get only one shot at life, and then face an eternity in hell because of bad luck or bad living. Or alternatively you create a system in which you afforded them as many chances as they needed until every single one of them realized it, not just in their heads but in their hearts and in their actions, that the only thing that works is love—I put it to you that, without a moment's hesitation, you would create the latter model.

Damn it all, when you are playing soccer with your own two children and are training them how to score a goal from a penalty kick, don't you give the younger one as many chances as he needs to succeed, so that when mom shouts, "dinner is ready!" each of them can run in breathlessly and announce, "Mom I scored a goal from a penalty!"

Wouldn't it be great if God were as nice a person as you.

(F) You are your own grandpa!

Years ago I heard a song with a convoluted plot but an extremely clever and memorable conclusion. Leading you through a complex series of blended families, incest, marital infidelity and social agreements, the climax was the line, "And so, you are your own grandpa." Well, a few days ago, while walking in the forest, I suddenly invented model number six, and realized that you are indeed your own ancestor and your own descendent. The "now you" is a product of the "then you" of 10 minutes ago; and the "now you" is the creator of the "soon to be you" of 10 minutes hence. When you lengthen the timeline, then the "this lifetime you" is the product of the "those lifetimes you" of accumulated past incarnations; and the "this lifetime you" is the creator of the "next lifetimes you" of incarnations to come.

Like a teenage girl, with her makeup and clothes, you are second-by-second changing your "spacesuit." You shed and re-grow your entire skin membrane each month; most of the dust in your house is dead skin cells. You shed and re-grow your stomach lining every six weeks; you shed and re-grow your entire skeleton every six months. And you shed and re-grow your entire body every seven years.

But, less obviously, you are constantly changing your astral (emotional) body, your mental (ideas) body and your causal (psychic gifts) body as well. You are a masterpiece-in-the-continual-making. If it is true that you can't step into the same river twice, it is equally true that you can't step into the same *you* twice. Do you remember who you are? Good, because you are no longer that whom you remember—unless, of course, you remember

your ultimate identity, that of a bite-sized piece of God. Go back now to
the Hindu wisdom,

> Sow a thought and reap an act,
> Sow an act and reap a habit,
> Sow a habit and reap a character,
> Sow a character and reap destiny.

You are the destiny of the thoughts you thought when you were your
own ancestor; and even more exciting, you can genetically engineer your
future self by modifying your present thinking. Jesus spoke very wisely
when he said, "You shall be held accountable for every idle thought." He
was not threatening us with a father who was a cosmic certified public
accountant recording all of our misdeeds for future punishment, rather
he meant, "Since your thoughts create your experiences, your reality and
your future self—think love."

An even more exciting corollary is that this teaching is as true of the
global human community as it is of the individual member. We are the
descendants of whom we have been and the ancestors of who we will
become. So practice birth control—birth only descendents conceived in
love.

(G) Parallel Lives

I often say that I believe thought creates. Gratefully, however, in the
physical realms there is always a buffer zone, a time lag between the thought
and the manifestation. This is not so in the non-physical realms, where
thoughts instantly manifest as reality, mainly because, in the non-physical
realms, our brain power is much greater and we receive immediate feedback
about the outcomes of possible thoughts before we entertain them, and
evaluate whether the thoughts are worth having. Because of our limited
human brainpower as humans, we need to try out our thoughts and use a
lot of trial-and-error to fine-tune our performance. So before we incarnate
we put some safety devices into place: thoughts that are not given as
much conscious attention or revisited as frequently tend to take longer to
manifest; and the emotions following on our thoughts instantly clue us in
to the quality of our thoughts. Abraham, a collective of other-dimensional
teachers that speaks through Esther Hicks, addresses the latter truth.
Abraham rightly and eloquently points out that there are basically just
two kinds of emotions, feel-good ones and feel-bad ones. "They" claim
that this constitutes a pre-planned emotional guidance system. Since it is
difficult to constantly monitor our thoughts, but we can easily be aware

of our feelings at any time, we have an early warning system built into our spacesuits. If I am feeling bad right now, it's because I have been consciously or unconsciously entertaining negative thoughts. So I can, instead think positive thoughts. If I am feeling good right now, it's because I have been consciously or unconsciously entertaining positive thoughts. So keep them coming.

Emotions, then, create the buffer zone, the time-lag, the opportunity to alter the blueprint before I start to construct the house. The house however *is* going to be built. And, as I have written elsewhere it is built in one of three "locations;" firstly, at a later stage of this life; or secondly, in a future incarnation; or thirdly, in a parallel life in a parallel universe, "right now." And there are more than enough universes to allow everyone to live as many parallel lives as wanted. According to a quantum physics formula there are more universes than there are grains of sand on all the beaches of all the oceans on all the planets in all the solar systems in all the galaxies of this one universe in which we consciously live right now.

(H) Simultaneous Lives

A soul never commits all of its energy to an incarnation, or even to several simultaneous incarnations in parallel universes. Vast as it is, there is always a huge amount of soul energy at home base no matter how many parallel lives it is living in the physical realms. That soul-at-home-base part of you honors the pre-arrangement by which it continues to inspire and assist the soul-on-safari part of you which is wrapped in amnesia for the arrangement and locked in a titanic struggle with vicissitude and limitation in this fragile and not very talented spacesuit. This "leaking" of information and insight via déjà vu, psychic abilities, unexpected moments of ecstasy and, according to Abraham, emotional guidance system, significantly lightens the burden once you begin to trust it.

All of which sets the stage for my eighth theory of life: you are not merely living simultaneously lives in this universe right now. Not only are you your own (dead) grandfather, you are your own (living) cousin and lover, child and mother—right now! But to realize this you have to dis-identify with all of the false identities to which you currently cling: you are not your persona, you are not your ego, you are not your gross, etheric, astral, mental, causal or even atma-body; you are God having a human experience as *all* humans. In order for this reality to take hold, you cannot call yourself Bob or Mary, but you must hold a non-dual awareness of "Self" in which, as a discrete point of consciousness, you *are* Bob or Mary, but as cosmic consciousness you cannot be confined to Bob or Mary. If I ask you who you are and you reply, "I am a Murphy," then your identity has transcended mere individual personhood; you are not just Bob Murphy, you are "a Murphy." If I ask you who you are and you reply, "I am an Irishman" then your identity has transcended mere Murphy-hood. If I ask you who you are and you reply, "I am a human being," then your identity has transcended mere Irishness. If I ask you who you are and you reply, "I am a creature of planet Earth," then your identity has transcended mere humanness. If I ask you who you are and you reply, "I am a sentient being of the Milky Way Galaxy," then your identity has transcended mere Earthliness. And if I ask you who you are and you reply, "I am a word of God made flesh," then, finally you are simultaneously, right at the moment, just now, your self, your cousin, your lover and your enemy. Now you are free to love your neighbor as yourself, and you are free to love your enemy because there is only You, the observer, the observed and the observing. Good God!

Let me offer another movie metaphor for this. A few years ago I saw a hilarious movie starring Eddie Murphy. It was called, "The Nutty Professor." In one brilliantly funny scene the professor and his grandmother and his grandfather are having a meal together, except that Eddie Murphy is playing all three parts! Of course, this is a trick of editing. The point is that as a visual experience all three characters are on camera together and interacting with each other. However, it gets even "curiouser": *You* manage an even more astounding performance every night when you dream because you decide the plot, write the script, pick the locations, choose the costumes, direct it, produce it, take charge of makeup, special effects, and then you play all of the parts, but with such realism that you fool yourself into thinking you are only one of the characters, and have had no part in creating the production and are genuinely convinced that you have no idea how it is going to turn out. You do this so effectively that you constantly surprise yourself and occasionally frighten yourself.

And for an encore you create a brand new production later in the night. You toss off multi-million dollar movies at the rate of five or six a night. Steven Spielberg give up your Oscars, you are not in the same league.

In effect you have managed parallel lives, simultaneous lives and reincarnation, all within eight hours. Now do you believe you are God?

Now that you realize you are even weirder than you thought, you are free to live a much more exciting "waking life." You are poised to become the mystic you always ARE.

31

The Dog who Grew up to be a Tree
(January 8, 2007)

I've named it, "Slí na Sidhe" or "The Pathway of the Fairy Folk." I only named it that today. In fact, I really only discovered it last week, 'though I've walked past it hundreds of times in the last twelve years. But you know the way the sun sometimes backlights a vista at a particular time of the day and at a special time of the year, and you notice silhouettes and juxtapositionings and shadows and shades? Your gaze softens and every blade of grass, every bed of moss, every whisker of lichen and every craggy rock catches, absorbs and releases the golden light in such a mystical fashion that you instantly see beyond "the veil"; and reality invites you into a much deeper level of her creation.

Well, that's what happened to me today. I went to visit that little rock-strewn, mossy dell with its lichen-laden trees that hold their gnarly limbs perfectly still for hours at a time, to see if they can fool you into thinking that they do not dance and sing and sway to the subtlest cues from the cosmic conductor, when you are not looking. But, today, I refused to be fooled. I sat on a mossy rock, with the setting sun off to my left and four oak trees in frozen, yogic mudras standing below me on the hillside. They tried to be as still as possible, hoping I'd go away, so they could converse with the setting sun and greet the Evening Star. But I was determined to be every bit as patient as they. And when they could no longer hold their breath, they showed me a miracle. I wasn't quite sure what kind of a miracle I was going to see, but I knew that if I waited long enough on this day, at this hour, during this season, I would surely see one.

Slowly it came into view. To be more accurate, it was as if the camouflage that it had been wearing began to slowly dissolve, and the hidden figure beneath became less invisible by the minute. At the foot of the farthest tree, pressed tightly against the trunk, sat a very large dog. He remained perfectly still; so still that my own dog, Kayla, lying beside me, never noticed. Then I began to realize that the dog wasn't actually sitting by the tree or even pressed against the trunk, rather the dog *was* the tree, and the tree *was* a dog!

I was determined not to be shocked, or even surprised, but to be awe-filled. I didn't move a muscle. The big dog remained perfectly still but was becoming less indistinct by the second, until, finally, I could see the patchwork colors of his coat, his great floppy ears and his full profile. In my mind I said to him, "I see you" and by then he knew that the "jig was up." So, very slowly, still sitting where he was, he turned his great head and our eyes met. His were round and deep brown, and mine were smiling blue. I knew that I was not allowed to approach him and that our dialogue would be telepathic at thirty feet.

"Hi!" I said, "My name is Seán."
"I know who you are" he calmly replied,
"I've been watching you pass this way for twelve years."
"Can I ask what *your* name is?" I ventured.
"My name is 'the-dog-who-grew-up-to-be-a-tree,'"
he said, matter-of-factly.
I must admit this answer gave me pause.
Finally, I said, "I would love you to tell me how you got that name."
He pondered my request for a moment and said, "Okay, I will tell you."

The sun dipped closer to the hilltop across Pena Creek; its light took on a more mystical hue. This seemed to deepen the telepathic modality, for now I could not just see him and hear him, I could sense his feelings.

"Well," he began "a long, long time ago, I was a little puppy dog. I don't mean a little sapling-dog; I mean your common-or-garden variety of furry, pre-potty-trained, bouncing, please-will-you-play-with-me bundle of unconditional love. My master decided I needed to attend puppy-training school, so to please him, I agreed. It was actually lots of fun. They taught us ridiculous little antics to the tune of "fetch" and "sit" and "stay" and because humans are so insecure we do what they ask.

"But mainly we talked among ourselves, and, of course, the major topic of conversation always was, 'What do you want to be when you grow up?' I changed my mind every week as I heard about new possibilities. One Husky said, 'I'm going to be a sled dog and run exciting races in Alaska. Why, I hear that Amundsen even took us to the South Pole, and we were the reason he beat Scott by a month!' A great, ponderous bloodhound whose ears constantly tripped him up said, 'I'm going to work for a psychic and help her trace missing persons. We will be an unbeatable team!' An Alsatian puppy said, 'I am going to be a police dog and ride around with sirens blazing and lights flashing, chase criminals and wrestle them to the ground.' To tell you the truth I wasn't too impressed with that option. A Golden Lab puppy said, 'I'm going to go to school and be a Guide Dog for the Blind. I'll be trained for traffic lights and curbs and Zebra crossings. I'll recognize car sounds, crosswalks, and, eventually, be the eyes for a really grateful owner.' A St. Bernard who was as big as any five of us put together said, 'I'll carry a keg of brandy to bring instant warmth to some frozen, lost mountain climber. I considered this option for a bit, but there was alcoholism in my family and I thought it better not to tempt fate by shlepping a barrel of liquor around under my chin. So I let go of that one.

"Then one day I went walking with my master in the forest. While he walked the trails, I scurried about in the undergrowth picking up invaluable information with my nose. 'Aha, wild pig, turkeys, bobcats, deer, rabbits and, uh oh! a mountain lion have all passed this way in the last week.' I decided to hurry back to my master, but as an act of defiance, I decided to mark the spot, just to show them I wasn't afraid. I lifted my leg and I appended my John Handcock to an old Madrone. For good measure, I underlined it, and added two exclamation points. I was just finishing and was about to root up some tufts of earth, as the ultimate sign of my disdain for the locals, when a voice said, 'Wow, they must be giving *you* lots of B vitamins in your food; your pee stinks!' Startled, I looked around; there was no one in sight. I did a 360 degrees pirouette; nope, nere a one. I thought it very peculiar and slightly disconcerting. Mountain lions and disembodied voices were a deadly combo, so I tucked in my tail, lowered my ears and was just about to break into a gallop when the same voice said, 'How do you think it feels to have someone piddle on you?' I stopped dead in my tracks. I thought, perhaps, it might have been a small squirrel or a banana slug on whom I had inadvertently micturated, but on closer inspection, I was the only critter in sight. By now I was utterly puzzled. Then the voice spoke a third time, 'Muttt! Ya you, don't these humans you hang out with teach you *any* manners? You ignore me, pretend I don't exist, then you piddle on my trunk, and to add insult to injury you tear up my lawn.' 'Holy Go-go-god', I stammered, 'it's a ta-ta-talking tree!!' 'Well, you canino-centric chauvinistic mongrel, why should a talking tree be any more surprising than a talking dog?' I must admit he had a point. I was tongue-tied for a bit and then I said, 'I'm really sorry. I'm basically only a kid; nobody ever told me that trees had emotions; and nobody ever, ever told me that trees could speak. I'm really sorry for, you know, doing wee-wees on you, and rooting up your garden.

"The tree visibly relaxed and his tone changed significantly. 'I pity you guys. Humans live 60 or 70 years. I see them come, be full of themselves; then they age and weaken and suddenly they're gone. Dogs live 10 or 15 years. I see *them* come, be full of curiosity, chase rabbits, piddle diabetically and then *they're* gone. It must be hard to be a dog.' This took me by surprise. I had never considered life hard. I'd rather enjoyed it so far, and planned to continue doing so. I didn't want to disappoint him by telling him that, so instead I asked, 'Do you mind me asking how old *you* are?' 'Not at all' he said, 'I'm 285 years old; and I have seen a lot of changes in my time, I can tell you.' This boggled my mind; 285 years old; that means he was born in 1637. I wasn't quite sure if trees were born, if the stork delivered them or if they were found under a cabbage; but however he got here, he was easily the oldest and wisest creature I had ever come across. My master smoked a pipe and was good at crossword puzzles, but he was only 71, and didn't seem to be able to pick up any information with his nose; or else he had little curiosity, for on our walks together he would blissfully ignore spoor of all kinds, and I have yet to see him sniff intelligently at a lamp post.

'That was the day I decided I wanted to be a tree when I grew up. The other dogs in puppy school laughed derisively at this, so after one or two attempts to explain my thinking I gave up and kept it to myself. I graduated puppy school "summa cum laude" and life took on a more regular and mundane aspect. I still wasn't sure how to break the news to my master; I knew he'd be heart-broken if I left him, but it's a terrible thing not to follow your bliss. I got to visit my tree friend fairly regularly and, eventually, I told him of my ambition. He was proud that I wanted to be like him and didn't want to rain on my parade, but he did gently point out some obvious problems. Seeing the disappointment in my face, however, he was quick to add that he had seen much stranger things than that in his 285 years. I knew then that I could do it. I wasn't quite prepared, though, for the way in which I was released to embrace my dream. My master was involved in an auto accident and he didn't survive. His only child inherited the house, which she came and emptied, cleaned and sold within a period of a month. Whatever furniture she wanted to keep, she loaded into a truck and drove away leaving me at the gate with no food, no water and no key to the front door.

"For a while I felt very sad, and then I realized I was finally free; free to be a tree. It took me about 18 hours to negotiate the city traffic, and head for the countryside until I was, once more, with my friend, whom I now called, 'Oakheart' and I quickly began my apprenticeship. I sat squarely on a level patch of ground, fixed my tail for an anchor, back paws horizontal, front paws vertical and head pridefully erect. At first, I could keep this up for no more than an hour at a time, but soon I became good at it. I found I needed less and less food, and was able to draw energy directly from the sun. One windy day a swirl of fallen leaves danced about me and formed a multi-layered coat that wrapped me from head to tail. A few days later another zephyr added several more layers. These matted together, and before you could say, 'Jack Robinson' I had the beginnings of a bark. And it was just in time. A great snowstorm came and blanketed me. I was well insulated. By now I had learned to make roots and branches. I practiced this for several months because I knew that when the snow melted I'd need to grow roots and branches in earnest. Through thick and thin, Oakheart offered encouragement. With the advent of springtime, I was ready, and slowly I mastered the craft. Within three years, I grew to a respectable height and my root system was so well developed that I was able to dance in the wind and not lose my balance. I was also learning how to feed myself through these roots.

"Many happy years passed and one day I realized that, of course, all of my puppy friends were long since dead. I wondered how many of them had realized *their* dreams; I certainly had. I was now 72 years of age, counting the two and a half years as a dog. I nodded wisely to a flock of pigeons who were doing a fly by, and then I heard Oakheart whisper, 'Dogwood (for that is the nickname he had given me), today is the day.' I didn't quite get it. 'Today is *what* day?' I asked. 'Today is the day I must let go,' said Oakheart. 'Let go of what?' I asked, still puzzled. 'Let go of my roots; let go of my life,' said Oakheart. 'I'm 357 years old. I've lived a great life. I'm tired. I need to go back to my father.' 'Your father?' I said, 'You've never talked about your *father* before.' 'Who do you think I have been waving at, all these years?' he said. 'When I meditate in the long winter months, with whom do you think I am in communion? When I draw water up from the earth and convert it to sap, offer it to my leaves and present them to the light, for whom do you think I am celebrating the marriage of soil and sky? And when the birds arrive and chatter among my branches, whose loving message do you think they are bringing to me? There was a long pause as I let all of this wisdom into my heart. Then Oakheart continued, 'I have enjoyed being a tree; I have *really* enjoyed being a tree; and one of the highlights of my life has been our friendship. I must leave you now; do not be frightened or saddened by the manner of my passing. You and I are soul mates. We will stand side by side in another adventure, another form, at another time. Farewell, dear Dogwood!'

"A sizzling, searing, dazzling shaft of lightning fissured the perfectly blue vault of the heavens and Oakheart reached up and grabbed it. There was a loud crash, and he fell over, snapping his ancient roots. Then, there was a small groan that sounded like, 'It is completed. Father, into your hands I commend my spirit.' Those were the last words I ever heard Oakheart speak. That was 13 years ago. On Midsummer Day that same year, I saw *you* for the first time. I knew eventually I would tell someone this story. And when I saw you that day, I knew it would be to you. I'm glad you finally saw me; and I'm glad you had the patience to wait."

I pondered this compliment. The sun, by now, had sunken behind the hilltop, west of Pena Creek. It became more difficult to make out Dogwood's contour in the fading light.

But I clearly heard his last remark,
"Would you like to grow up to be a tree?"

32

Buddha-Brain or Bubba-Brain?

"Our deeds determine us as much as we determine our deeds."
George Elliot

What do you think is the best measure of creativity: the ability to find new uses for old technology or the ability to find old uses for new technology? Let me give you an example of both, from my experience in Kenya, and then you get to decide the answer.

For many years the toughest car rally in the world was the East African Safari. Normally about 120 cars started the weeklong event, and by the end, perhaps 15 or 20 made it to the finish line. It used to be held at Easter time, when the rains are likely to dump inches of rain on the dusty roads, turning them into seas of mud. The race snaked its way through Tanzania, Uganda and Kenya, typically ending in Nairobi on Easter Monday.

In an era when only men, crazy men, would even think of doing something so dumb and so dangerous, an Irish-woman called Rosemary Smith was a frequent competitor. Though she never won it, she finished it on several occasions, which is enough to put her in the history books. One year in the middle of the safari, in a very remote section, a long way from the backup crew of mechanics and spare parts, she broke a fan belt. Within seconds she thought of a solution. She took off her panty hose and made a fan belt of it, and raced the rest of the day with it in place.

Now there is an example of old technology being pressed into service to replace new technology.

And here is the second example. For seven years I lived among the Tugen people in Kenya, in some very remote areas, literally on the equator. Some of these regions were still untouched by western civilization in the 1970s. The Tugen had been, for millennia, nomadic pastoralists, wandering the arid areas of Baringo with goats, cattle and sheep. And your typical Tugen elder had only three possessions all of which he carried on his person. A small three-legged stool, carved from a single piece of wood which he tied to his wrist by a piece of rawhide thong. It was a seat on which to perch while he was in conference with fellow elders, and a pillow on which to lay his head for naps. The second item was a spear, consisting of a long narrow wooden shaft and a foot-long, three-inch-broad beaten-metal blade. He normally carried this across his shoulders, behind his head, with his two hands draped over it and hanging down the front. And the third item was a tobacco pouch, also made of leather. He loved to chew tobacco and could expectorate as accurately as a spitting cobra and nail any target of his choice within ten feet.

Well, one day, such an elder, a man called Kimaleel Arap Tuimising was minding his own business, languidly strolling through the bush when he came across a cassette-player-radio which must have fallen out of a land rover. The long antenna had snapped off and lay a few feet away. Of course he had never seen or even heard of a cassette player or even of a radio. He stopped in amazement and couldn't believe his luck. "Kumbe" he exclaimed "Ng'cheret!" (Wow! It's a stool") and he promptly sat down on it. As he did so, he pressed the eject button and the cassette section opened up. "Kumbe!" he exclaimed again "Oldap tumbako" ("Wow, a place for tobacco"). What he took to be a spear did not impress him because it was far too skinny and fragile, and the blade non-existent; so he threw it away. Once more he sat down on the "stool," and this time he sat on the radio play button. Immediately cacophonous sounds of foreign music and lyrics in an unintelligible language screamed out right under his tuckus. He jumped up shouting "Chemosit! Chemosit!" (A mythical Tugen monster) and abandoned his find and galloped away to share this strange story with his fellows.

Now that is a case of foisting old uses on new technology. So you get to answer the question. Which is more creative: the ability to find new uses for old technology or the ability to find old uses for new technology.

Recently I came into the 21st century myself. For over 13 years I've lived half of each week in the forested hills west of Healdsburg in northern California. There is a five-mile dirt track leading to a cabin, which is a holdover from the 1880s when it was homesteaded by the

Derrick family. It hadn't been lived in for nearly 20 years when I began to use it. So initially there was a lot of work needed to make it habitable. Eventually I decided I wanted to build a "real" house, so I set about it in a very organized way. I cleared an area of the chamise and scrub that are abundant in the area. Then five years ago I put in a septic system; four years ago I dug a well and laid a water line; three years ago I put in solar panels and created a power supply; two years ago I began building and I moved in September 2006; then I thought about internet access. Since the nearest phone lines were a few miles away, I opted to "go satellite." Then came a pleasant surprise, the satellite connection was a high-speed connection, whereas in my Palo Alto apartment I used a landline and an old 14k modem. The shift from the modem to DSL was dramatic. I felt like a cross-fertilization of Rosemary Smith and Kimaleel Arap Tuimising! And that is the metaphor with which I wish to introduce the topic of this chapter: "Buddha-brain or Bubba-brain," "The History of the Brain" and "The Future of the Brain."

(A) Buddha-brain or Bubba-brain

By "Buddha-brain" I mean full-potential brain. Sir John Eccles, the Australian neurologist and Nobel laureate, claims that we use less than ten percent of its capacity. This ten percent brain, I call "Bubba brain." Alternatively, I call these two brains, "Christ consciousness" and "Cruise consciousness" respectively.

If you've made the transition from an old 14K modem to a high-speed DSL, you'll know what I'm talking about. The "Buddha brain" is to the "Bubba brain" as DSL is to 14K modem. The Buddha brain is capable of downloading much more information, much faster from cosmic consciousness than a Bubba brain.

But there are two problems. The first is that most of us are still relying on the old modem; and the second is that when we get the stuff on our desktop, most of us have only two folders to store it. They are labeled, "good" and "bad." Even mystical experiences, and we all download some, are forced into one or the other. The never-repeating creativity of cosmic consciousness is forced into one of these two holders. The autoerotic, multiple-orgasm-producing ecstasy of life's love affair with life is simply reduced to a boring choice between good and bad. Abraham Maslow said, "When all you have is a hammer, everything begins to look like a nail."

But the true test of spiritual evolution is the ability to adopt a multiplicity of perspectives. I don't have to go along with them, or even agree with them, but I must be able to walk in another's moccasins in order to understand him, be in meaningful dialogue, learn and grow with him. I don't have the right to confront or contradict any position that I can't articulate as clearly as the holder of the position.

Not only is this a true test of spiritual evolution but it is also the basis for all moral decisions. Morality, ultimately is the ability to make choices that deal compassionately with human and animal suffering, and I can only do this, if I can walk in the other's shoes and see and feel life through his eyes and his heart.

All too often pigheadedness masquerades as principle and a closed mind dresses itself up, self-righteously, as a virtuous heart.

What you *do* is not at all as important as the *awareness* of what you are doing. An action is only moral if it is done with awareness. And any action done with awareness is "ipso facto," a moral action. "Ah! You object," does that mean that a murder committed with awareness is a moral action? No, it doesn't, because awareness does not merely mean the immediate knowledge of what I am doing just now; rather awareness is the ability to operate from a truly cosmic consciousness that I then apply to a specific situation. No one with awareness, then, can commit a murder; and no one who commits a murder can be operating with awareness.

According to Carl Jung, the collective unconscious is the repository of the entire cultural heritage of humanity. What does this actually mean? It can mean one of two possibilities, it seems to me. Either, first, that an individual can only manifest in his own psyche, via dreams, altered states etc., what is in his own *direct* ancestry. This is also how the immune system in any individual operates. To deal with a bacterial infection, I can only call upon antibodies in my DNA from my ancestral line. If no one in my direct lineage has previously encountered a particular strain of bacteria, then I won't have immunity for it. By analogy, then, my psyche can only produce archetypes that emanate from my own psychic lineage, the cultural experiences of direct ancestors of mine. Or, secondly, Jung's collective unconscious could mean that any experience of any individual in any culture could get "uploaded" to the field of human consciousness, forming a morphogenetic field, from which any other individual in any other culture could "download" it to personal experience in his dreams or in altered states of consciousness. This would mean that I don't need a direct ancestral lineage to be the recipient of an archetypal motif. To use a biological analogy, any cell of the body can have an experience, learn something and then communicate (upload) this information to the brain (the field of consciousness) and thus make it immediately available to any other cell which subsequently may have to deal with a similar situation.

To round off my thesis then, every experience of every being on every planet in every dimension is uploaded to cosmic consciousness, and thus is available to any individual mind plugged into that field, provided that

that mind has the requisite hardware (brain). In other words, anybody can upload information to the web and that information can then be downloaded by any one else who has the appropriate computer and software.

But if you only have a black and white monitor (only two categories: good, bad) then you can only interpret/display the infinite creativity of God in fundamentalist categories such as with-us/against-us, true/false, axis-of-evil/allies, saved/damned, raptured/left-behind.

Prophets and visionaries, then, are those who see what is, as it is, without cultural filters or denominational prejudices. They plug into the field and upgrade both their hardware and their software through prayer and meditation, through clear thought and through right action.

The next section then, is about both the hardware and the software, that the field creates, and uses as channels for uploading and downloading material to assist the evolutionary process.

Imagine a multi-talented artisan who counts among his gifts craftsmanship and music. First, he handpicks the best woods and lovingly manufactures a beautiful guitar. Then in his mind he composes deeply moving music. And, finally, he plays it on the guitar. The artisan is cosmic consciousness (or God, Source, Ineffable Ground of Being, Tao . . .), the guitar is the human brain, and the music is the life-experiences, which run the entire gamut from pre-birth to trans-personal.

The really good news is that the guitar is capable of producing even more extraordinary music, than has heretofore been coaxed out of it—in other words the hardware, which is the human brain, is already configured to receive and transmit encounters way beyond what we have yet experienced. Psychic abilities, unitive states and spiritual ecstasy are merely the prologue to the main scripture; they are the aperitif to the main course.

(B) The History of the Brain

Just as the body is not one but exists at seven different levels, so, too, the brain is not really one, but at least three—as Paul MacLean, a neurologist opined some 60 years ago calling it the "Triune Brain." Anatomically and functionally speaking, we appear to have three levels of brain, which have evolved over the last 500 million years; the brain stem or the "reptilian" brain; the paleo-mammalian brain; and the neo-mammalian brain. Let me, briefly, give an account of each of them.

The "reptilian" brain actually began with fish about 500 million years ago. It continued to evolve in the amphibians (who came after the fish), but reached its most advanced state with the reptiles (who came after the amphibians) around 250 million years ago. So it was evolving for 250 million years before it "perfected" itself in the reptiles. Anatomically it consists of the brain stem and the cerebellum, and it is active even when we are in deep sleep. Its basic function is to ensure survival of the individual animal, and so 100 percent of its consciousness is devoted to competition. It does this in four ways, feeding, fleeing danger, fighting and breeding. Apart from humans and mammals who contain this reptilian brain as a "sub-brain," species for whom it continues to be its *only* brain are snakes, lizards, turtles, crocodiles and alligators.

In its time it was a great advance, and indeed highly successful, because these species continue to thrive after 500 million years. What they lack, however, if we compare them with the mammals, are the following abilities. They have no emotions, do not dream, do not play (even as youngsters), have no social life, cannot cooperate with others of their species, and do not nurture, raise or teach their offspring. Their total commitment to parenthood is to lay their eggs and split.

Their behavior is rigid, obsessive, compulsive, and repetitious; they have no memory and cannot learn from past experiences. Don't you sometimes wonder if we humans revert to this brain in our individual and national behavior, all too often?

Evolution, in its never-ceasing zest for creative expression, then decided to try a more advanced model, but, so as not to waste any of the development and effort that went into manufacturing the reptilian brain, it proceeded epigenetically i.e., it transcended *and* included what had gone before.

It began with the first small mammals about 150 million years ago. This brain goes by a few different names. It is called, "the mammalian brain" or the "paleo (old) mammal brain," or the "limbic system." Anatomically it consists of the amygdala, the hippocampus and the hypothalamus. What it adds to the reptilian brain are the following features; it can dream, feel emotions, engage in social behavior and cooperate; it can raise, nurture and teach its offspring; it can play (and loves to!); it is big into "family values"; since it has memory, it can learn; it also makes unconscious value judgments, ascribing valence to available options and events.

This brain is 50 percent competitive consciousness and 50 percent cooperative consciousness; in a new environment it may revert, without conscious choice, to reptilian brain behavior. If you surgically remove the limbic system, you greatly reduce social interactions.

The third brain to evolve also goes by many names. It is known as the "neo-mammalian brain," the "primate brain," the "cerebral cortex" or the "neo-cortex." This is a very "new" development and began with the first primates, about three million years ago. It is the crinkly, convoluted matter, which manages to cram a lot of surface area (and therefore "building sites,") into a small cubic space. It surrounds both the limbic and reptilian brains, and, in humans, it accounts for over 65 percent of the entire brain. This increase of "real estate" has enabled the building of very sophisticated structures that allow much more complicated social interactions, like human language, art, music, mathematics; it is the seat of imagination and abstract thought, self-consciousness, creativity, planning, insight; it enables us to "create" and manipulate time, to exercise foresight, to predict and solve issues *before* problems arise. It allows us to be concerned with issues outside and beyond the personal self, to understand cause and effect, to see the total, environmental connectedness; and, ultimately, to have transcendent experiences.

It is a part of the brain that is 100 percent available for cooperative consciousness. It brings both survival (the concern of the reptilian brain) and emotions (the domain of the mammalian brain) under conscious, volitional control.

All in all this super computer of ours occupies about 1350 cubic centimeters of space, and has increased threefold in size in just the last three million years. It is claimed that it is the most complex structure in the universe! I fear this is a wild exaggeration, and like the flat-Earth, creationism, and Earth-as-center-of-the-solar-system, it will become another arrogant myth of the infancy of our thinking. We are the brightest we know only because we are not bright enough to know any better; the human brain is a medium-sized fish in a tiny puddle; the star student in a rustic, single-roomed schoolhouse, who, alas, will one day meet post-graduate geniuses from an ivy-league university.

(C) The Future of the Brain

The good news is that nature always develops the hardware first, so that when we eventually have experiences, we can create the software to manage them. We have the hardware not just to engage in more complex social behavior, not just to exercise ever-increasing levels of cooperation (with other humans and other species), not just greater abilities to think abstractly and use mathematics evermore brilliantly, but, much more importantly, we have the hardware in place to have radically transpersonal, mystical encounters with cosmic consciousness. And we know we have that hardware because we've been having those experiences for almost 50,000 years. Over the last five-thousand years, sages have been examining those experiences so as to create rituals to induce them and cosmologies to understand them. One such cosmology is the seven-levels-of-body, of which I have previously written. I briefly want to show how these bodies correlate with the three strata of brain.

The reptilian brain was the hardware created for the emergence of the gross body, and is the seat of the intelligence that sustains it. The mammalian brain was the hardware created for the emergence of the astral body, and is the seat of the intelligence that sustains it. Hence the astral level is the place of both dreams and emotions. The neo-cortex is the hardware created for the emergence of the next four levels of body. Thus, it is truly a quantum leap in terms both of timeline and capabilities. It took 250 million years to make the modest gains of a brain (the reptilian) that could guarantee physical survival; the next 150 million years (60 percent of the time) saw huge advances: play, dreams, emotions, cooperation, child raising, memory, value-judgments, learning. Now in just three million years (just over one percent of the time) we added, language, math, science, art, time, abstract thought, and self-consciousness. We could map most of these advances onto the "mental" body of the spiritual cosmology, but the neo-cortex *also* has in place the hardware to go beyond these capabilities into the transpersonal and the mystical realms. All we lack is the software and the practice to turn this incredible machine into the medium for creating paradise on Earth. And this precisely, has been the mission of the avatars (the ascended masters), the super software engineers of a mystical technology that has truly cosmic implications for life and peace on planet Earth. Gaia has spent 4.5 billion years developing this hardware. The avatars announced the IPO 2,500 years ago; now there is a Christmas blowout sale on this software. You can have it over-nighted to you—and nobody will ask you for a credit card or even a shipping address. Santa knows where you live, and he has long since deleted his naughty-and-nice list. There is only one condition. You have to install it in your own PC (personal cosmology); you have to re-boot your hard drive and then, sit back and enjoy your life.

33

The Wingéd Eye of Spirit
(April 24, 2001)

House fly,
butterfly,
dragonfly,
expert eye-makers.
Borrowers of chitin from the lowly trilobite,
How do you see?
How do you fly?
Do you pity me for my myopia?
Do you sympathize with *me*
for this dense, earthbound spacesuit of mine?

Teach *me* to see.
Teach *me* to fly.
Teach *me* to shed this clumsy body
and soar.

Winged Eye of Spirit,
let *me* be free.

34

I Dreamt That I Couldn't Get To Sleep

"When one sees eternity in things that pass away and infinity
in finite things, then one has pure knowledge."
Bhagavad Gita

I think I finally figured out why a sage said, "Go west young man!" The reason is that going west is much easier on the body-clock than going east. I visit my family in Ireland each year. I fly from San Francisco to London and then from London to Cork, and for the first four or five days my body-clock is very much out of sorts. I toss and turn at night, but no matter how exhausted I am, sleep eludes me. Normally I am a great sleeper; 360 out of 365 nights of the year, I put my head on the pillow and it's "lights out" immediately. If I didn't prime my alarm clock, I'd sleep each day until 10 o'clock But on my annual Irish trip, this blessing is interrupted. By the fifth or sixth night the problem has sorted itself out and Greenwich Mean Time and Seán time are re-aligned.

A few years ago I figured out that it must be the change in diet. It is a family tradition to meet me at the airport and whisk me home to a huge feast of Irish cream pastries and mugs of caffeine-laden, sugar-soaked, milk-saturated tea. Here in California I never drink tea that has caffeine, and I won't look twice at the anemic efforts that get touted as creamy pastries. So I figured I had finally solved the problem. The next year, much to the family's consternation I broke with this 30-year-long tradition and was content with merely salivating as I watched hordes of nieces and nephews, grand-nieces and grand-nephews, brothers and sisters and uncles and aunts demolish the mountains of creamy pastries and teapots of "real tea" that should have been mine. The result of my heroic asceticism was—five nights of sleeplessness. In the much-abused wisdom-belief that "Rome wasn't built in a day" I decided to repeat my Herculean effort the next year, and this time the payoff was—five nights of sleeplessness. So this year I gave up my life of virtue and returned to my old criminal ways. As was to be expected, I spent the first five nights of my visit wondering how long it would take the first five nights of my visit to be over, so I could get some sleep.

The funny thing is I never have any problems coming west. I land in San Francisco airport after reversing the same journey, taking just as long to cover the 5,712 miles from Cork to London to San Francisco, stay up the remainder of the daylight hours, go to bed shortly after sundown and sleep the sleep of the just. My body-clock immediately adjusts.

One year I wanted to be in Ireland for my 60th birthday on October 8, so I left SFO around noon on Monday, October 2, and arrived in Cork on Tuesday October 3. A feast of dairy delights greeted my lightning-storm-in-Chicago-eight-hours-delayed arrival, and when I could no longer keep my eyes open, I went to bed, where I found it very easy to keep my eyes open, all night long until about 9 o'clock on October 4 when I finally dozed off. The night of October 4 was a repeat, and the night of October 5 was a three-peat; but the night of October 6 was the pits; I was going for the four-in-a-row, a famous feat of 1940s Cork hurling. By now I was really, really frustrated; I tossed and turned physically, then I calmed my body so that I could simply toss and turn mentally; decided one good turn deserves another and went back to tossing and turning mentally *and* physically. I was now getting cranky and irritated about not being able to sleep, only to wake up and realize that I had been *dreaming* about not being able to sleep! With this realization, I smiled wryly, put my head on the pillow again and promptly went back to sleep. When I woke up fully, around midday, I grabbed a pen and paper and started jotting down notes about dreaming, sleeping, waking, and how you'd know the difference.

And those ideas will form the basis of this chapter.

(A) Is this a dream?

How do you know if you are awake or dreaming? You can be fooled, in either state, into thinking you're in the other. At night we are totally convinced that the encounter with the anaconda in Africa is really happening; and during the day, in traumatic events of which we are a part or to which we are merely witnesses, there is a surrealism that often gets expressed as, "I feel as if I am in a dream." Is this a learned phrase? I don't believe so; rather it is the best spontaneous articulation of the experiential quality of the event.

To wake up in the morning and say, "That was only a dream," does not mean that dreams are not real. Dreams are every bit as real as events in "waking" consciousness. They have exactly the same psychic feel to them while they are happening. They are simply arising in a different state of consciousness. In fact, all events in all states of consciousness are merely experiences arising within the awareness of the Witness. So for the "realist" or "materialist" or "reductionist," to say dismissively that, "it was *only* a dream" is to miss the truth.

Equally, those wannabe esotericists, who sit in a lotus position and proclaim, "life is an illusion," miss the truth. Life is real, though it is not the only reality, not the most important reality nor even the first reality. "Life," too, is simply an experience arising in the awareness of the witness.

So how do we escape from this dilemma of answering, "Am I awake or in a dream right now?" One way is by going into deep, dreamless sleep. This can be directly accessed, either from dreaming-sleep or from the "waking state," typically via a hypnogogic antechamber. The second way to escape this dilemma is to enter into "Samadhi," and this is mostly accessed via meditation, though it can happen spontaneously. The core of dreamless sleep and formless Samadhi is the experience of content-less consciousness.

Let me use an image to illustrate how dreams and waking perform differently. Imagine a railway station with a central platform that has tracks on both sides of it. One set of tracks is for the dream train and the other set for the wake train. As soon as you step aboard the dream train (i.e. you begin to dream), the train itself stops moving and all the action takes place inside the train. When you get off this train (i.e. a dream ends and you wake up), the train itself moves and leaves the station. If you step aboard the dream train later that night (i.e. dream again) you are actually stepping into a brand-new train. It, too, grinds to a halt as soon as you enter, and now all of the new action takes place inside *this* train. So the essence of a dream train is that it stops as soon as you embark and moves off as soon as you disembark. Thus, the scenes, events and experiences are disjointed. There is no continuity among the dreams because they have happened *inside* the trains, and they were different trains, each with a *different* interior design. It's rather like going to a cinema that has five or six different theaters. You buy a ticket, popcorn, chocolate and a 64-ounce soda and head for the movie on your ticket. You get totally absorbed and climb aboard the roller-coaster of the plot, characters and emotions. When it is over, you go back to the concession stand load up on the goodies, have a quick look around to make sure no "official" is watching and then run into a second theater to watch a totally different movie, with different characters, plot, location and costumes. The only continuity between the movies is you and the butter stains on your trouser leg from the first bag of popcorn.

On the other side of the tracks is the wake train. When you climb aboard this train (i.e., wake up) it pulls out of the station. Now, the action takes place *outside*; you are looking through the windows as scenes and people and events rush by. When you get off this train (i.e., fall asleep) the action ceases, the train stops and remains in the station until you need it again. If you wake up during the night, or in the morning (i.e., step aboard this train again) everything is just as you left it. So the essence of the wake train is that it moves as soon as you embark and stops as soon as you disembark. Hence, there is continuity to the scenes and events.

(B) Lucid Dreaming, Lucid Waking

Let me introduce this section with a little matrix (a window, for the mathematically challenged).

	Dream	Wake
I think I'm awake	**(Foolish) Normal dreaming**	**(Foolish) Normal waking**
I know this is a dream	**Lucid dreaming**	**Lucid waking**

Normal dreaming, or what might be called "foolish" dreaming happens when I'm in REM sleep watching a great movie while being convinced that I am actually awake and this is "really" happening. For most of us this is our dream experience 100 percent of the time. It is so "obvious" to us that we are "awake" and that this is "really happening" that we don't feel the need to say or even think, "I am awake and this is really happening." Yet morning after morning we open our eyes and declare, "that was merely a dream," only to close our eyes again that night and go right back into the illusion.

Normal living, or what might be called "foolish" living happens when I am in alpha or beta brainwave mode, eyes open, driving my car to work after breakfast and thinking, "Now I am truly awake; this is the real thing, and last night was merely a dream." Yet night after night we forget this credo and become, once more engrossed in the midnight matinee, only to hear the shrill sound of the alarm clock at six o'clock and slip right back into the illusion, that now, at last, once again I am truly awake and this *is* the real thing.

Lucid dreaming is the ability, during REM sleep, to watch the movie, and come to the realization, "I am dreaming!" This may result in (a) the dream ending, opening my eyes and coming "awake," or (b) I may decide to allow the dream to proceed, go along for the ride and thoroughly enjoy it, or (c) even to "consciously" become the director of it. Since I now realize, "it is a dream," whose plot, characters, location, script and costumes I myself have created, I am aware that I am quite safe to experiment even further, and so I push the dream into areas or topics of my choice. Some people experience this occasionally and quite spontaneously; but there are traditions which cultivate this ability e.g., Tibetan Buddhism. As you might expect from such a deep spiritual system as Buddhism, this is not meant to be merely a source of entertainment but an aid to impress upon the experiencer that all experiences in all states are simply arising in "witness consciousness" and that no state is more privileged than any other state, and that no experience is "more real" than any other.

Naturally, in the West, because of our fascination with and genius at figuring out the "how questions," we have developed tests for lucid dreaming. In elegant experimentation done at Stanford, people with a self-reported ability to dream lucidly were rigged up to an electro-encephalograph and allowed to sleep. In order to prove their claim they agreed that when they became lucid during a dream they would raise a finger. Meanwhile, the researchers could verify from the brainwaves that the sleeper was actually in REM sleep.

Lucid waking or lucid living is the ability to realize during this alleged "waking state" of ours that it is, itself, merely another kind of "dreaming." Once I get this, I am free to (a) now truly "wake up" to Witness Consciousness, (b) flow with "normal life" and enjoy it, while not falling into the illusion that it's the only reality or (c) even "direct" it and push it where I want it to go, while still resisting the temptation to believe it's ultimate reality.

The ability to say, "This is only a dream," in *any* state, is the essence of Witness Consciousness, which is the awareness, the Self, in which all experiences and all other states of consciousness arise; whereas the conviction that allows me to say, "This is reality" of any other state I am experiencing is the illusion of identifying these states of consciousness or these experiences with Self. It's the equivalent of saying "I am angry" and identifying a passing state (anger) with my essence ("I Am-ness). There are languages such as Swahili, Kalenjin and Hebrew in which there is no present tense of the verb "to be;" we have to get around it by a linguistic trick called, "predication without a verb." The value of this lack of a present tense of the verb "to be" is that I cannot identify a passing state, such as anger, hunger, sadness etc. with the Self. Most languages however, make it possible or even connive to produce this confusion. We can then conflate whimsical emotions e.g., "I am really irritated," or temporary ideation e.g., "I am fully convinced," or a physical attribute e.g., "I am too fat" with core essence. Similarly, we tend to conflate experiences that arise in a state of consciousness with the Self. Hinduism reminds us,

> *"I have a body, but I am not my body;*
> *I have emotions but I am not my emotions;*
> *I have ideas but I am not my ideas."*

The only time I can truly say, "I am awake and this is reality," is when the "I" is the Witnessing Awareness within which all states of consciousness and all experiences arise.

(C) Making the Maps

A particular state of consciousness has hijacked the terms, "I am awake" and "This is reality." It's rather like the confusion generated by the term "real presence" in Catholic liturgical theology. By "real presence" Catholic theologians mean that, as a post-consecration wafer, Jesus Christ is truly present to an experience of communion. In popular thinking, however, the other liturgical divine presences are downgraded as "lesser realities"; so, for instance, the reality of an encounter with God in the community (" . . . where two or three are gathered together, there am I in their midst") or in the scripture (" . . . the word of God") is regarded as not of the same quality.

So, it is with the idea that ultimate reality and true awakening only occur between opening my eyes in bed in the morning and closing them in bed at night. This mistake is of the same order as regarding the Earth as the center of the solar system, or even of the universe; of seeing humans as the apex of creation, if one is a fundamentalist Christian, or as the apex of evolution if one is a materialistic, reductionistic scientist; or regarding humans as the only intelligent species in the cosmos; or regarding a particular race, culture, nation or religion as "chosen." It is an error of the same magnitude as regarding the ego as the center or even the totality of the psyche, rather than merely exercising an executive role in a particular state of consciousness.

This was the huge psychic, spiritual and social adjustment to which Gautama Siddhartha pointed in choosing his name: "Buddha" means, "one who is awake." This was the radical shift to Christ consciousness that Jesus of Nazareth advocated when he insisted that we "stay awake" e.g., the saying, "Blessed is that servant [ego] whom the master [Self] finds awake upon his return;" or again, "If the householder [Self] had known at what time the thief [ego-illusion] intended to break in and steal, he would have remained awake."

To cut through the language confusion, I will simply refer to what happens between sunup and sundown as "day time consciousness," because to call it the "waking state of consciousness" is chutzpah, hubris and grossly inaccurate. The term, "waking state of consciousness" needs to be reserved for that state of consciousness in which I identify with my God-Self, which is also *your* God-Self, the God-Self of the daffodil and the dinosaur, the God-Self of poodles and of poets.

Each state of consciousness has a different cartography, different laws, different time usages, different space-continuums and different kinds of causation. So we need to be multi-lingual; we need to be aux fait with these different levels of reality, and not hide our insecurity behind a compensatory superiority complex in which we arrogantly strut our daytime consciousness state as the only or real generator of truth and fact.

Any cartography of the other states created from any state other than the true waking state leads to poor maps. In particular, the maps that have been created during the daytime state have led to caricatures of the laws and terrain of those other states. It's a bit like looking at an early 16th century map of America; it is pitifully inexact by today's standards. It's as if I knew nothing of the United States of America except what I read in Charlie Brown or Doonesbury, and then set out to write the definitive history of this country on the basis of those comic strips.

Yet, the bulk of our map-making is done by people who really think that the daytime state is the state of reality and of wakefulness. Not only does this give us poor maps of the other states, it gives us poor maps of the daytime state itself. It gives a two-dimensional, flatland rendition of a multi-dimensional reality. And any attempt to map the other states from there leads to pathetic, childish stick figures. If we want accurate maps of all the states, including the daytime state, we must look at those cartographers who have done their map-making from the truly awake state or God-state; the avatars and mystics.

(D) The United States of Consciousness

A sampling of states of consciousness is the following: daytime state, of which I have written; dream state which we experience five or six times during the night; deep sleep, which has its own sub-states, readily discernible on an EEG; the hypnotic state, which researchers claim is a state unto itself; and, according to the avatars, four states of mysticism. The first of these is Nature Mysticism, a state in which a unitive experience, an ecstatic sense of union with nature, pervades consciousness. Then comes Deity Mysticism, a state in which the same results as in nature mysticism are achieved by devotion to a divine figure, or the incarnated version of a divinity e.g., Jesus within Christianity. Thirdly, comes Formless Mysticism, a state in which all content, imagery, sensation and ideation cease, and there is union with Source. Some avatars claim, however, that this is merely the penultimate stage. They speak of a fourth state, called Non-dual Mysticism, in which identity is *held* at the level of content-less, unitive source while it is simultaneously incarnated and *lived* in these spacesuits of ours. It is walking the spiritual path with "both of God's legs," the transcendent, ineffable origin and the immanent, manifested journey.

However, all incarnations end; all manifestation ceases; whatever is born will grow, change and die. Only that which is "prior" to manifestation, what is unborn and uncreated, does *not* die. So finally, when we are done with all incarnating and all manifesting, the "game of God" folds back into what "preceded" form. The good news is that we practice this process nightly. Dreamless sleep is a return to the content-less consciousness which we can also experience through other advanced way stations on this spiritual safari. The first of these advanced way stations is a deep meditative, radically transformative experience that goes by many names e.g., Samadhi, Kensho, Ananda and is experienced in the middle of the clutter and noise of incarnation. It shifts perception so completely that it results in the creation of very different maps of the human experiment.

And the second of these advanced way stations is death. Interestingly, in the Hindu tradition, where "Samadhi" literally means, "with the Lord," the name given to death is, "Maha Samadhi," where Maha" means "Great." Death, then, is seen as the great union with God. It's the reason why death and sleep are sometimes confused and often used metaphorically of each other. The term, "he fell into his final sleep" is not just a euphemism for the trauma of death, it is a recognition that it is a condition which the soul experiences nightly. "To die, to sleep no more" said Shakespeare; before he went on to talk about Hamlet's fears, "For in that sleep of death what dreams may come, when we have shuffled off this mortal coil, must give us pause."

In one beautiful story, Jesus is urged by Jairus, a synagogue official, to come and heal his 12-year-old daughter, who is seriously ill. By the time he arrives, the child has expired and the mourners are bending to their keening with gusto. He reprimands them and says, "Be gone! The child is not dead, she is sleeping." and then proceeds to "wake" her and present her to her recently bereaved and now-reprieved parents. So death and sleep are not just cruel or evasive word tricks to deny or vilify a human experience; rather they are real experiences, one embraced nightly and the other at the end of each incarnation. Sleep is a series of practice laps for death, while death is a more radical and transformative rendition of the sleep.

In fact, death is a very profound state of consciousness or more accurately death is a collective term for many states of consciousness, all the way from the confused states of some newly-departed, to the fear-based addictive clinging-to-Earth states of others of the newly-departed, to the recognition and embrace of the white light of many more, to the gentle but thorough life-review in the presence of a heavenly mentor, to the healing-space state of consciousness in which "departed" souls recuperate from the vicissitude of incarnation, to the de-briefing with the higher Self (the atman of my returning jiva) and with the soul-group, to the next, enthusiastic phase of ongoing disincarnate evolution, to the taking of the bodhisattva vow, to total "extinction" of union-with-Source. All of these stages involve different states of consciousness, states from which our daytime maps of incarnated "reality" are pitifully inexact.

For grins, I want to do a simple three by five matrix (for the mathematically-challenged, a 15-paned window). In it, I want to briefly indicate how three of the bodies (gross, astral and mental) behave in five of the states of consciousness (daytime, dream, sleep, meditation and death.) Obviously, it is a rather simplistic model of a much more complex reality.

		Bodies		
		Gross	Astral	Mental
	Daytime:	Active	Active	Active
States	Dream:	Inactive	Active	Active
of	Sleep:	Inactive	Inactive	Inactive
Consciousness	Meditation:	Less Active	Less Active	Less Active
	Death:	Inactive	Active	Active

Of course the spectrum from "active" to "less active" to "inactive" has an infinite number of possibilities. So, even the gross body which appears to be totally inactive after death is actually orchestrating the re-distribution of its own molecular structure to the surrounding eco-system, through its "Shiva intelligence." Also, the "less active" category in meditation for all three bodies goes all the way from a formless mystical state in which all three bodies are "inactive," to beginner mediators for whom all three bodies will continue to be rather active. And in "death," of course, depending on the evolutionary stage of an individual soul, the astral body will shift significantly to positive emotions, while the mental body will have the power and the clarity to manifest outcomes immediately, without the buffer zone of confusing, competing agendas.

And finally to lighten up this analytical discussion, I want to end with a piece I wrote in July 1997. It gives a creative experiential flavor to what happens when we shift gears and shift states of consciousness. I named it after a real, mystical location in County Cork, Ireland.

Tobairín na Súil

Loch Oighin, some six miles from Skibereen is, at 50 meters, the deepest lake in Ireland. Divers come from all over the world to sample its stratified flora and fauna. It is actually a sea-lake. A tiny opening in the rocks connects it to the Atlantic and the tides hissingly pour through it in great water torrents. When the tide is flowing, the sea level becomes higher than the lake level, because the ocean is attempting to squeeze itself into the lake through the small aperture. Eventually, of course, lake and sea reach the same level, but very soon the tide begins to ebb and then you have the same phenomenon in reverse. The water in the lake is not able to flow out as quickly as the sea level is falling, so there is another spectacular "waterfall" tumbling in the opposite direction. The lake level never quite catches up on this leg of the cycle. By low tide there is a discrepancy between the level of the lake and that of the ocean.

The lake contains fish and octopi that are not seen again in European waters until you go as far south as Portugal. It is altogether an extraordinary sight. I went there on July 27, 1997, with my father. I thought it as magic a place as I would see in my travels—but I was wrong! On our way back, my father remembered that there was a holy well nearby and, eventually, we found it. In fact, there are two holy wells, within 400 meters of each other. One was by the side of a little boreen and was gaudy, whitewashed and bedecked with rosary beads and holy pictures. The other was a little way into the woods. It was dark, unadorned and utterly mystical. The surface of this well only had the circumference of a large dinner plate, and it was only as deep as your average kitchen pot. It was surrounded by a few rickety flagstones and overhung by an oak tree. It was absolutely still there, with a tree-studded hill rising behind it—and I knew as soon as I saw it that I was in a "Caol Áit" (a "thin place"—the Irish name for a location where the veil separating the invisibly-sacred and visibly-secular orders of reality is diaphanous.)

I knelt on one of the rickety flag stones, peering into the well. A small hand-painted notice said "Tobairín na súil" which means "The little well of the eyes." It obviously had a reputation for healing diseases of the eye. I knelt there for perhaps 15 minutes, transfixed. I didn't know whether I was looking down or looking up. In the tiny pool, I could see the reflection of the branches of the oak tree, of the white fluffy clouds, and of the azure-blue sky far above my head. By changing my focus I could see mud and some fallen leaves at the bottom of the well. By refocusing again, I could look down through the well, through the center of the earth, out the other side of the globe and see the branches of an oak tree in the antipodes; I could see the fluffy clouds and the azure-blue of southern skies.

I refocused again and saw back into time—a time before Christianity had been invented, the time of Fionn MacCumhaill and the Fianna of Ireland. I saw Oisín and Niamh Chinn Óir, hopelessly in love, chasing each other in the waters of Tír na nÓg and then uniting in the cosmic bliss of soul mates, where bodies blend, hearts harmonize, minds merge, and there is only the oneness of Spirit loving itself.

And I prayed. I prayed for the gift of vision. I splashed the water on my eyes, and asked that I might have the ability to see beyond the veil, and bring back wisdom; that I might recognize "Caol Áiteanna" whether I encountered them in physical locations or in the person of another.

If ever I meet a woman I want to marry, that is where I would want to exchange vows. If ever I wanted to conceive a child that is where I would want it to happen. If I needed to be ordained a priest over again, that is where I would want the ceremony to take place.

I asked that I might recognize that each one of us is "the Word made flesh".

35

When Spiders Play Tennis
(1/12/1999)

Everybody knows that there is no such thing as an "ordinary walk." There's only "sleepwalking" and "real walking." Anybody who doesn't gasp for breath at Nature's profligacy, several times during an evening's stroll, isn't awake. Oisín walked regularly in the mountains, but there was nothing "regular" about his walks. Mostly, he didn't cover huge distances—five or six miles total, perhaps—but each walk lasted three or four hours. There was so much to be seen. And seeing is what Oisín did best.

Take last Tuesday for instance. It had been raining heavily for several hours, but then the sun came out and the hillsides steamed themselves dry, birthing mists and fogs and vapor clouds, that playful zephyrs spun into exquisite diaphanous gowns, sensually semi-concealing the shapes of the mountains underneath. Oisín sat on a rock overlooking the valley five hundred feet below, with its silver stream, newly fortified, twisting its way among the Scrub Oak, Madrone and Redwoods. The hillsides opposite were pitted with the labyrinthine paths of the wild pig trails. And the sunlight was splitting itself into rainbows through every droplet of water on every spider's web.

And that was when he noticed the "tennis racket." It wasn't really a tennis racket of course. It was much cleverer than that. Some enterprising arachnid had used a tall, slender stalk of grass to construct a web. The stalk, three feet high, drooped over in a parabola. A spider fastened the dangling stalk with her silk and pulled it tightly until it was joined to its own stem. Then she built her entire web within the resultant peaked ellipse! It was a perfect "tennis racket.'

And in the lure of this misty rainbow-racket, Oisín had a vision. He saw where the mist was coming from; he saw that it was the steam off the cooking pots of the Faery Folk who were having a party under the mountains. And because he saw, they invited him in. Never had he seen a merrier, and yet more industrious, group. Faeries scurried about fetching, carrying, preparing and cooking the most exotic array of foodstuffs he had ever seen. Hundreds of huge, black, three-legged, iron cauldrons bubbled furiously, and the steam filtered through the high ceilings and out into the human world. Faeries were chatting, laughing, singing, dancing—and one old faery was watching Oisín intently. Since he was the only faery who didn't appear to be "doing anything," Oisín approached him.

Dia dhuit! (God be with you!")
said Oisín.

Dia 's Muire dhuit! (God and Mary be with you!)
replied the old faery pleasantly.

So they fell to talking.

I didn't realize that there were faery folk outside of Ireland,
said Oisín

Oh yeh! We're everywhere.
But only children and mystics ever see us.
The rest are too busy—and too self-concerned.

I don't mean to be rude,
said Oisín,
but what do yee do all day?

Well, our primary task is to clean up the planet after humans trash it.
Ye see all the cooking that's going on here?
It's actually food for Gaia—Gaia is what the Greek faeries call her.
And the chatting, laughing, singing and dancing?
—all that revives her Spirit.
It's really hard work, ye know, being a planet I mean.
Great souls come onto the Earth

as prophets, poets and enlightened masters
—but only the greatest souls of all get to become planets.
Gaia is a great soul, what the Hindu faeries call a "Mahatma,"
but she's having a rough time of it lately.
So we help out.

Then why don't yee reveal yeerselves to the leaders?
Bishops and politicians and scientists and the like?

They wouldn't be able to see us!
Ye have to be able to stoop very low to spot a faery.
The people ye mentioned are mostly myopic and self-important.
They can't see what's real,
they're too busy chasing totally fictitious illusions.
It saddens us a lot to see them.
And what upsets us even more is to see what they do to the children
—it's terrible entirely to watch the deep, awefilled, curious eyes of a child
glaze over as a result of "education."

Gee, I'm sorry. I didn't realize things were so bad!

They're not.
Every now and then an adult wakes up, and then we throw a party.
This one's for yerself.

Really?? Thanks a million! How can I stay awake, though?

Spend a lot of time with children.
And walk a lot
—with yer eyes open.
All of yer eyes.

I remember last August in Ireland, I baptized the baby of a
friend of mine, in Dingle, County Kerry.
We did the baptism in the ruins of an eleventh century church,
called Kilmakeadar, overlooking the wild Atlantic.
She wanted her baby baptized there,
because that's where her own father is buried.
On his tombstone is the Gaelic statement:
"Níl sa tsaol ach naoscoil na Síoraíochta"
(Earthly life is merely the Kindergarten for Eternity).
So my question for ye is this:
Which place am I in, now?

Ye're in the antechamber, between the two places
—what we call a "Caol Áit" (thin place).
We make shoes here.

Yee make shoes!?

Yeh. We make shoes here.
Didn't ye ever hear tell of the Leprechauns?

Sure I did, and their pots of gold.
But is it true?

As true as God's blue heavens!
But their gold isn't the stuff ye'd find in Fort Knox.
It's the treasures of the Spirit.
And the shoes they make, they're not leather for the sole of yer boot
but wings for the soul of yer spacesuit.

Could I ever get a pair, myself, d'ye think?

That's precisely why we enticed ye in here; to fit ye for a pair.
Séamus over there,
said he pointing to a wizened old-timer bending assiduously to his task,
is just putting the finishing touches to them for ye.

There was a long, wistfully-satisfying pause, and then he asked:
D'ye have any wish ye'd like me to grant?

Gosh no. I'm just totally mesmerized.
I never thought I'd be talking with a real faery.
And getting a pair of shoes into the bargain!

Well, I have one more wish to grant ye, anyway,
whether ye ask for it or not.
And here 'tis:
When people listen to ye speak,
may they be overcome with nostalgia for home
—not for their earthly home, mind ye, but for their real home.
May they know that there's someplace else.

May they become a little sad,
but may it be a good sadness,
that'll make them begin the search themselves.
And, eventually, may they all find us.
That's my wish for ye now!

I knew what he meant. I feel it myself sometimes.

When he finished his prayer for me, I fell into a kind of reverie. I don't know how long I was in it. When I came to, there was the spider checking out the strings on her racket. I winked at her. She pretended she didn't understand.

But I knew she did.

36

Embrace Entanglement

"The spiritual path needs a certain amount of realism; one has to see the real value of things that are, which is very little except as steps in evolution."
Sri Aurobindo

My nephew, Seán óg, is a brilliant young man who is a very original thinker and deeply compassionate. Long after midnight on Christmas Eve, he and a friend of his came to my apartment and we talked about the homily which I has just given. Then, next day, I had Christmas dinner with him, hosted by his sister, Dawn, and her husband, Seth. Seán óg and I continued our discussion. Those discussions prompted me to hunker down and think my ideas through in more detail. The result is the chapter you are now reading. It has to do with the notions of reality, of who creates or co-creates it, of states of consciousness and of mapping these. So let's dive in.

(A) Reality

What most of us define as "reality" is merely our personal trance as it is created and supported by the cultural trance of the society and times in which we live. So "reality" changes for an individual throughout the course of a lifetime and is influenced hugely by reading, travel, the media, time spent thinking and experiences of altered states of consciousness. Similarly, each culture changes its models of reality from epoch to epoch, depending on the memes it creates, the charismatic figures it throws up and its meeting with other cultures (through war, commerce, tourism or religious conversion.) And "reality" is very different from culture to culture even at the same period of human history e.g., a Bushman in the Kalahari, a fundamentalist Christian in Alabama and a European bureaucrat in Brussels, have radically different notions of reality.

Within the cultural trance (or consensual reality), we each create our own private trance (or individual reality). These two play off each other. The individual reality was born of the cultural trance but then donated blood to it on a regular basis to keep it alive and vibrant so that it could continue to inform the private reality. For we are social animals who need group approval but who, also, value personal difference. So no two human experiences are identical. If I tell you I have a toothache, don't tell me you fully understand, because my experience of my toothache is not the same as your experience of your toothache. We live in this paradox of wanting to be part of a community, be accepted and approved, while, at the same time, wanting to be one of a kind. So, yes, you create your own reality as a unique strand in the tapestry of the global reality.

It can be fun to sometimes concentrate on what we have in common, and, at other times, to concentrate on our differences. So, for instance, we humans share 98.6 percent of our DNA with chimps and 60 percent of our DNA with bananas! What do you choose to focus on?

Science, too, that somber sentinel of "real reality," has radically shifted its position several times even in the course of the 20th Century. So, reality is not cut-and-dried, unchanging, obvious and out-there-for-all-to-see.

(B) Truth and Fact

"Factoids" do not create reality, and truth is not synonymous with data. I define truth as that which transforms and aligns us with our core essence. And Absolute Truth is that which transforms us radically and aligns us permanently with our core essence. Absolute Truth is beyond the scope of science, of culture, even of religion; it can only be handled by mysticism.

Since even Pure Mathematics, the queen of all the sciences, operates by reducing the observed cosmos to its best approximations, so as to be able to handle it with the simple equations in its tool-kit, then the scientific method is destined to answer "how questions" with, hopefully, increasing specificity, while acknowledging that it is utterly inadequate to ask any of the values-based "why questions," which alone can create a cartography of reality.

(C) The Four Steps of Reductionism

This reduction of Absolute Truth to mere cultural trance proceeds in four steps. First, we ignore the fact that there are many states of human consciousness, and pretend that there is only one, which we, grandiosely, call, "Waking consciousness." Since this is a bastard fathered by chutzpah and carried by hubris, I will, instead, refer to this state of consciousness as, "the Diurnal state of consciousness" or, more simply, "the daytime state of consciousness." The second step of the reduction is to focus on a tiny, utterly non-representative sample of daytime-consciousness-generated data and pretend that that is the total picture. Of the billions of sensory experiences your average human being has in a single day, s/he has been trained and frightened into ignoring the vast bulk of these miraculous experiences (e.g., a healthy body, fun friends, great sunsets, wonderful food), and, instead, to focus exclusively on the few discordant daily data (e.g., traffic jams, terrorists attacks, the bird flu).

Step number three is to then spin the sample in the most fearful fashion, so that minor events are turned into global tragedies, occupying the full screen of our consciousness and of our TV sets. It's the opposite of the Occam's Razor criterion, which says, "the most simple and elegant explanation for the data is probably the most accurate one." Instead we operate from the adult version of the "monsters under the bed" syndrome. Now the explanation of choice is the one that creates the most xenophobia and the greatest possible panic; "If it bleeds, it leads."

And the final step is to tell us plainly, frequently, and oh so sincerely, that there is only one possible response, and our trusted leaders have already begun to execute it on our behalf. Once the damage has been done, the story swallowed hook, line and sinker, and relieved sighs of satisfaction heaved that we are in the care of leaders with such perspicacity, the icing on this arsenic-riddled cake is that they conduct a survey to poll the populace on their wishes in this matter. This has all the integrity of forecasting a hurricane the week after it has happened.

(D) States of Consciousness

So, is there merely one state of consciousness? No, there isn't. There are at least nine, each with its own specific signature on an electroencephalograph. We have Daytime consciousness, Dream consciousness, Dreamless Sleep consciousness, Hypnotic consciousness, Meditation consciousness, Nature Mysticism consciousness, Deity Mysticism consciousness, Formless Mysticism consciousness and Non-dual Mysticism consciousness. The last two I will call the God-state consciousness, or the Higher-Self-state consciousness. And each of these states comes with it own system of laws, in which time, space and causation are different. Thus an experience in any one of these states generates very different data from an experience in another state.

(E) Thinkers and Talkers

And now the rub. Our thinkers, scientists, theologians, cosmologists and philosophers decide which of these states are real and worthy of our attention, and which are imaginary and belong in the same nursery as Santa and the Tooth Fairy. Then those who control the dissemination of information decide what exposure we get and how many of the reduction-steps get collapsed into "facts and actions" for simple minds who want to be entertained and not bothered by any effort that might cause mental stretch marks.

(F) Responses

Most of us buy dumbly into all four steps of this reduction. Occasionally, a contrary bastard will come along and baulk at step four, the action plan. Many of these protesters have both compassion and courage and stick to the task with tenacity, but almost none of them realize that they have been hugely hoodwinked. They have no appreciation of the other steps of the reduction process, and so have gulped them down. No matter how loudly they protest, no matter how long they struggle, no matter what apparent successes they have, ultimately, they have merely re-arranged the furniture on the deck of the sinking Titanic.

The dumb majority, that accepts all the steps, is like the children who are ordered to bed at 7:00 each night and never protest. Instead they think, "It's 7:00 PM, I'm a child, it's bedtime, it's the law." The objectors, those who take issue only with step four, are easily outfoxed by a parent who says, instead, "It's 6:45 PM, before you go to bed do you want milk and cookies or a bedtime story?" The child, thinking it is exercising choice, free will and independence, doesn't realize it's still going to be in bed at 7:00 PM.

The prophets, typically, recognize and inveigh against steps two and three, and so are more troublesome to the authorities and may achieve more radical and longer-lasting changes. But these will not endure because even the prophet doesn't realize that the very first step, the one *he* failed to spot, was the most eviscerating of all. So prophets may change institutions temporarily and thus lead to happier and more peaceful times, in the short term, but the transformation has not reached the soul level and the old cycle has not really been broken. That is the job of the mystic. Only the mystic and the avatar recognize the first step and undo it. They will know all of the states of consciousness and re-install the God-state, or the Higher-Self-state as the primary reality and as the Operating System for an incarnational experience on planet Earth.

Let me illustrate all of this with a simple analogy. There is a puddle of water on the kitchen floor. The authorities say it was caused by the maid who dropped a full glass she was carelessly carrying. They tell us that *she* is the problem and must be fired. Most of us, on seeing the puddle and hearing the explanation, go along with the plan to fire her. Some contrary individual, however, will want to give her another chance. The prophet will question the explanation, ask, "Did anybody actually *see* her drop the glass?" and then point out that the puddle is being caused by a drip from the ceiling. We look up and see that he is right. So we trudge upstairs and notice that the puddle downstairs is being fed by a puddle upstairs in the bathroom under the basin. We look underneath the basin and notice a drop of water on the copper pipe that feeds the hot-water line. So we all agree that the pipe is the real cause of both puddles. We replace this pipe and mop up the puddles. But within a week both puddles have reappeared. If we had asked the mystic he would have shown us that the true source of the problems is that there is a leak in the roof, over the bathroom, which is running down inside the wall and emerging right over the hot-water pipe from which it drips until it has created a big-enough puddle to export its excess through the bathroom floor and through the kitchen ceiling onto the kitchen floor. But we almost never take the mystics seriously and so we simply fire the maid, and, occasionally, replace the water pipe.

When we do listen to the mystics, we don't have to fire the maid or replace the pipes. Instead we follow a simple protocol: fix the roof; mop up the bathroom puddle; and mop up the kitchen puddle. When we don't consult the mystics we focus so intently on the kitchen puddle that our worldview revolves about it; it becomes our "reality." Any effort to point out a sunset or the comfortable chairs in the sitting room or little Johnny's great school report, are seen as "ignoring the real issue." Preoccupation and anxiety soon lead to anger, so we fire the maid, mop up the kitchen floor and then look around for somebody else (the new maid, the gardener, grandma's nurse) to blame once the puddle recreates itself.

(G) Who, then, Creates Reality?

For example, am I responsible for the war in Iraq? Let me say what responsible might mean. In truth, responsible literally means Response-able i.e., I am able to make a response. In that sense, yes of course, I am responsible; it behooves me to make a response to such an event. But, when we use the word responsible, we mean, "I am the cause of." So, am I the cause of the war in Iraq? I am responsible for agreeing to the four reductions and thus allowing the event to have an importance totally out of proportion. I am also responsible for giving it a huge amount of my conscious focus and unconscious ruminations—and it doesn't particularly matter, at the energetic level, whether I am totally in favor of it or passionately against it. It is my *focus* that energizes. Naturally, the cultural trance, by which human beings have accepted the four reductions and allowed their focus to be trained on Iraq, is much more powerful and immediate in its impact than the focus of any one individual. But despite this, there are people for whom the war in Iraq is not their reality e.g., the mystics. They are not saying that there isn't a war going on in Iraq, but simply operate in a totally different game in a radically different venue with absolutely different rules. And the result of this different game is that they hold the Iraqi situation in a different way; and since they are mostly bodhisattvas, it will be an embrace of love that manifests in practical ways, while never making it their reality. It is a small feature in a huge landscape, and the mystic's perspective and energy will do far more to create peace than any protests will do. He will take practical steps also, but always grounded in the number one perspective, the God-state of consciousness with its vast eternal view that ensures that practical steps are elegant and permanent.

And so the warmongers will continue to wage war; the protesters will continue to give energy to the war by protesting it and, therefore, focusing their attention and that of others on the violence; the prophets will draw attention only to changing the middle stages; but the mystics will provide the only lasting solution.

Those who bury their heads in the sand are not those who *don't* give attention to the war, but rather those who *do* give their attention to the war. These people have buried their heads in the quicksand of unworkable solutions, to false interpretations of non-representative samples from a less-than-basic state of consciousness. And then we wonder why the cycle has continued for the last 5,000 years; why just wars to end all wars have always thrown up more just wars that merely breed new wars.

And so, any energy, no matter how well intentioned or peaceful, will continue to invigorate the very phenomenon it seeks to extinguish, because it is the energy of attention, especially when blind to the four reductions, that created the war in the first place.

The protesters are like a man who planted a flower garden at the other side of the fence from a weed-dominated garden. Each day, however, he waters the weeds but not the flowers. And each day he complains bitterly that the flowers are dying while the weeds are thriving.

So, then, do I create my own reality? Yes! But I am not the cause of the factoids, data or events that fill the columns of our news reports and video footage. I do attract into my experience the objects of my thoughts, the contents of the screen onto which I project the light of my awareness; and I feed and nurture this reality of mine by the energy I continue to direct to it.

And what of the atrocities yet to come? Even now, anxious minds are hatching new tragedies which they will conceive, carry, birth and suckle. Am I responsible for these? Am I anxious about the future? Do I put graphic imagery to fear-filled thoughts? Am I now planning ways to deal with them when they happen? If my answer to any of these last three questions is yes, then I am responsible, together with millions of other co-creators, for the future. The bomber and the voyeur have different degrees of responsibility, but they are both responsible. If I am a mystic who could honestly answer no to all three questions, does this mean that shit won't happen? Not necessarily. The Law of Allowing ensures that people be free to create their own experience, and once a critical mass is reached they will manage to co-create an outcome which will occupy the center stage of their cultural and personal reality. And even then, it will still not be the reality of the mystic, who will see it as a time-circumscribed incident in a tiny corner of the timeless masterpiece of the God-state consciousness.

(H) Immediate Solutions

Some critical situations demand immediate, practical responses (the man-in-the-schoolyard-with-a-machinegun scenario), but merely "taking him out" to save the children will never solve the problem of murder unless we also ask why we need/permit weapons at all. And he wouldn't have been in the schoolyard in the first place, with his Uzi, if in the past we had thought differently as a culture.

It is always interesting to me that the people who are most insistent on proposing this critical scenario to justify violent intervention are the very ones who then initiate violent interventions as their long-term policy to solve disputes. Violent national self-aggrandizement then sneaks into foreign policy while wearing a badge earned by a pretense of interest only in chivalrous altruism.

Every critical present situation is the product of faulty past thinking and myopic policy-making. And any immediate response to a present critical situation that is not also accompanied by a radical shift in thinking is going to lead to an endless chain of other critical situations.

Sure, put a bucket under the downstairs and the upstairs drips to slow the damage, but if the roof isn't fixed, those buckets will fill up again and the puddles will increase in volume, and the damage increase in severity.

(I) Co-creators

So, do we create individually or are we co-creators? Both. We are the individual creators of our own personal reality while we contribute, also, as co-creators of the cultural trance or consensual reality. In both conditions we elevate factoids to truth, and thus reality is the illusion of perceptions and focus masquerading as how things really are. We co-create this radically impoverished version of reality that is so distressing, so engrossing and so central to our conscious lives, that we actually perpetuate it and expand it, even as we claim to be horrified by it. And this is precisely because we focus on it and play their game, on their field with their rules.

(J) The Map-makers

Our maps of reality are almost all produced by cartographers who are convinced that daytime consciousness is the waking state and the true reality. With such pathetic maps, is it any wonder that we find ourselves lost so often? Only maps of reality that emanate from the non-dual application of God-state experiences can really provide us with an adequate guidance system. At this stage of human evolution, we need to recognize and undo the four reductions and then create accurate maps from real mystical experiences in the God-state. And please let's not confuse God-state with the dogmatic mindset of sectarian religion.

And the mystics, all of whom are deeply compassionate bodhisattvas, who have often forfeited their own Earthly spacesuits in violent deaths, these mystics and avatars all insist on a different map, a different game on a different field with different rules. And even their violent deaths were not forced upon them, thus disproving their world-view; they accepted this level of violence against their person voluntarily as a way of teaching ignorant people, stuck in a different game, that killing them would not quash the new map. So, for example, Jesus said, on the last day of his Earthly life, to Pilate, who was about to condemn him to crucifixion, "Nobody takes my life from me. I lay it down freely. I could appeal to my Heavenly Father and he would send legions of angels to rescue me." And later, on the cross, he proclaimed, "It is completed! Father, into your hands I commend my spirit."

All of these bodhisattvas, knowing the way this cosmos works, could have chosen to spend idyllic lives in meditation. Some of them did precisely that, and it was *their* contribution. Others chose a different path, but always with the realization that they were creating their own reality, so as to intersect with the cultural trance and seek to un-stick it. Both kinds of avatars recognized the four reductions; they recognized the laws of attraction, deliberate intention, allowing, karma etc., some of which I will speak of in the next section. Most importantly they recognized the God-consciousness as the ultimate, primary and basic state of all—the one that births the mystical, dreamless, dreaming and daytime states of consciousness; the only state from which accurate maps of all the other states can be created; and the only launching pad from which lasting solutions to the world's pain can be initiated.

(K) Some Cosmic Laws

In order to move to an action plan of my own, based on this thesis, I want, briefly, to touch upon some of what I consider to be the laws of the Cosmos. These eleven laws are the laws of love, unity, attraction, karma, deferred outcomes, impermanence, deliberate intention, allowing, manifestation, entanglement and interdimensional communication.

Love is the fabric of the universe, the source, the warp and woof, and the final end. And so, the law of love states that when we come into alignment with love, we rest in our own true core; and our reality is serenity, patience and tolerance for all sentient beings. We are imperturbably compassionate.

The law of unity states that when we do discover our true identity it will not be in discrete selfhood, not in our bodies, emotions, ideas, names, reputations, affiliations or achievements, but, rather, in our God-Self. And so every creature is a manifestation of this essence; I AM THAT. This identity-by-unity translates the law of love into practical relationships.

The law of attraction states that since everything in the universe is composed of energy vibrating in a myriad of frequencies in a multiplicity of created things, from galaxies to kidneys and from squids to thoughts, then similar frequencies attract, resonate with and amplify each other. Each discrete energy-emitter is like a tiny snowball rolling down a mountain until it becomes the nucleus of an avalanche. It is both an attractor and a manifester.

The law of karma says that causes beget consequences and no result is fatherless. Thoughts lead to words that spawn actions that create habits which birth characters who reap destinies. It is a law without either guile or malice.

The law of deferred outcomes works in the following way. In the non-physical realms, where we are operating in a less dense environment and are far brighter, thoughts *immediately* result in outcomes. For physical beings, however, in acknowledgement of their lesser intellects and impulsive behavior, there is a time buffer between the thought and the outcome. This can be minutes, days or even years; or it can even be deferred to another incarnation or to a parallel universe. It allows us to revise, revamp and re-configure our trajectory before planting both of our feet in the future. We have a proverb in Irish, "Is minic a bhris béal duine a shrón" ('tis often a person's mouth broke his nose.) Well, on the occasions when his mouth didn't break his nose, it's either because he spoke lovingly or he "bit his tongue." A bit tongue is a great improvement over a broken nose. The latter two possibilities would be evidence of the law of deferred outcomes.

The law of impermanence states that everything that is born will die; anything which was created will change and pass away; growth and development and evolution demand the constant, creative re-configuring of all of the elements of all that exists in form. This is the law that allows all of English literature to come from a mere 26 alphabetical symbols; it is the law that allows all of the musical masterpieces to emerge from a mere seven notes; it is the law that allows all life-forms on planet Earth to be constructed of just four elements: A, C, T and G; and it is the law that allows all mathematically-encoded computer language to be born from merely two digits: Zero and One.

The law of deliberate intention states that when we live consciously, with full awareness, we are, indeed, masters of our own destiny. At this stage of planetary evolution, it is this law that invites us into the driving seat of the automobile, in which, up to now, we were merely passengers. This law confers on each one of us the formal license to mindfully command the car given us at incarnation.

And the law of allowing reminds us that each one of us creates his/her own reality and that I will save myself a lot of frustration when I do not insist, or even hope, that you could be like me if only you could wake up.

The law of manifestation means that all created things are a manifestation or articulation from unmanifest, uncreated Source. All forms come from emptiness and when we examine the essence of any form it is emptiness. Should you visit emptiness, you would find that it is the womb from which all forms might emanate. So you, your cat, the mailman and the gladiola in your garden are a "hard copy," a printout of an online program.

The law of entanglement follows on from that, for truly the online original is never destroyed but continues to hold energy for the hard copy. Put more simply, when you incarnated and took on a spacesuit, you did not commit all of your soul-energy to the project; rather a significant amount of this soul-energy remained at home base, where it remains actively entangled in your incarnational experience.

And the final law I want to mention, the law of interdimensional communication, follows on from that. It means that spirit energy and spacesuit energy continue to communicate with each other EVEN when the four reductions circumscribe your cosmology and reduce it a flatland of scientism. The spirit part of you speaks to the spacesuit part of you via dreams, déjà vu experiences, intuitions, sudden inspirations, synchronicities, chance encounters and, in your Emotional Guidance System that shows the basic emotional categories "I feel good" and "I feel bad" are an agreed-upon signal from the Higher Self to alert you to the quality of your thoughts, so you can use the time buffer to deliberately choose an outcome.

The Catholic version of this interdimensional communication is called, "The Communion of Saints," and it says that the three groups: post-incarnated souls (those in heaven), transitioning souls (those in purgatory) and incarnated souls (those of us currently in spacesuits) all influence each other's experience and pray for each other.

All of these laws interact and together they provide the rules for this cosmic game; rules that apply whether or not we are aware of them; rules that create even when we fall into the trap of the four reductions and invent other games with different rules. These cosmic rules trump all man made rules and permeate all man made games. It is the reason that most of our games lead to misery, warfare, anxiety and despair, even for the inventors and medal-winners.

(L) An Action Plan

On the basis of my entire thesis in this chapter, I made a list of things that I believe, if followed, will bring you into enlightenment and could contribute to peace and serenity in our times.

1. Learn how to access the God-state consciousness e.g., Meditation.
2. Visit there often.
3. Learn to use maps of daytime consciousness created in God-state consciousness to walk with its compassionate truth in a non-dual awareness during incarnation.
4. Hang out with other God-staters.
5. Immerse yourself in books, journals, videos, audios and movies that treat of incarnation from a God-state stance.
6. Don't get seduced into the four reductions.
7. Frequently shift your locus of identity along the spectrum that spans individual cell to Cosmic Creator.
8. Since like energies attract each other, BE the energy you want to attract.

9. Use the karmic feedback loop, within and among incarnations, to improve your creations
10. Use the buffer zone and the Emotional Guidance System to create deliberately and positively.
11. See impermanence as your friend.
12. Don't create either unconsciously or negatively.
13. Don't fear or oppose the cultural reality but do add your own creativity to the mix.
14. Marshal your own emotional energy to amplify and accelerate your creations.
15. Avoid focusing on a negative in present time, rather be the creator of a love-filled future-time.
16. Allow others their reality.
17. Embrace entanglement.
18. Welcome interdimensional communication when it occurs spontaneously and develop ways to initiate it from your end.
19. Begin and end each day in love.

37

Will There Be Life?
(3/20/01)

A lichen-whiskered oak tree stands on the river bank,
uninhibitedly naked.
He watches a spider sling a single strand of silken web
across the creek,
ten feet above the water.
A breeze blows his long beard over his shoulder,
and makes the acrobatics of the spider-walk
even more breathtaking.
She is the daredevil of Niagara
and he the silent mystic who watches.
How many times has she done this?
And how many times has he watched?
How many spiders
and how many oak trees
have done this dance
since Earth was an infant?
How many times will they do it again?
How many times will we notice them do it,
and gaze in awe?
How many times will we allow them?

The setting sun has found the silken strand,
fifty feet of fiber optic,
in which to create an undulating rainbow.
Prism strand, rainbow strand,
a long, multi-colored tendril
connecting the two riverbanks in a tender embrace.
Work of art.
Art of work.
Nature of life.
Life of nature.
Will we see?
Will we participate?
Will there be lichen-whiskered oak trees
and will there be silken-strand-spinning spiders
in the forests of our children?
Will there be children in our forests?
Will there be forests?
Will there be children?
Will there be Life?

Will there be—Life?

38

So, How Do I Become Enlightened?

"You are simply being lived through in order to discover that you are the divine."
Tony Parsons

Have you ever seen an Aran sweater? Perhaps you have and didn't know the name of it. It is a type of heavy, hand-knit woolen sweater peculiar to the Aran Islands, a cluster of three, that lie off the west coast of Ireland, just across from County Galway. If you are a stranger to these sweaters and are seeing one for the first time, you'll be very impressed with the quality and intricate design of them.

If you are Irish you'll immediately recognize them and be able to say, "Yes, this is an Aran sweater. They are hand-knit on the Aran Islands off the west coast of County Galway."

But if you are actually an Aran Islander, you'll know a lot more about them. You'll know that each family has a different design; and when you see a man wearing one, you'll recognize the family from which he comes and say, "Yes, he must be one of the Conneelly boys." When you see a different design, you'll know that the wearer is one of the ÓFaoláin men.

However, if you're a *woman* from the Aran Islands, you'll be privy to an even more esoteric piece of information. Originally it was the men who knit them, and to this day, it is normally only men who wear them. But at one stage of history the women took over the task of the knitting. And when they took over, they didn't just make more intricate designs; and they didn't just honor the family code of the pattern; they knit-in secret signs, for other women, to alert them to the fact that the wearer was either a single man or a married man.

So now, if a man went to another island (and these men are mostly fishermen who brave the wild Atlantic in their curraghs which are light wooden-framed canoes with tarred canvas stretched over the frame) and he took a fancy to a girl in that place, all she had to do was have a quick peek at his sweater and she would know whether or not he were really available. Many an intended tryst died prematurely on the basis of such hastily gleaned information. And for years the man never twigged it.

Now the scriptures of the world are a bit like that. People can only see or hear what they are capable of, for we don't see things as *they* are, rather we see things as *we* are. So there are people who meet a bible story, and if they are from a religious tradition other than the Judeo-Christian one, they think, "That's a good tale!" And that is the end of it. They are like the stranger seeing the Aran sweater for the first time.

At a second level are the "ordinary" Christians who have a passing familiarity and can tell you, "This is a bible story; it's not from Shakespeare." But apart from that, they can't tell you a whole lot about it. These are like the Irish who know the sweater is from Aran.

At a third level, is the devout Christian who reads the bible regularly and is familiar with the stories, the genres and even the exact part of the bible from which they come. But he tends to interpret them in a literal fashion. He is like the Aran Islander man.

But at the fourth level is the mystic who can hear the scriptural message in its deepest essence; experiencing the symbols of the story in the core of her own soul. She is like the Aran Islander woman.

Let me tell you of a totally different situation that teaches the same lesson. The Kalenjin people, among whom I lived in Kenya for 14 years, were, traditionally, polygamists. A man might have three, four, seven or even 50 wives, depending on his cattle-wealth. The Kalenjin didn't live in villages; they gave each other lots of space, for they had originally been nomadic pastoralists. When you came across what looked like a small village of 15 or so houses, it was simply a single family. The man had his own hut in the center, surrounded by the huts of his wives. And when each boy reached puberty he, too, would build his own hut.

Now, when one of the wives got pregnant and was four or five months along, conjugal relations would cease. She would go full term, birth her baby and nurse it for about two and a half years. Eventually she was ready to re-engage sexually with her husband, and she would send him the following signal. She would entrust a bowl of soup to the toddler and say, "Bring that across to your daddy's house. The little fellow would teeter across, spilling most of it and having the dogs sample it directly from the bowl en route. He felt really proud at this important commission. And a non-Kalenjin adult onlooker would simply see a young child carrying food to his father, and wonder at the wisdom of entrusting this task to one so young and so unsteady on his feet.

Daddy, of course, got the message and whatever remained of the soup, and was pleased that another of his harem was available for intimacy.

And the scriptures are like that; they are filled with signs and symbols that are interpreted at many levels—from the literal to the critical to the inner levels. Again, we can only see what we can see.

(A) From Mystical Teachers to Institutional Leaders

"They will beat their spears into pruning hooks and their swords into ploughshares." Such are among the signs of the Messiah's arrival, says Isaiah in Chapter 2. It was a prophecy uttered in the year 741 BCE (we know this from other references in the text which mention events that can be cross-checked with records in secular history.) So we have waited 2,748 years and not only is peace not happening, the scale, frequency and viciousness of war are increasing. Why is God playing games with us? He's not. We simply look in the wrong places for the promised Messiah.

Paul's letter to the Romans, written about 57 CE enthuses, "It is now the time to wake from sleep, for our salvation is closer than when we first believed." Closer? How much closer? Not very, it seems, for it's been 1,950 years since Paul uttered his cry, and there still is no sign of our salvation happening. Once again, we are looking in the wrong places.

And Matthew's gospel puts these words into the mouth of Jesus, "Stay awake, you cannot know the hour your Lord is coming." Well, we have been hyper-alert and radically sleep-deprived for 1977 years since that clarion call, but the Lord hasn't come. Or has he? Of course he has; to those who know where to look.

And he told us as much. He specifically gave his teachings in the parables and metaphors that would allow each of his listeners to relate to them from his/her own level of spirituality. He would say, in reply to his interlocutors, "I speak in parables so that seeing you may see and not understand, hearing you may hear and not comprehend." In a final ringing rejoinder he added. "He, who has ears to hear, let him hear!"

But the responses to and interpretations of his appeal were all over the map. The bored mob simply found his stories and his miracles entertaining. It didn't go any deeper than that. The religious authorities found his views heretical and even blasphemous and tried valiantly, but vainly, to discredit him in debate. His disciples, for the most part, saw in him a ticket to prestige. He would be the Messiah, the priest-king and they his inner core of advisors. Perhaps only his mother, Mary of Magdala and maybe John really understood the mystical meaning of his message.

And his message was quite simple, The Kingdom of God in "en mesoi," meaning within each one of us; it is our core nature, our birthplace, our origin and our home. And it is among us; it is what happens when we recognize God in each other—all others: friends, family, neighbors, enemies, foreigners, animals, nature.

During all these times—Isaiah's, Paul's and Jesus' time—we have been looking in the wrong places; waiting for a conquering king, a partisan messiah, an angry God-man to return and rapture the elect while he punishes the rest. "You are the light of the world. But if your light be darkness, how very great will that darkness be." The light given us was love, it was God-life and, instead, we have turned it into anger and prejudice, violence and warfare, crusades and inquisitions. Our light has become darkness, a darkness that has become profound in our times.

Generation by generation, leader by leader we have twisted the message of love into an instrument of fear. Each mystical teacher has said, "the way is north, come follow me." And, initially, we set out enthusiastically. Eventually the teacher always leaves and though we have been given great directions, we find ourselves alone. Our first response is to create organizations where there had been family and institutions where there had been community. We set out a mission statement; erect by-laws; draw up a code of necessary beliefs, orthodox credos; designate the enemy; and elect leaders who will get us to heaven. Self-importantly, with great gravity and fully aware of their own august personhood, the leaders soon advise us, "We have pondered the teachings of the master and we have come to the conclusion that he didn't mean north, he actually meant North North East (NNE). So we need to tweak our direction a little!"

Satisfied and a little relieved the band sets out in a NNE direction; only to be advised by another generation of leaders, that on a closer inspection of the texts, the correct direction is not in fact NNE but NE. We grunt in agreement and veer a little more to the right.

This re-interpretation of the master's message undergoes many iterations, each one the result of much prayer, deep meditation and soul-searching on the part of the current leaders, and the results are that NE becomes ENE, ENE becomes E, E becomes ESE, ESE becomes SE, SE becomes SSE and SSE becomes S. Now we are literally going south; going in exactly the opposite direction from the master's teaching.

How else can Jesus' injunction to love our enemies have become global war? "Ah yes, we are followers of Jesus, but the real way to love our enemies is to kill them, because they are really not good for themselves." How do we know that we are *his* followers? Because he said, "Outsiders will know you are my disciples because of the love you show each other." And, indeed, we have shown this love to our fellow Christians by murdering lots of the outsiders for their own good; we have then killed fellow Christians, because the ultimate sign of love is to eradicate a brother's heresy by pulling him asunder on a rack. The ultimate form of compassion is torture.

(B) From Raw Data to Spirit-on-Mission

Data are meaningless. I arbitrarily define data as signals, and believe they are meaningless in and of themselves. Once data are assigned meaning then they become information. So information = data + meaning. For example, a dot and a dash are data and they have no significance; but if I assign them each a different meaning, then I can string them together in lines and, by assigning meaning to various groupings, e.g., .— . . . or -.-. or— . . . etc; I can create language. One such language is Morse code—dots and dashes, that are assigned meanings and then become capable of delivering information. And where does meaning come from? From two sources—imagination and memory. And imagination is not the faculty of making up stuff that doesn't exist rather it is the faculty that allows us to channel stuff that already exists in a different dimension or in a different state of consciousness and manifest it in this dimension in our normal waking state of consciousness. Imagination is plagiarism-writ-cosmic, and its greatest practitioners have become the architects of our sciences and our arts—Einstein, Newton, Descartes, Shakespeare, Da Vinci to name just a few.

Memory comes in two kinds—genetic and learned. Genetic memory is the record-of-Earth-life first collected four billion years ago, by bacteria. Everything that is alive today desperately depends on those archives for detailed descriptions on how to build, maintain and reproduce itself. Within those archives each species focuses on a particular aisle of bookcases. And in that aisle each race or tribe is particularly interested in one bookcase. Then, each family concentrates its research on one shelf on that bookcase; and, you, as an individual member of that family, will focus on one book on that shelf. It will contain the information specific to your configuration of genes.

Though we like to focus on the information that separates us, we hold the vast bulk of our DNA in union with the most unlikely of cousins. For example, as humans we share 80 percent of our genes with the oak tree; and a whopping 98.6 percent with the grub-eating chimps. All of these levels of DNA generate memories that allow us to assign meaning to raw data.

The other kind of memory is learned memory. This is not hardwired into us but taken aboard, unconsciously and consciously. It comes from the culture, from societal norms, from religious and scientific stories and beliefs, from family imprinting, from education and from our own experiences and discoveries. All of these create a rich tapestry of truths and untruths which become our model of reality that allows us, nay constrains us to assign meaning to data.

Once this movement has itself established and created its data-based language of meaning, it co-opts both physiology and emotions to strengthen its case and set its meaning in stone. Faced with any life situation, the body will react in accordance with the given wisdom of information-bearing data. Stimulus, interpretation, body reaction and emotional response will all go into an instant, excellently choreographed dance, with each part perfectly playing its assigned role. There are basically three movements to the dance—towards, away from and against. When the assigned/interpreted meaning is love, the movement of body and emotions is towards. Sometimes it gets stuck in towards and becomes addiction. When the meaning is fear, the movement is away from; and when this becomes stuck it becomes chronic anxiety. And when the meaning is anger, the movement is against. A stuck version of this is persistent rage.

So the movement, to date, is: data to information via imagination and memory to physiological and emotional responses. But this entire process is largely instinctual so to provide us with more options and the ability to sometimes override instinct, nature evolved, reason. This allowed us to create consistency in our models of reality and in our reactions to reality. It was a huge leap forward, coming, as it did, with the advent of the neo-mammalian brain (or the neo-cortex). Unfortunately, over time, this great gift has been hijacked by greed. It still masquerades as reason but has become a harlot in the service of selfishness. How else can we explain millions of people dying of hunger while food is hoarded by government policy, or farmers paid to not grow crops? How else could you justify trillion-dollar wars when the money it takes to make war for one day would be enough to give clean water to every person on planet Earth for a year? Or, on a more mundane personal level, how do we make sense of cigarette smoking, when the research shows that, each year, 750,000 Americans die of tobacco-related illnesses? Addiction/attachment quickly learned to press rational thought into the service of emotional need.

Every brilliant invention of this newly developed faculty of reason has been turned into a technology for war. We invented fire about 800,000 years ago. It allowed us to warm ourselves, cook our food, give us light, protect us against wild animals, who never figured out how to create it, and continue to fear it. And it was probably the beginning of story telling! But in time, fire would become guns and bombs and intercontinental ballistic missiles.

When we learned to make canoes, what a wonderful achievement that was. It allowed us, however feebly, to imitate our older marine brothers. We could fish in deep waters, and travel over vast seas to new lands. But in time, these became battleships and destroyers, nuclear submarines and torpedoes.

And when the last frontier was cracked and we learned to fly, hopping from landmass to landmass and, with the Apollo Program, even leaving Gaia entirely to visit her sister Luna, it seemed that now, at last, we might behave like a global family. But instead, we developed fighter planes and bombers and the SDI, a costly program to export our violence into outer space and turn it back on ourselves. We are willing to blast ET's and fellow Earthlings with equal dispassion.

So nature had to think again. And it came up with the idea of self-reflection, the faculty to rein in prostituted reason and allow us to critique our own individual and our culture's behavior, thinking and motives. It's still a young faculty and gets punished frequently when it's directed at the status quo of politics, religion, economics or common sense.

Realizing what we had done with reason, nature quickly added another radically new phase to evolution, namely the discovery of soul. Up to now, everything had been bound by the space-time continuum. Soul brings a new kind of memory with it—not genetic and not learned, but the innate, eternal imprint of our God-origin. It is outside of time and independent of the spacesuit.

For the first time compassion, the movement towards actually feeling the pain of another, became possible physiologically, emotionally and mentally. It was the first crack in the ancient misidentification which claimed that ego = self.

But compassion, and even the soul, are predicated on the notion of separation so, in quick succession, having introduced self-reflection, and soul, nature now showed us Spirit—the original and ultimate source-destination of all evolution. Not only is Spirit outside of the space-time continuum, it also transcends both compassion and soul, and simply IS. All arise within this placeless place, in this timeless time—all creation, manifestation, experiences, the good, the bad and the ugly. It is the great I AM, and we touch it occasionally in our unitive consciousness. It is the most intoxicating state, so enticing that mystics who get there regularly are tempted to dive in fully and never to re-emerge. And, indeed, when the vast multi-versed experiment of souls is over, that is precisely what we will all do. But for the moment, you and I have volunteered for an incarnational mission. Actually, it's a two-phased mission. First, Spirit freely articulates into a myriad of souls; and, secondly, each soul volunteers for an incarnation in some dimension away from home base. Those who choose planet Earth then have to operate within a spacesuit that has physicality, emotionality, intellectuality and personality. By all accounts it's one of the toughest assignments of the lot, with dense material stuff, volatile emotions, a meager brain, an almost 50-50 tug between "good" and "evil" inclinations and, the topper, radical amnesia for our true nature, origin and purpose for being here. No wonder so few get it right!

True spirituality then, during incarnation, is a delicate dance between really getting it that there is no separate self (Buddha got it right!) and, on the other hand, realizing that I need a sense of separate self in order to operate as an individual point of consciousness in this particular spacesuit.

Let me try to illustrate what I mean by using an analogy. If my physical heart is to adequately perform its task within my body, it has to have a separate sense of self. If it thinks of itself as the entire body, then it fails to perform its specific cordial tasks, as it attempts to also perform the roles of eyes, kidneys, teeth and toenails.

So we have to differentiate between functional identity and ontological identity; between what I do and who I am. The heart needs the sense of its own unique function, but not make the mistake of thinking it's the entire organism. Similarly, an individual human needs a sense of its own unique incarnational mission, but not make the mistake of thinking it's separate from other beings.

(C) The Myth of the Given

The great benefit of memory is that it prevents us from the "Sissyphusian" task of continually pushing the same rock up the same mountain, or of having to reinvent the wheel, each generation. It allows us to stand on the shoulders of giants and go where no man has gone before. The antithesis of this is the person with an injury to the hippocampus who cannot form any long-term memories, and can read the same page of the same book eternally and not remember that he already has—or be introduced to his own wife every half an hour and not recall that he is married to her.

The big downside to memory are two-fold. First, we quickly become jaded to life and project all kinds of filters i.e., fear, expectations, prejudices onto each fresh encounter, often missing important distinctions between this item, event or experience and its look-alike from yester-year. The great gift of children and visionaries is that they restore this freshness to each observation, discovering both the joy and the newness of each experience. It is why children are so alive, until we teach them to go to sleep under the rubric of education; and why visionaries are paradigm-busters, revolutionaries and dangerous.

The second problem with memory is that, as we stand on the shoulders of giants, we build upon both their genius and their blind spots, their watertight methodologies and their unproven postulates. Physicist, Paul Davies, pointed out recently in an op-ed article entitled, "Taking Science on Faith," in the New York Times, that when one challenges scientists as to why the laws of physics are what they are, one is met with either, "that's not a scientific question," "nobody knows" or "they just are." In a telling final statement he says, " . . . until science comes up with a testable theory of the laws of the universe, its claim to be free of faith is manifestly bogus."

So memory reduces us into erecting edifices on experiences, beliefs and assumptions that are either inaccurate or false or non-representative e.g., prejudices. Eventually the building or, at least sections of it, collapses e.g., mythic theology and Newtonian physics.

We are back once again to the data-information divide. Our senses only feed us data; they do not give us information. Even when our eyes tell us the shape and color of a table and our tactile sense adds solidity to the picture, they are not telling us any of that; rather we are telling ourselves. The eyes are not feeding us color or shape, but simply some neutral data. Then the brain with its many kinds of memory banks ascribes meaning to these data and assigns attributes to them. Since all human senses and brains work alike, we then make the assumption that this is what is really out there. Assuming that there is a reality out there that our senses can simply record is a philosophical fallacy called, "the myth of the given." As humans, we are guilty of a species-wide arbitrary attribution of meaning to sense data and then we believe our own make belief. Our version of reality is no more intrinsic to what's out there than Morse code is to a bunch of dots and dashes.

Part of our huge problem as humans is that we believe our senses, then we force animals, in a reversed anthropomorphism, to inhabit our world. Having bought into this huge fabrication as a species, we then fine-tune it, and individual cultures, tribes, religions and scientific theories are convinced that their particular version of it is really real. When push comes to shove, it gets a lot more violent than mere pushing and shoving and we kill each other in great acts of genocidal self-righteousness.

(D) So How Do I Become Enlightened?

Well, it depends on who is asking the question. If it's the ego that's asking, the answer is, "You can't—ever!" Your function is not to become enlightened i.e., reach a meta-perspective; rather it is to be the CEO of this little cluster of consciousness, during the waking hours. If you could attain enlightenment, then another ego would have to be invented to take your place; because the ego's job is vital and can only be done by someone with ego qualities. The problem is that you want enlightenment because it sounds cool; it would be another feather in your cap; people would whisper in awe as you passed by, "Look, an enlightened master!" If you did reach enlightenment it would mean that you would dissolve; so who, then, would get the credit or bathe in the admiration? It would be like winning ten million dollars in the lottery, the day after you died. So you're stuck as ego. Thank you for what you are doing. Without you I couldn't tie my shoelaces, pay my taxes, stop at a red light or eat a good meal. However, please realize that you are merely the manager of the house, not the owner, or even the tenant

If it's the soul that asks the question, "How do I become enlightened?" the answer is the same, "You can't—ever;" but for a different reason. The reason the soul can't become enlightened, is that it already is enlightened. Enlightenment is its very state-of-being; it's ISNESS.

The soul initially receives this response with a tingling of pleasure, "God, I'm actually already enlightened? Wow!" But this quickly gives way to even more confusion, "If I am enlightened, how come I don't feel enlightened?" And the answer to that is, "You do feel enlightened, in between incarnations, as you rest in God-space. You know and feel your oneness at every moment, with every fiber of your being. However, when you decide to incarnate, all bets are off. Taking on a spacesuit creates both opportunities and problems. And one of the problems is this; you had to trade a great mind that is aligned with the cosmos, for a tiny mind crammed inside a three-pound brain. This little mind has to break up even the simplest truths into yet smaller pieces in order to be able to understand them and deal with them.

The ego quickly learned to hijack this little mind and use it for its own purposes. It assured its own preeminence by feeding fear-filled, victim messages to the mind, "You are being persecuted, taken advantage of, not being appreciated, being disrespected, not getting your deserved credit . . ." The ego's very survival and its sense of importance lie in the belief that it can rescue the self from all and every assault. The price, however, is blind obedience; the mind must believe everything the ego feeds it. The ego loves to have the mind endlessly rehearse scenarios, based on remembered or imagined hurts in which the mind can indulge its self-righteous anger with verbal gems that reduce the opposition to a sullen, though awed, silence.

Religion learned that from the group ego, and invented hell; and the politicians learned it and created the Patriot Act.

To expand the metaphor of the house, the ego is the manager, the mind is the tenant, while the soul is the owner of the house of incarnation. When Jesus warns us to stay awake, he means that the soul has to become self-realized and keep both mind and ego to their assigned roles. Once the soul has awakened, the ego is transformed from a tyrant to a servant, and the mind is able to transcend its own tiny thinking and facilitate the Earth-mission of the soul.

While the soul sleeps, the tenant and the manager believe they are the homeowners. And of all the foolish thoughts, the most foolish of all is that the little mind believes in the notion of a separate self. It believes itself to be separate from God; which it is not. It believes itself to be separate from other minds; which it is not. It believes itself to be separate from nature; which it is not.

The scared little mind is rather like a child who invents the game, "Let's see if there are monsters in the closet." Furtively, tentatively it squeaks open the closet door, peers into the darkness, frightens itself silly, is terrified by his own creation, and keeps returning to the game.

How, then, might you feel your own enlightened state during incarnation? I have three quick suggestions. First, keep the ego in its place, gratefully but firmly; second, don't believe everything you think; and, third, trust the unitive experiences i.e., compassion, love, meditation, deep prayer, a wonderful sunset, the eyes of a baby—for these allow us to trust our true nature and our God within.

When we take the spiritual path seriously we may pray, "Dear God, I will take anything you throw at me; anything—if only I can wake up and become enlightened."

And the ego and the mind immediately draw up the worst case scenario and scare themselves silly, "What if God makes me homeless, or sends me to prison for a crime I didn't commit; or what if he sends me insanity, or I get in an auto accident and have to have both legs amputated; or I get divorced, or if my child dies . . . ???"

So the prayer is taken back and the offer rescinded. But why, in God's name, would we imagine that the ultimate Godhead, the ineffable ground of all being is sitting in his office just waiting for some naive fool to offer Him a blank check? Do we really think God operates like that, "Aha, another wannabe mystic. I'll have fun with this one, like I did with Job."

It is more useful, accurate and grounding to pray, "Dear God, I accept everything, every situation that is in my life right now. And I promise to work with it in a state of patience, compassion and creativity. I will live fully in the now, in order to fashion a future of even greater love and harmony in myself, in my world and in my times."

If I can pray this, I am already on the edge of enlightenment.

39

Logos of Light
(May 26, 2001)

Playful river of Cosmic light,
I see you spearing Space;
tumbling over the rocks
of galaxy-clusters;
dancing deftly around the pebbles
of individual solar systems;
on your mystic journey
from the vast, vacant void;
on your sacred safari
back to the fertile womb
of No-Thing-Ness.

Sound of creation,
I hear the harmony of the heavens;
Om from my home.
Liquid Light,
liquid Logos;
the Word,
the Silence.
Sometimes, the Word.
Always, the Silence.

Made in the USA
Middletown, DE
10 May 2019